The Corporates Strike Back

Lucas Sauberschwarz • Lysander Weiss

The Corporates Strike Back

How Large Companies Win the Innovation Race Against Disruptive Start-ups

Translated from German by Lynn Urch C

Springer

Lucas Sauberschwarz
Venture Idea GmbH
Düsseldorf, Germany

Lysander Weiss
Venture Idea GmbH
Düsseldorf, Germany

Original German edition published by Verlag Franz Vahlen GmbH, Munich, Germany, 2018

ISBN 978-3-030-79113-1 ISBN 978-3-030-79114-8 (eBook)
https://doi.org/10.1007/978-3-030-79114-8

This Springer imprint is published by the registered company Springer Nature Switzerland AG
The registered company address is: Gewerbestrasse 11, 6330 Cham, Switzerland

Foreword

Some 10 years ago now, I managed one of the first design thinking projects at SAP. Together with a cross-functional team of colleagues from Walldorf and Palo Alto, we were commissioned to develop an 'innovative' prototype using the design thinking method and then present this to SAP co-founder Hasso Plattner. The project was backdated from the date of this presentation. We had 2 months. Our Eventus project – in the form of a collaborative platform for event-based supply chain management – was a complete success. It was not only praised by Hasso Plattner, but also embraced by the then CEO of SAP in his keynote speech at the customer conference. It was then presented to customers in a live demonstration as a future SAP product vision. This was how we received the official commission to 'productise' our innovative prototype and bring it to market. Unfortunately, it quickly became apparent that there were no development resources available, and the development departments involved also had varying degrees of interest in implementing the prototype. The 'innovation' was therefore discussed, but ultimately failed in its implementation.

That was an important insight for me. In large corporations, real innovation in the form of new products and services means far more than developing a prototype which presents an innovative solution to an existing problem. Corporations need to organise their innovation processes systematically and integrate the numerous innovation methods in a goal-orientated way, especially in these times of digitisation and rapidly changing economic conditions. This is the only way that long-term success and competitive edge can be achieved through efficient innovation.

An important aspect of my research and lecturing at the Karlsruhe Institute of Technology is therefore to deal with as holistic a perspective as possible with regard to the process of designing innovative software and digital services. Many methods coexist independently today. This therefore raises the question of how we can integrate and scale methods for agile software development (for example, Scrum) as synergistically as possible using design thinking or other user-centred design methods. We are already passing on this knowledge to our students during their studies while at the same time focusing on a scientific basis for further development in our research work and also on a targeted integration of different methodological approaches, in particular.

A wide range of innovation methods have also been developed for large corporations in recent years although lacking any overarching integration of the individual approaches. This lack of integration has resulted in applying individual innovation methods which definitely deliver good outcomes locally but become enmeshed in the 'machinery' of large corporations and end up not being brought to market in the form of innovative products or services. While start-ups react to changing economic conditions and can implement new ideas quickly, corporates are naturally slower and less agile. At the same time, corporates have a clear advantage over start-ups with their established brands and their ability to scale up in all functional areas. It is therefore necessary to overcome the known weaknesses of large companies while also harnessing their strengths.

This book addresses the above challenges and introduces the 5C process for efficient innovation from a practice-orientated perspective. The authors have developed an integrated innovation methodology and the relevant tools specifically for the target group of large corporations based on their experience gained from more than 60 innovation projects in more than 20 different industries. With their 5C process, they are filling a gap in the practice-orientated innovation literature and delivering an integrated approach for efficient innovations in corporates.

Alexander Mädche
Karlsruhe Institute of Technology (KIT), Karlsruhe, Germany

That's a really great idea, but...

... the business case is too small.
... that doesn't fit our corporate philosophy.
... it's not our job.
... we don't have the competence for that.
... that won't work.
... we don't have the resources for that.
... that's impossible for legal reasons.
... we don't have time for distractions right now.
... it won't scale.
... no one will buy it.
... our industry doesn't work like that.
... that's too risky.
... we haven't got the people for that.
... I've already tried that.
... that's still too far in the future.
... is that really necessary?
... we don't have the budget for that.
... will that also work without any investment?
... it won't go down well with investors.
... where's the impact?
... it's not the right time.

You could continue this list indefinitely, of course. No wonder employees in corporations feel as if they are sitting in a rigid 'tanker'.

Under these conditions, how are they supposed to react quickly and successfully to social changes, new technologies and changing customer needs? And will this tanker still be able to keep up with all the start-up speedboats in future?

Corporates are looking to Silicon Valley increasingly often these days as a result. After all, successful start-ups like Uber, Airbnb, Dropbox or Pinterest seem to emerge there as if they were exiting a production line. Many corporates began employing the customer-centric innovation methods of successful start-ups for their own innovation development years ago. The problem with this is that large companies are not start-ups! And so ideas developed using start-up methods such as *design thinking* or *lean start-up* usually cannot be implemented in large companies. The complexity within these companies is simply too high. As a result, innovation is outsourced – out of frustration and as a supposed solution – to separate units whose value addition is simply not significant enough for the corporation. Instead of processing strategically new, significant opportunities, innovation often degenerates into innovation theatre.

When looking for solutions to this problem, we asked ourselves, what if the corporation isn't the problem, but the idea instead? And how can we develop ideas that can be implemented successfully in large companies without any ifs or buts? After all, established companies actually possess the best preconditions for successful innovations with their resources, expertise, customers, network and strong brands. So why do they not manage to exploit them?

Throughout more than 8 years of theoretical and practical research, we have studied why current customer-centric methods – such as *design thinking* and *lean start-up*, or the outsourcing of innovation to separate units, like innovation hubs and labs – achieve no significant impact in corporates. And what a new methodology must look like to ensure that large companies are able to innovate successfully.

The result is the 5C process for efficient innovation. We have continuously developed and tested this process with the experience we have gained from more than 60 projects in over 20 industries. In this book, we intend to describe our insights and the underlying 5C process in detail to provide new impulses and approaches for practical use. Our aim is to see innovation regain its status in established companies as a strategic tool for future corporate success. Decision makers in corporations and small and medium-sized enterprises should be made aware of their internal innovation challenges and external, often disruptive, threats and be equipped with the tools and methods needed to counter them successfully. In this way, established companies can win the innovation race against disruptive start-ups.

We hope to inspire plenty of good ideas when you read this book and we look forward to receiving your feedback.

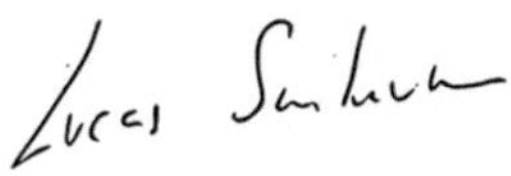

Lucas Sauberschwarz

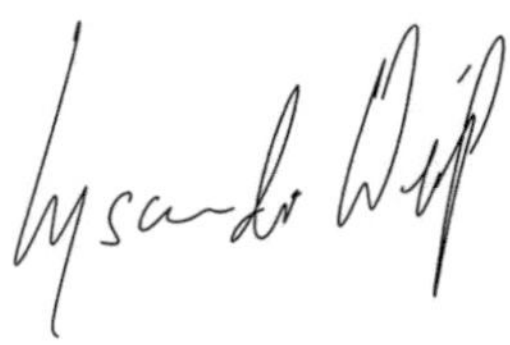

Lysander Weiss

Acknowledgements

This book and the 5C methodology described in it are the culmination of years of research and work so far. This would not have been possible without Florian Lanzer and Alexander Kornelsen. Our collective work on this process forms the basis of this book which they have supported with their valuable advice and active support.

A special thanks goes to Lynn Urch for translating the book and thus making it possible to publish it beyond the borders of the German language.

A project like this can only succeed if, in addition to support at work, the process is also accompanied by help, understanding and motivation in your private life. I (Lucas) would therefore like to thank my wife, Lisa, who has always given me the courage to follow my heart. My thanks also go to my two sons, Leo and Rafael, who show me every day just how much there is still to discover in this world and who have enriched my life in so many ways.

I (Lysander) would like to thank Charlotte who has always made me feel I can achieve anything. I would hardly have had the strength to write this book without her support, whether this was her understanding and support for the phases of my work or the joy and relaxation in between them.

In addition, we are happy, grateful and also a little proud that we were able to win over so many people to support us in writing this book. We would first of all like to thank Wolfgang Böcking, Maximilian Schön, Dennis Wedderkop, Matthias Hampel, Josef Stoll, Britta Gayko and many others for our valuable discussions about the content of this book. We would also like to thank the many test readers who helped us with their valuable feedback and great ideas, Jörg Limberg, Björn Sprotte, Andreas Seitz, Dr Werner Sauberschwarz, Oliver Sauberschwarz, Tim Merforth, Dr Florian Muschaweck and Philipp Blasberg, as well as David Dorn, Josephine Bayazid, Marc Parat and Thorben Rückert for their support with research and corrections.

We were also impressed by the willingness of the many companies and their representatives to help us with comments and case studies to make the book as practical and lively as possible. Many thanks to all the companies and individuals mentioned in the book and to all the other companies which have placed their trust in us over the years.

Last but not least, we are grateful for our publisher Springer, namely Christian Rauscher and his team, to make this our first international book on the market. Thank you very much for your many helpful tips, assistance and editing.

We could thank so many other people in our private and professional lives who have helped us to achieve this goal. So, thank you to anyone we have not mentioned here, but who played an important part for us. We are eternally grateful that our dream has now become reality, and that the comprehensive book which has brought our work and our passion for innovation into the world is now sitting on our desk.

Guest Commentaries and Case studies

Chapter 1:

Guest Commentary: Uwe Wagner, Chief Technology Officer, Schaeffler
Guest Commentary: Britta Gayko, Managing Partner Commerz Business Consulting, Commerzbank
Guest Commentary: Michael Weppler, Executive Vice President of Systems at German Certification Body TÜV Rheinland

Chapter 2:

Guest Commentary: Nicolas Biagosch, Managing Director, Digitalhafen, former CEO, Simyo, former Executive Board member, E-Plus
Guest Commentary: Olivier Krüger, Chief Executive Officer, Lufthansa Systems
Guest Commentary: Luke Mansfield, Vice President Innovation, PepsiCo Beverages
Case Study: Estée Lauder Companies
Case Study: Telekom Innovation Laboratories
Case Study: A Container Shipping Company
Guest Commentary: Nicolai Andersen, EMEA Lead Innovation and Head of Deloitte Garage, Deloitte
Guest Commentary: Dr. Klaus Suwelack, Senior Manager New Business Development and Innovation Management, Janssen Deutschland, Johnson & Johnson
Case Study: Hermes Arzneimittel
Guest Commentary: Reyk Radojewski, Chief Financial Officer, Beiersdorf South East Asia
Case Study: FTI Group
Guest Commentary: Till Bauer, Head of Strategic Projects and Commercial Innovation, MSD Sharp & Dohme (Subsidiary of Merck & Co.)
Case Study: Hymer

Chapter 3:

Guest Commentary: Klaus Burmeister, Founder and Managing Director, Z_punkt, The Foresight Company, Foresightlab and Initiative D2030 (Germany 2030)
Guest Commentary: Jörg Limberg, Vice President Europe Research Solutions Sales and Marketing, Elsevier, Former Vice President and General Manager Software and Solutions, Hewlett Packard
Guest Commentary: Timo Emmert, Head of e-Commerce, MediaMarktSaturn
Guest Commentary: Dr. Hans-Joachim Popp, Chief Information Officer, Dt. Luft- und Raumfahrt (German Aerospace Centre)
Guest Commentary: Dave Birss, Author of "A *User Guide to the Creative Mind* and Chief Thinker, RIGHT thinking
Guest Commentary: Björn Sprotte, Chief Executive Officer, OSM Maritime Group
Guest Commentary: Thomas Weiler, Vice President Innovation Portfolio and Strategic Programs, Deutsche Telekom

Contents

About the Authors

Lucas Sauberschwarz
is managing director of the strategy consultancy Venture Idea and director of the Center for Innovation at the SGMI Management Institute St. Gallen, Switzerland.

Lysander Weiss
is partner of the strategy consultancy Venture Idea, a doctoral student at the HHL Leipzig Graduate School of Management and a lecturer on strategy, innovation and new work.

Lucas Sauberschwarz and Lysander Weiss are best-selling authors and leading experts in the fields of strategy, innovation and new work. Together, they run the management consultancy Venture Idea, which was awarded as Germany's best medium-sized consultancy for Innovation & Growth (2018) and Strategy (2019) by Germany's leading business magazine WirtschaftsWoche. They regularly share their expertise through publications, teaching and as keynote speakers.

Additional materials can be downloaded on www.the-corporates-strike-back.com

Innovate or Die: Efficient Innovation Instead of Inefficient Start-Up Thinking

Contents

L. Sauberschwarz, L. Weiss, *The Corporates Strike Back*,
https://doi.org/10.1007/978-3-030-79114-8_1

Innovation is essential for the survival of established companies today. Increasingly rapid innovation cycles and competition from convergent and new industries ensure that the life expectancy of the 500 largest, publicly listed companies is now only 18 years, instead of 60 years as it was in the middle of the twentieth century (Rettig, 2017a). Today, 90% of the Fortune 500 companies around in 1955 have disappeared from the list. Consequently, 65% of the CEOs of global corporations are afraid of being overtaken by disruptive start-ups (KPMG, 2016).

Compared to the past when technology and consumer goods companies in particular were focused on innovation, innovations can now begin to reveal their impact as guarantors of growth and revenue accelerators in all industries, according to a global PWC innovation study (Gackstatter, 2015).

With no, or with too small, an innovative capacity, growth targets scarcely seem to be achievable today. Over 80% of participants in the study therefore regarded innovation as being either important or very important for the success of the company. This fundamental problem creates the framework for the first part of this book, namely, how do successful, established companies become caught in this innovation dilemma? And are all tankers now effectively being overtaken by far more successful speedboats? What are they currently doing about it, why do they need new solutions and what do these need to achieve?

The role of innovations changed drastically from the twentieth to the twenty-first century. In the twentieth century, the life of a medium-sized and large company usually followed one simple pattern, namely, patent-based product innovations, made by either pioneers and inventors or research and development departments. These were the basis of many companies, and it made them large and successful for many years. Today, twenty-first century start-ups no longer follow this principle. With methods like *design thinking* or *lean start-up*, they develop customer-centric innovations on the greenfield in line with the wishes of their customers and can then build new companies around these innovations.

This is how start-ups attack established markets and companies. Without regard to existing core competencies and business models, start-ups are able to innovate faster and more cheaply, and are more customer-orientated. They exploit this advantage to attack established companies and markets and destroy or conquer them, i.e. disrupt them. Disruptive start-ups no longer limit themselves just to traditional product innovations. Instead, they focus primarily on completely new services and business models, based mostly on new, digital technologies in which large companies do not (yet) have any core competencies.

For corporates, this new, disruptive competition is a problem. Against a wave of start-ups with innovative business models and customer-centric (digital) products and services, patents alone usually no longer offer protection (Anthony, 2012). Instead of playing the familiar game with clear opponents and rules, established companies suddenly have to compete against new opponents under new rules, making the old tactics useless.

As a result, large companies are increasingly resorting to the methods used by start-ups, trying to join in the new game. New innovations are now also being developed using greenfield, customer-centric design. Unlike start-ups, in the traditional structures of large companies, these ideas cannot be implemented in greenfields, however, and so they quickly reach their limits. Companies' existing brownfields which were originally successful with their available resources, processes, structures and a wide variety of stakeholders thus become a barrier to implementation which causes most customer-centric ideas to fail or to change beyond recognition. Corporates seem to be left with only incremental product improvements, while start-ups reign supreme over radical or even disruptive innovations.

Fortunately, however, there seems to be a solution to this innovation dilemma, as the 'inventor' of disruption theory, Clayton Christensen, describes. It is not just the search for ideas, but the implementation of customer-centric, and preferably disruptive innovations too, which are being outsourced to greenfields. Innovation takes place in separate units, such as innovation hubs, incubators or future labs instead of in a large company's brownfield.

But this supposed 'innovator's solution' where large companies act like start-ups is unfortunately a fatal decision. Naturally, as the strengths of the core business no longer play a role in these separate units, the chances of success roughly equal those of the start-ups they are now competing against. And, even if the same (supposedly) successful models—such as Uber, Tesla or Airbnb—like to hide this, these chances of success are very small. Considering relevant figures for established companies, the opportunity to create significant value added USD 100 million is **1:500**. For a value added of USD 500 million and long-term, profitable growth, the chances even decrease to **1:17,000** (Zook, 2016).

In the start-up industry, this is not a problem as start-ups have little to lose at the beginning and are often considered successful even with a revenue of a few million euros. With patient venture capitalists (VCs), they can also survive long, unprofitable periods, as the Uber example shows. When large companies rely on this success rate though, it is suddenly a matter of the survival of billion-dollar companies with a corresponding responsibility towards investors which are not venture capitalists, as well as customers, employees and partners, and ultimately the entire economy.

Yet there is hope if large companies can manage to exploit their strengths. **If the core business and scalability advantages of an established company can be exploited for innovations, the chances of success increase by more than 2,000-fold to 1:8** (Zook, 2016). These innovations cannot be achieved by design thinking and other start-up tactics alone though. New methods developed specifically for large companies must incorporate the company's brownfield in the innovation development in addition to the wholly important customer perspective, thus achieving a successful implementation with significant value added.

The **5C process (*Configuration, Customisation, Compilation, Construction and Conversion*) has exactly this goal**, namely, of developing and implementing brownfield innovations which—in contrast to most incremental innovations—also ensure an excellent fit to future customer needs. With the resulting 'efficient innovations', the company's existing structures, processes, resources, networks, customers and other success factors can be used to successfully place innovations in the market and scale them. Thus, large companies and small- and medium-sized enterprises don't need to fear disruptive start-ups in a future characterised by new technologies, high levels of complexity, strong convergence, cost pressure and global competition, but can win the innovation battle against them. This is also required urgently in this kind of future since it is often only established companies which have enough critical success factors and power to lead innovations to the success which everyone can ultimately profit from.

At this point, we recommend that readers who are just interested in the practical 5C process jump to the part two of the book. We invite everyone else to continue reading here first. In the next two sections, we will examine the exact background to the changes described in the innovation battle and the current challenges with start-up methods before developing the fundamentals of efficient innovation as a new approach to a solution.

Summary

Innovate or Die: Efficient Innovations Instead of Inefficient Start-Up Thinking

With the 5C process, corporations can develop efficient innovations by combining customer fit with the company's strengths to win the innovation battle against disruptive start-ups.

- Innovation has now become crucial for future growth and corporate success in all industries.
- New disruptive start-ups have changed the rules of the game and are winning against traditional corporations with their agile, customer-centric methods.
- As a countermeasure, corporations try to copy start-up methods.
- The result: plenty of ideas, but poor implementation which fails due to restrictions.
- The solution to this innovation dilemma: outsource innovation to separate units.
- Chances of success with start-ups from separate units is only 1:17,000.
- Combining customer fit with the company's strengths offers a chance of success of 1:8.
- We have created the 5C process to develop efficient innovations like this.

1.1 Corporates Yesterday: From Patent Factories to the Innovation Dilemma

Let us start again with our initial questions. Why have many corporates and small- and medium-sized enterprises such enormous problems with developing innovations in this new millennium? With all their scarcity of resources, why do start-ups seem to zoom past corporates like speedboats overtaking huge tankers? To understand why the fear of being overtaken by disruptive start-ups has grown so strongly in large companies in recent years, and why so many managers are departing for Silicon Valley to learn from start-ups in learning journeys, it is worth taking a look at the development of innovation in large companies—and the changes which have led to today's situation.

Guest Commentary: Uwe Wagner, Chief Technology Officer, Schaeffler

"As a member of the executive committee of Schaeffler AG, a leading global supplier to the automotive and industrial sectors, I am responsible for research and development. In that role I am directly affected by the rapid changes in these sectors. Trends such as new mobility, climate change, autonomous production, data economy or demographic change create a complex and volatile environment. The R&D unit needs to address these constant changes in a way that leads to relevant solutions for our product and business sectors. Therefore, we are constantly scanning and assessing the changing environment and its impact on the business to define relevant focus clusters for R&D.

In total, around 8000 employees at 40 R&D locations develop new products, technologies, processes and procedures for market-driven solutions. Consequently, Schaeffler is one of the innovation leaders in the industry with more than 2400 patent applications annually. This underlines the inventive spirit of Schaeffler, which itself was founded 70 years ago based on relevant inventions, and today still stands not only for quality and technology but also for innovation. However, the art of engineering alone is no longer enough to carry this promise into the future. The rapid changes also demand new, digitally capable products and services with suitable business models and a comprehensive system understanding. For this reason, we are using our core competencies to expand the company's role as a holistic solution provider for our clients combined with an improved innovation process that takes into account the speed of digital change and enables the existing core competencies to be expanded in a targeted manner for new solutions.

With our industrial product OPTIME, for example, the company offers an efficient and easy-to-use low-cost solution designed specifically for comprehensive condition monitoring of machine and equipment parks. It combines wireless sensors with a gateway and an app to constantly analyse and visualize all indirectly process-critical assets with specifically developed algorithms—an innovation that would not have been possible without, on the one hand, the technologies developed in research and, on the other hand, the complementary digital services and business models, combined with the technical expertise and extensive storehouse of physical models from the existing bearing servicing operations. This combination of existing strengths with new, exciting possibilities brings successful innovations to the market. Therefore, traditional R&D is still indispensable for innovative products and processes, but it is no longer sufficient to shape the future in the market, in which a holistic, integrated view is the key for future success."

For centuries, the predominant form of innovation was product innovation. Before the advent of large-scale mass production, individual inventors, in particular, were responsible for innovations. Whether that is the car, the generator, the light bulb or the telephone, we are usually thinking about the people behind them, like Carl Benz, Werner von Siemens, Thomas Edison and Alexander Bell. These inventors looked like pioneers on a sailing boat, battling their way slowly and determinedly towards an unknown destination. However, it was here that the foundation stone was laid for the tankers which soon replaced sailing boats. Many of the innovations at that time also represented the origins of corporates—in the above cases, Daimler-Benz (cars), Siemens (telegraphs), General Electric (electrical appliances) and AT&T (telephones).

The era of great inventors soon ended. The increase in complexity and innovation costs, on the one hand, and the institutionalisation of inventiveness in companies, on the other, which accompanied mass production from 1915 onwards, made the development of successful innovations by individual inventors increasingly difficult. Instead, the inventors have been multiplied in companies' research and development (R&D) departments. Companies now experimented on a large scale, researching increasing numbers of products and technologies and bringing them to the market. Thanks to patent protection, those were long-term, competitive advantages and thus justified the investment (Beige, 2017). While these now established companies were, in fact, generating more and more product innovations and new technological achievements, they also had to manage and improve their successful products, becoming more complex and bureaucratic with time.

In the 1970s and 1980s, we saw a brief resurgence again of a wave of inventors on the back of the new computer technology. Large companies encountered new competition from pioneers, like Bill Gates and Steve Jobs. They established a new breed, the Silicon Valley start-up, which was similarly dedicated to technological product innovation and attracted the innovators (and investors) for whom progress was now too slow in the large 'tankers'. However, companies like Microsoft and Apple rapidly became large patent factories themselves, which IBM, 3M, etc. battled with until eventually there was a veritable forest of patents.

It became clear no later than the dotcom bubble in 2000 that patents and technologies alone were not (or were no longer) a long-term recipe for success if ultimately nobody bought the products (Surowiecki, 2016). Large as well as small companies suddenly recalled what economist Joseph Schumpeter had established as early as 1912 that the success of a company depends not just on patents but also on the clever use of resources for more productive purposes—or as he termed it 'creative destruction' (Schumpeter, 2006). As a result, productivity growth no longer depended on technology and patents alone, but above all, on their useful implementation, that is, the innovation. Besides technology, entrepreneurship as a skill is also needed to repeatedly implement new inventions on the open market and sell them to the customer. In particular, since technologies and resources were increasingly available, these were no longer the sole competitive advantage in the new millennium (Beige, 2017).

In this phase, innovation research flourished outside research and development. This now dictated that the best technologies and patents would not necessarily always be guaranteed success with customers or in the market if there is a lack of entrepreneurship or no benefit to customers. Competitive advantages, i.e. the main focus of innovation, were no longer just technologies, patents and products, but new, customer-orientated, business model innovations too. Global growth in financial resources made talent and ideas the dominant currency for companies which also fought increasingly fiercely for market share. As a Bain & Company study shows, a mere one to two companies in each market then shared 80% of the profits

(Rettig, 2017b). Suddenly most companies found themselves too far from their customers, had the wrong expertise and were too slow.

A new category of start-ups successfully countered these new requirements. With their clever ideas and agile, customer-centric methods, like lean start-up and design thinking (see the overview on the next page), these experienced a new heyday. Suddenly it seemed possible to set up new companies with the most limited resources and test them close to the customer without incurring the large investments and risks which led to the dotcom bubble.

This change stretched over a long period, in fact, but still took many large companies by surprise. Previously innovation leaders with limitless resources and inventions in the form of patents and process improvements, these large tankers were suddenly overtaken left and right by agile speedboats launched onto the water almost effortlessly on the strength of new, customer-centric innovations.

The most successful companies of all times were facing their greatest challenge. The skills and resources which they had built up over the years now seemed to become a burden, their product improvements seemed to pass the customer by, and their business models no longer seemed cutting edge. At the same time, however, these were the very success factors and core competencies of the company, and they could not simply abandon them. A large company cannot just be rebuilt around new ideas, particularly as long as it is still successful.

So it was time for a rethink for the corporates. It just needed someone who could put the uneasy feelings of large companies into words and document them to facilitate change in large companies on a grand scale. Harvard (George, 2016) Business School professor Clayton Christensen took on this task and achieved a big hit with his work *The Innovator's Dilemma* (1997), not least because he immediately introduced a new buzzword, 'disruptive innovation' or later on 'disruption' (Christensen, 1997).

The concept of disruption is initially plausible. Christensen studied corporates to understand where they were failing and recognised that many large companies were unable to detect or to exploit new technologies and business early enough when they did not meet high standards of success at the outset, for example, if they were still not very efficient or profitable.

Excursus: Overview of Selected Innovation Methods

Agile Development

Agile development is a philosophy which has its origins in software development. It is to be understood as a response to increased speed of the growing complexity in the business world. In the context of process or product innovations, this development leads to traditional procedures increasingly failing, because detailed development plans only provide illusory accuracy and result in too many influencing factors changing in the course of a project. The goal is therefore to attempt to manage with little bureaucratic effort and few rules and to adapt quickly to changes without increasing the risk of errors.

Design Thinking

Design thinking is a process developed by the innovation agency IDEO to produce innovations which focus on the needs of users. This approach is centred on the way in which designers work and sees itself as a process consisting of understanding, observing, brainstorming, refining, executing and learning. The approach is based on the assumption that problems can be solved better if people from different disciplines work together in a creative, stimulating environment. Issues are identified jointly in a clearly structured process, taking into account people's needs and motivations in order to then develop concepts which are tested and optimised in several loops.

Lean Start-Up

Lean start-up describes an approach to founding a company in which the focus is on making all of the processes as lean as possible. People attempt to set up a company with a small amount of capital and reduced processes and to bring a prototype or beta version to the market as quickly as possible. The focus is on flexibility and learning-by-doing effects and on attempting to keep the product life cycle as short as possible so as to be able to respond quickly and effectively to desires and suggestions for change as a result of customer feedback.

Business Model Canvas

The business model canvas is used to visualise a business model or a start-up idea clearly, check the strategic logic and then design it in a profitable and goal-orientated way. The basis is a one-page canvas which has been divided into nine different spaces. These spaces represent the most important factors to be considered and hence clarify interrelationships, thus helping to develop a business idea into a business model in a structured way.

Stage-Gate

The stage-gate model is a process for structuring and optimising linear innovation and development processes. The goal is to achieve better focus as well as faster process handling. For this, processes are divided into individual 'gates' (sections). First of all, an innovation is checked with regard to its technical and commercial quality before it is brought from development to production maturity and finally to market launch. The number of individual gates may vary depending on the industry and the innovation. It is characteristic that individual gates are always supervised by mixed project teams, and a decision is made for each gate about whether the project will pass through the gate onto the next level or will be terminated.

These established companies had to simultaneously concentrate on competing to sell their existing products and services and keep on improving them through incremental innovations, making them increasingly complex and expensive, and therefore at some point either not or no longer relevant to whole market segments. According to Christensen, start-ups can exploit such opportunities and serve these market segments with new (cheaper) technologies and business models or even create completely new markets which grow step-by-step. Eventually, they can pene-

Fig. 1.1 Disruptive innovation. (Adapted: Christensen 1997)

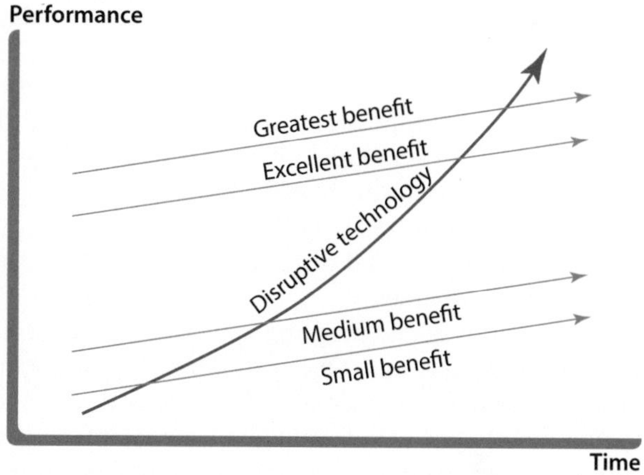

trate the existing markets of large companies and either destroy or replace them, in other words, disrupt them (see Fig. 1.1).

A good example of *disruptive technologies* is the development of the computer market. Here, powerful mainframe computers initially dominated and were used by many companies. Minicomputers manufactured by newcomer firms, such as DEC, were initially ignored by established mainframe manufacturers, because they were significantly less powerful and profitable than professional mainframes. Over time, however, they were able to conquer (or create) the private customer market and ultimately threaten the corporate market for mainframe computers too. So, for example, in 1981, 4 years after the Apple II, IBM introduced its own minicomputer (the IBM PC) to ward off disruption at the last moment but never believed in its success (Spector, 2016). No other established mainframe manufacturer became a leading manufacturer of minicomputers or PCs.

In time, Christensen and other academics expanded the theory to cover other aspects of innovation. They hence discovered that disruption can also emerge from *new business models* (e.g. low-cost airlines, discount stores or online education) or technological innovation which creates entirely *new markets* (e.g. mobile phones). As a result, the term was then changed from 'disruptive technologies' to 'disruptive innovations'—so creating the basis for its widespread use.

The term 'disruption' has become increasingly popular in practice since 2004 and been transferred to more and more phenomena. The original, quite narrow definition hardly has a role to play today which has also resulted in extensive criticism of the theory. Disruption has thus become a buzzword for all kinds of innovation efforts. The German newspaper *Frankfurter Allgemeine Zeitung* named 'disruption' as its economic word of the year for 2015, whereas authors were voting to retire what they termed 'Silicon Valley's emptiest buzzword' (Meck & Weiguny, 2015).

This term and the basic theory underlying it are still enjoying great popularity in large companies, in particular. No wonder, especially because with faster and faster technological changes as a result of the Internet, 3D printing, artificial intelligence, wearables, the Internet of Things, blockchain or virtual reality, established companies are facing exponentially growing technologies which they are no longer able to counter using previous innovation methods alone.

Christensen's **innovation dilemma aptly describes the situation of large companies**, namely, the impossible balancing act between their existing, successful core business and the simultaneous challenge posed by disruptive start-ups and new customer needs. In trying to support one side, they lose the other. In contrast, start-ups which did not yet have customers, resources, processes or structures could, and had to, act as riskily and disruptively as possible to have any chance at all against established companies.

The result was that corporates turned their attention to the methods employed by disruptive start-ups. Due to the innovation dilemma and the disruption risk, large companies were increasingly concerned with the myth of Silicon Valley and spent a lot of time with learning journeys, and start-up and design thinking workshops in order to copy the supposed recipes for success of disruptive start-ups.

However, as the next section shows, these methods are not yet the solution to the innovation dilemma for large companies.

Summary

Corporates Yesterday: From Patent Factories to the Innovation Dilemma

The corporates which were successful in the twentieth century as a result of patent-driven product innovations find themselves today caught in an innovation dilemma between disruptive, customer-centric innovations and their own successful core business.

- Yesterday's innovation successes came from inventors or research and development (R&D) units.
- R&D units secured a long-term competitive edge for companies through patent rights.
- Technologies and resources have become increasingly widely available and therefore more irrelevant.
- Tech start-ups changed the rules of the game by conquering corporates' markets with their new, customer-centric services and business models.
- The innovation dilemma of large companies is the challenge which exists between the successful core business and new, disruptive innovations, and broadly falls under the heading of 'disruption'.

1.2 Corporates Today: Inefficient Start-Up Thinking in Separate Innovation Units

Corporates and small- and medium-sized entities are countering the threat posed by disruptive, customer-centric and agile start-ups with a tactic which seems clever at first glance. They are trying to beat them at their own game. **As a solution to the innovation dilemma, corporates are focusing on supposedly promising start-up thinking**. To achieve excellent customer fit, customer-centric innovation relies on a greenfield search for ideas which is as free as possible, but is customer-led. Restrictions resulting from companies' brownfields are initially ignored as far as possible. 'Design thinking consultants' are engaged to provide training in the methodology and to create the right 'customer-centric mindset'. Companies purchase furniture, Post-it notes, bean bags and whiteboards for design thinking or, in the extreme scenario, even establish entire design thinking departments, e.g. at Deutsche Bank, SAP or Deutsche Telekom.

Once the right underlying conditions have been successfully established, nothing more should stand in the way of customer-centric, preferably disruptive ideas and innovations. In contrast to R&D or the incremental development processes in individual departments, the customer now becomes the core of the innovation process, and observations and surveys reveal specific customer problems. Creative brainstorming sessions, supported by rapid prototyping and role-playing games, provide promising ideas. Additionally, lean start-up methodology is added to test the developments with direct customer feedback (Ries, 2011). This methodology takes the same line as design thinking with an iterative, customer-centric process to implement ideas. Initial solutions are built as prototypes and developed directly with the customer in keeping with the old adage, '70% is good enough'. This allows customer-orientated testing of the idea as a minimum viable product (MVP) as well as tailored development in line with customer requirements. Using agile methods, this flexible, lean process can then also be continued during the further implementation. Self-organised teams, iterative and incremental processes as well as the right office equipment provide the required the start-up feeling.

Companies should now have achieved the goal of producing their own customer-centric innovations. Instead of continuing to develop existing products and services over customers' heads, they have created ideas and solutions with excellent customer fit that new or existing customers actually need. The result is that established companies can produce new customer-centric and—in the best scenario—disruptive innovations, just like start-ups.

The problem with this is the implementation. This is because you cannot usually implement all of the innovations in a company which look promising in theory or from tests or experiments. Concepts with excellent customer fit are handed over for implementation to departments which have other priorities, objectives and criteria. Implementers tend to show little understanding of the need to trouble themselves with the details of implementing out-of-the-box ideas, whereas creatives seem to have had all the fun earlier on (Gothelb, 2017).

The innovations therefore usually stay at the stage of Post-it notes on the wall or prototypes in a drawer and become the 'random product of this battle of the methods'. (Kleske, 2016) Even in the best-case scenario, ideas are mostly changed in retrospect and made to fit the company until they can finally be implemented. By then, there is usually not much left of the basic idea, and customer centricity and the potential for disruption have been lost.

The reason for this implementation problem is not really a surprise. The applied methods were developed for start-ups which are the exact opposite of corporates. Although they usually have very few resources at the beginning, on the other hand, they have no limitations or restrictions from a current business either. So they can, and must, build the entire new company around the customer-centric, disruptive idea. You cannot redesign a large company around every new idea though. At the same time, ideas developed on greenfields rarely fit the existing company brownfield with all its specific structures, processes, goals and resources as these have been ignored in the search for ideas in the pursuit of 'thinking freely'. It is no wonder, therefore, that most ideas never see the light of day (Wolfangel, 2016). The only thing they completely fit are the needs of the customer. However, in the end these needs are not met if the ideas are never implemented. **Start-up methods consequently bring a new problem with their solutions. The innovations of corporates are no longer failing because the customer does not want them, but because they cannot be implemented in large companies**.

Clayton Christensen noticed this too, and a few years after *The Innovator's Dilemma*, he presented **his answer to this problem with** *The Innovator's Solution* (Christensen, 2013)**:** If you cannot implement the 'greenfield' ideas which were developed, you must also create a 'greenfield' for your implementation so that you can complement the underlying start-up conditions.

Consequently, like many of their international counterparts, most of the large companies now adhere to the mantra 'disrupt or be disrupted' (Gans, 2016) **and try to behave like start-ups**. They act on the (controversial) case studies presented by Christensen in which firms develop and implement disruptive innovations in separate units (Christensen, 1997). These do not pursue the core business' goals and criteria, but instead are organisationally separate from it—and preferably, have a separate location too. In this way, they can experiment freely with new business models and emerging technologies, ideally implementing them in new start-ups which can then either drive the tanker forward like a speedboat or become a tanker themselves. It is clear what the underlying hope is—that they will be able to discover and develop disruptive innovations in these separate units before another start-up disrupts the market. And so, companies optimistically set up innovation hubs, future labs, accelerators or incubators to find 'the next big thing' (Paap & Katz, 2004a) (authors' note: these are all referred to below as 'separate units' or 'innovation hubs', despite their differences in practical use). This way, corporates can handle the implementation problems in their brownfields and develop and implement disruptive innovations. That is the theory.

But how does it look in practice? The solution sounds great at first, and will in many cases even successfully produce some new start-ups and reassure investors that the threat of disruption is being addressed. Unfortunately though, it will not help corporates to solve the innovation dilemma in the long term. This solution is often even a fatal decision, because it 'feels' as if the innovation dilemma has been solved—although in practice it has not.

How many companies really want to be disrupted and lose their successful core business within a short space of time? Probably very few. Using separate units for disruptive (digital) innovations runs counter to the goal of integrating them into the core business of the company later on, or even actively works against the core business (Iansiti et al., 2003). This leads to a problem which is not obvious in the short term. Although innovations from these innovation units can be tested and implemented quickly at the start, they will experience problems later with actually having a significant impact on the market. That would require the support of the corporate with all its resources, processes and structures—but this is initially deliberately ignored by the spin-offs which are intended to function as independent start-ups (Kohler, 2016).

Separate innovation units are practically a bet on the innovation success of their own start-ups therefore. If the goal of separate units is to disrupt the core business, this bet only pays off if the start-up achieves a value added which ultimately replaces or significantly adds to the core business. Successfully disruptive innovation for the large company therefore needs to generate a significant new value added and represent a long-term competitive advantage ('unfair advantage') over time. In this scenario, the separate start-ups could actually replace a core business which already has these features.

The chances of achieving this innovation success with separate start-ups are vanishingly small though. If you consider how small the chances are of a start-up surviving at all, there is only a marginal probability of actually developing innovations in innovation hubs which even come close to the core business' profit and revenue figures. This is because if innovations are developed and implemented on greenfields just like any other start-up—and can only be scaled back to the large company again with great difficulty too—then these innovations ultimately have the same chances of success as any other start-up. Unfortunately, however, these chances are not as great as you might assume from the few—usually identical—success stories following a 'learning journey' to Silicon Valley.

The difficulties of actually implementing transformative greenfield business models have been extensively investigated and described in numerous studies. Moules, for example, investigated 600,000 start-ups in Great Britain, only 1% of which managed to achieve the status of 'scale up', defined as achieving growth of at least 20% for revenue or staff numbers over a 3-year period (Moules, 2016). The statistics do not look good in the USA either. In an analysis of all US start-ups, Bain & Company established that the chances of a start-up achieving long-term value added (of USD 500 million and 10 years of profitable growth) is 1:17,000. If you are satisfied with a value added of USD 100 million, the chances are 1:500. The long-term value added considered here may seem high at first, but it is only having such 'big cogs' which will ultimately help corporates if they want to survive (Viki, 2017). In 2016, there were only 165 'unicorns' worldwide, that is, start-ups with a valuation of at least USD 1 billion. And as Managing Director of SevenVentures Sascha van Holt expects, of these even every 50 unicorn will die or fall below the EUR 1 billion mark, because in the long term it will not generate an annual revenue of at least EUR 100 million to justify such a valuation. Companies like Fitbit, WeWork or GoPro as well as the shares in Rocket Internet are already showing today that a long-term impact is difficult even for much-hyped start-up stars.

In short, **there is a war raging on the greenfields**. The resources of customers, time and money are limited, and everyone wants some of them, but no one has a head start. The factors which make start-ups strong at the beginning—like speed, simplicity and the lack of complex structures or processes—present them with problems in the course of scaling. They are immediately copied, must face tough global competition and often fail due to overly strict regulations or finance requirements (George, 2016). In regulated or consumer-critical sectors in particular, such as energy, finance or healthcare, they often even experience problems asserting themselves at all against established companies, and if they do manage to stay in the market, they remain on low or negative profits.

For start-ups, this is not a problem. They do not (usually) need to generate a value added of USD 500 million to be considered successful or to satisfy founders and venture capitalists. Added to that, entrepreneurs and start-ups begin with few resources. If they fail, it has only minor consequences, and others can follow suit until there is another success story at some point.

This is not so for corporates, though, as they are already bringing an existing business with them. If the innovation hubs with their start-ups really intend to ensure the future of the company, they need to see significant success. If this fails to materialise after several years of experimentation, it is not only the innovation hub which fails, but the core business too as it has relied heavily on the separate units. Especially as the company may be overtaken by a disruptive start-up which is not located inside the innovation hub.

Innovation hubs therefore have the same small chances of success as all other start-ups due to their separation from the core business and its innovation activity (O'Hare, 2008). They are highly likely to be unable to compensate for losses in the core business and, in the worst scenario, may even contribute to them. Still, they cannot prevent other disruptive start-ups to emerge outside.

It is no wonder, then, that a recent study by the journal 'Capital' on the 'best' innovation hubs in Germany found that none of the 17 digital hubs surveyed had really made any money so far—not even those which had existed for some time. 'It is striking that almost nothing has been achieved so far in business terms', said Julian Kawohl, Professor at the University of Applied Sciences (HTW) Berlin who helped with the study, when commenting on the outcomes. 'No company has built up a significant new business from its lab.' However, 'What works is generating ideas. Labs have made fantastic progress there'. (Kreimeier, 2017)

These insights must raise strong doubts about the probability of success of separate innovation units. Many of the innovation hubs currently springing up seem to be more like 'innovation theatres' created primarily for investors and the press. In the worst scenario, separate innovation units cause a migration of talent and resources, because their journey from the core business into unsuccessful, or barely successful, start-ups rarely leads back to the corporation (Blank, 2014).

How does the current performance look in practice? The economic success identified in the 'Capital' study is failing to materialise. That is currently not yet a problem for the existing, separate innovation units as those usually have medium- to long-term goals and often, have not been on the market for long. Later on though, most will probably go the same way as the early pioneers in this space, such as the labs and hubs belonging to Nordstrom, AOL, eBay, Coca-Cola, Microsoft, Disney or the *New York Times* which have since disappeared again (Berengian, 2017). And the Lufthansa innovation hub—which topped the rankings for digital labs in the 'Capital' study—has only managed a mere 14 employees and 3 'lighthouse projects' after 2 years: an airline check-in app, a compensation platform for flight delays and a travel bookings app (Hoffmann, 2017). Those were all good services, but none were disruptive ideas nor, probably, the next revenue generators for the corporation either.

Added to that, even if the idea of separate innovation units is in vogue right now, it is by no means new. And as is so often the case, a glance back to the past would protect you from making mistakes both now and in the future. As early as 1970, Xerox founded the famous Palo Alto Research Center (Xerox PARC) with the aim of developing new technologies and innovations outside its core photocopier business. With its strong focus on research, several revolutionary technologies were indeed developed there. Ethernet network technology and the graphical user interface (GUI) for operating a PC with a mouse, for example, originated from their innovation laboratory. Did this mean success for Xerox? By no means. Except for the laser copier (which was very close to the core business), Xerox was unable to implement any of the innovations itself as that would have required completely new processes and structures. Instead, the inventors founded their own firms like 3Com and Adobe, or the competition grabbed their ideas. Many companies with separate innovation units are experiencing similar problems to Xerox again today too.

The second largest German bank, Commerzbank, was also able to gather the relevant experience with separate innovation units at an early stage. In 2000, it founded a wholly owned subsidiary, Commerz NetBusiness AG, an Internet consulting service provider and a future lab for the banking of the future. Provided with a large budget, the 30-strong team was tasked with developing greenfield banking innovations and participating in new Internet business models. 'It was a great time, like being in a start-up!', recalls co-founder Britta Gayko, '…until the money eventually ran out and it dawned on us that the technology and our customers were not that far along yet. We were just too early for internet-based business models. In short, the implementation was missing'. The future lab went to its grave without adding any long-term value to the customer or the company, and from that team they developed an internal management consultancy which even today still takes care of strategic topics close to the core business, from the idea through to the implementation.

Guest Commentary: Britta Gayko, Managing Partner Commerz Business Consulting, Commerzbank

"Design thinking is not a universal secret weapon—and it doesn't work as 'cool kids in the corner' in the ivory towers of their innovation hubs or future labs. The result of that is often a whole heap of ideas and a lot of fun had by the team, but no real value added for the company and its customers.

Instead, it needs much more than 'just' creativity and a cool environment. It needs freedom and the constant will to keep learning, testing and questioning and hands-on trying out things conceived theoretically—often jointly with end customers and developers. Innovation also requires the operational ability to carry out ideas until they are implemented. To achieve that, you need joined-up thinking and action inside and outside the corporation. Why the corporation? Because it possesses the relevant success factors combined with the necessary critical mass, that is, customers, trust, security and an understanding of the regulations required."

1

In academic research, too, there are major reservations about separate innovation units. Many scientists have already established that the 'innovator's solution' is not a panacea and that large companies should by no means rely solely on separate innovation units in the innovation competition. Wadhwa explains, for example, that Christensen's theory is now completely outdated: 'Disruption is no longer a small field consisting of new technologies or business models that can be solved by a new entity. Innovation is happening all the time, everywhere' (Wadhwa, 2015). This 'continuous disruption' requires the strength of the entire company in order to survive in the battle against new competition from completely different or new industries (Blank, 2014).

Even Clayton Christensen has been trying to steer away from this since, saying: 'Established companies should respond to disruption when it occurs. But they should not overreact by giving up their profitable business' (Schwerdtfeger, 2016).

'Change guru' John Kotter (*Leading Change*) also noted that the 'balance sheet of the two worlds [is] sobering' and instead proposes that companies anchor the search for new opportunities better and process them themselves within the company (Kotter, 2016).

So why do companies continue relying on innovation hubs and similar separate units then? Mostly, because they have no alternative. Corporates only seem to have the choice between customer-centric, disruptive innovations with a small chance of implementation, or incremental innovations with easy implementation, but poor customer centricity and very little potential for disruption. The huge task in innovation management is now to build a bridge between these two extremes.

Summary

Corporates Today: Inefficient Start-Up Thinking in Separate Innovation Units

Corporations try to beat start-ups at their own game. Customer-centric innovations in the company or start-ups from separate innovation units therefore only have a small chance of success.

- Corporations try to solve the innovation dilemma by developing customer-centric innovations like start-ups, using design thinking and lean start-up methods.
- The problem is that these methods usually do not take into account the complex corporate environment so implementation of the ideas usually fails.
- As a supposed 'innovator's solution', innovations are relocated into separate units in order to set up start-ups on greenfields.
- The chances of success of these start-ups are vanishingly small as the company's strengths can no longer be exploited for traction and scaling.
- Both theory and practice show that separate innovation hubs, etc. do not yet provide the solution to successful innovations. There has been no alternative to this so far.

1.3 Corporates Tomorrow: Efficient Innovation with Customer Fit and Traction

The current and future challenge for corporates is that new innovation methods need to close the gap between incremental innovation with a strong focus on implementation in their core business, on the one hand, and disruptive innovation with a weak focus on implementation in start-ups or separate units, on the other. In contrast to the start-up methods currently used, the main task of future innovation methods is to combine new, customer-centric innovation with the existing implementation strengths. Even though the mantra of design thinking—'customer centricity'—is extremely important, this is not enough by itself to achieve significant innovation success. That only happens when customer-centric innovation is also accepted in the market in the long term and generates significant value added for the company. **For a corporate, successful innovation must therefore also achieve excellent traction in addition to customer fit. We call this 'efficient innovation'**. Put simply,

$$\textit{Efficient innovation} = \textit{customer fit} + \textit{traction}$$

One thing is clear. **Unless it has customer fit, it will not work**. Competition is on the rise in an increasingly global market, and companies can simply no longer afford to ignore their customers' needs. Whether we think about energy, finance, telecommunications, transport or logistics, even industries which were previously clear suppliers' markets as a result of strong state regulation and quasi-monopolies now need to not only respond to demand but anticipate it even. In addition, customers have long been accustomed to a high degree of orientation to their needs in other commodity groups, like food, clothing or IT, and simply expect the same today—at home, as well as at work. When Amazon Prime promises 'same-day delivery' and customers can customise their Adidas shoes with their own colours and patterns, it becomes difficult to present customers with waiting times or standardisation. Individualisation, on-demand services and customer experience, these are not just buzzwords. They are trends which are here to stay.

These insights have rightly made customer-centric innovation methods—such as design thinking—great. It has created an awareness about involving the customer right at the start of the innovation process and always keeping them in mind. All too often, development has been carried out internally at first, only to discover that customer and market needs were either nonexistent or completely different.

Starting from this perspective, the probing look by corporates at start-ups is understandable. With start-ups being able to—or even, having to—build their companies around greenfield, customer-centric ideas, they have a very high degree of customer centricity, especially in the early years. This gives the impression that they are much more innovative in contrast to cumbersome corporates. But we now know that this is only *one* part of the equation, because traction (or in start-ups, scaling) is rarely successful (even if such cases are memorable). From the Bain & Company study cited in the previous section, we can even put a precise figure on

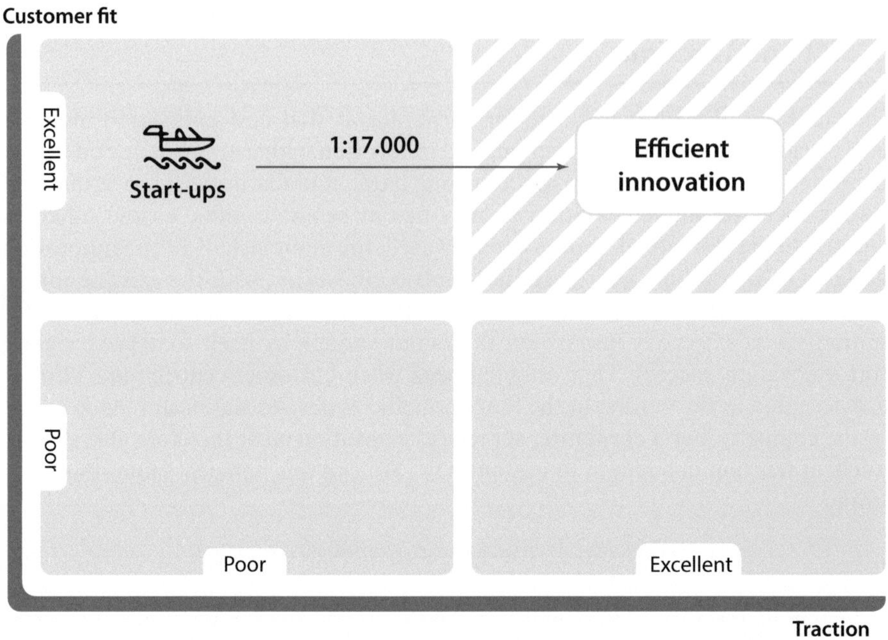

■ **Fig. 1.2** Innovation in start-ups: excellent customer fit, poor traction (author's own figure)

the chances of achieving excellent traction in addition to customer fit, a mere 1:17,000 depending on the target figures (see ■ Fig. 1.2). And the more that companies develop customer-centric innovations on greenfields, the harder these attractive innovations compete for customers, and the more that successful implementation and traction counts.

For corporates, traction is as important a success factor as customer fit. Traction describes the effect of an innovation in the market and hence its implementation success almost. How many people or companies are actually using the innovation? How large is the growth in the market? How much revenue, profit, etc. does the innovation generate for the company and for the economy?

Successful traction requires unique and appropriate resources and skills which normally go beyond those possessed by start-ups or which they can only achieve with a great deal of effort (Kostopoulos, 2002). In management theory, the performance prerequisites for strong growth are described in a resource-based view (RBV). This approach addresses the question of why companies are successful and how they can achieve a competitive advantage in the long run (Kostopoulos, 2002). The general wisdom is that companies need resources which are as valuable, rare or difficult to imitate or replace as possible in the competition, as well as the skills to use and coordinate them (Barney, 1991). It is obvious that these factors can also provide competitive advantages for innovations, and preferably produce an impact over the long run added to excellent growth and correspondingly excellent traction. In contrast to start-ups, established companies already possess core competences which have made their corporate success possible.

Even if these competencies change over time or are expanded or disappear, it is certainly not far-fetched to form the impression that they might be helpful in implementing innovations.

Guest Commentary: Michael Weppler, Executive Vice President of Systems at German Certification Body TÜV Rheinland

"TÜV Rheinland operates in a very complex environment. On the one hand, our customers are moving in a wide variety of markets. On the other hand, the majority of our services depend directly on regulations and legislation which we ourselves have no influence over. At the same time, we have numerous strengths—like our global presence and our expertise in a wide variety of industries. We build on this to develop new solutions and services.

We are therefore particularly interested in innovation methods which can exploit our strengths and lead to innovations which can be actually implemented in our complex corporate environment. Traditional methods do not offer a sufficiently systematic approach to this, though, meaning that ideas often fail due to one restriction or another, or can only be implemented in a small part of our business. But if we can succeed in finding the right lever for overarching innovations, this could deliver a significant value added."

But what exactly distinguishes traction? A closer look at successful corporates shows that such 'traction factors'—that is, those strengths which can be competitive advantages for innovations—tend to be found in the following categories: networks, brand strength, resources, customers and markets, as well as structures and processes (◘ Fig. 1.3) (Anthony, 2012).

1. *Networks:* this term refers to both access to competitors and suppliers as well as to valuable contacts with politics, research and other institutions. These 'partner relationships' make it possible to, for example, implement innovations even in highly regulated markets, to work together on innovations with other companies and universities in open innovations and to complement each other and profit from basic research or counter any criticism in advance. Car manufacturers, for example, benefit in this way from joint research projects. Energy suppliers and financial service providers benefit from links in politics, or large-scale

Network	Brand	Resources	Customers and markets	Structures and processes
Competitors	Visibility	Machines	Contact data	Customer service
Start-ups	Followers	Software	Merchants	Manufacturing
Universities	Campaigns	Buildings	Global presence	Quality assurance
Research institutes	Trust	Branches / stores	Local production	Decision-making clarity
Legislators	Ambassadors	Employees	Recommenders	Professional development
Regulators	Influencers	Expert knowledge	Ambassadors	Approval
Press contacts	Sponsorships	Patents / IP	Testimonials	Purchasing
...	...	...	...	...

◘ **Fig. 1.3** Example of traction factors (author's own figure)

consultations on links at all management levels (Bry, 2014). By contrast, you can see from the examples of Uber and Airbnb how difficult it is to implement an idea without an established political network. Bans in various countries and cities are still putting a stop to their services even today after many years, and even completely preventing the implementation of their innovative business model in some markets.

2. *Brand strength:* brand strength not only describes the visibility which can also be bought by start-ups with the appropriate financial resources. Much more important is trust and tried-and-tested communication as well as the associated convictions of 'gatekeepers'. Gatekeepers may, for example, be doctors, shopkeepers or financial advisors who want to run few risks when recommending products and services and prefer relying on tried-and-tested brands. This is particularly relevant not only for sensitive areas of life, such as finance and healthcare, but also for discriminating categories like luxury goods or travel. Even in 'simple' industries, like entertainment and toys, the advantages of brand strength are evident. With its successful brand, LEGO has been able to build up increasing numbers of new markets, such as films, amusement parks and video games, and now even successfully offers creative workshops for business customers with its LEGO Serious Play Kit.
3. *Resources:* a company's existing resources are certainly the most complex factor for traction. Whether this is expertise, IP, employees, production machines or other physical and virtual goods. Many of them are difficult to obtain even with considerable financial resources. Expertise, in particular, is often anchored within companies in the form of specialised teams of experts and can only be built up by new companies with difficulty. You cannot really master more complex innovations with great potential without resources which you have nurtured over many years. For example, IBM in its 'Smarter Cities' initiative is combining the knowledge it has gained from its numerous IT projects with cities and municipalities with the connectivity services and sensor technologies already available in the company. As an alternative to a 1-billion-dollar tunnel, IBM was able to create a smart, incentivised traffic management system for the city of Stockholm which cut traffic congestion delays by 50% without incurring any construction time and at one-tenth of the cost. In 2015, nearly 10 years after 'Smarter Cities' was established, that business unit contributed approximately USD 10 billion in revenue for IBM through the implementation of complex innovations in various metropolitan areas around the world (Anthony, 2012). These are numbers which current Internet of Things start-ups hardly dare to dream about.
4. *Customers and markets:* in many industries, existing customer relationships and markets are the most relevant success factors. Purely Internet-based offers can still relatively easily be offered globally—but they can also be copied similarly quickly. Physical products and personal services, on the other hand, require a far-reaching infrastructure to ultimately really reach customers. In addition, all of the offers are competing for a limited amount of time, money and customers. A suitable example here is the much-hyped financial start-ups (fintechs). With their automated, software-based investment advice, Betterment, FutureAdvisor

and Wealthfront, for example, are making a name for themselves in the USA. These 'robo-advisor' start-ups have been in the marketplace since 2010 and 2011, respectively. Vanguard, an established financial firm, decided to offer its customers a similar product in 2015 after 2 years of testing. In contrast to start-ups, however, it relied on its core competencies and, for example, used its financial advisors as optional telephone assistants. The company was able to offer the new service to its millions of customers without any major additional expense. By the end of 2015, the company was managing USD 31.3 billion with its robo-advisor—more than those three start-ups put together (Govindarajan, 2017).

5. *Structures and processes:* nowadays these are often the embodiment of innovation barriers in corporates. In reality, they are the secret weapons in the innovation battle. Even if too much bureaucracy or too little flexibility makes innovation difficult, it is worth including these factors. After all, they not only facilitate fast scaling and easy 'ramping up' for rolling out products and services but also high-quality and optimised logistic and organisational processes at the lowest possible cost. It is lengthy and difficult building up these structures and processes in new companies. It is no coincidence that many of the highly praised crowdfunding products never make it into mass production. That is because the devil lies in the detail. The famous Coolest Cooler—a record-breaking project with USD 13 million received in crowdfunding—was only delivered to a proportion of its investors after many delays. The company was simply not well enough prepared for mass production and had no financial reserves and no scalable structures and processes to serve tens of thousands of customers (News, 2016). Even, Pebble, one of the first smartwatch companies, was sold in 2016, significantly below its value because of its large debts resulting from unprofessional mass production (Wikipedia, 2017). And even a quick look at Tesla reveals the scaling problems of many start-ups. The company (felt like it) had a lead of many years over the automotive companies which were slowly waking up to reality. And yet, now that other companies have flipped the switch, Tesla is in permanent danger of becoming a niche supplier. As if at the push of a button, established manufacturers have announced numerous new electric vehicles and will probably deliver them in significantly greater quantities than Tesla over the next few years. Within 6 months, Volkswagen decided to build its own battery factory and switched a complete plant over to electric vehicles—structures and processes which Elon Musk had to fight for over many years to find the money needed. And in view of this, Tesla, with its focus on building up processes and physical resources, is already an exceptional case which at least has the opportunity to become profitable at some point. However, established automotive firms can build millions of high-quality cars quickly and 'only' need to supplement the missing technologies to be able to roll out their own innovations on the new market.

As these examples show, corporates hold all of the advantages in terms of traction. Unlike start-ups, they already possess networks, brand strength, resources

1

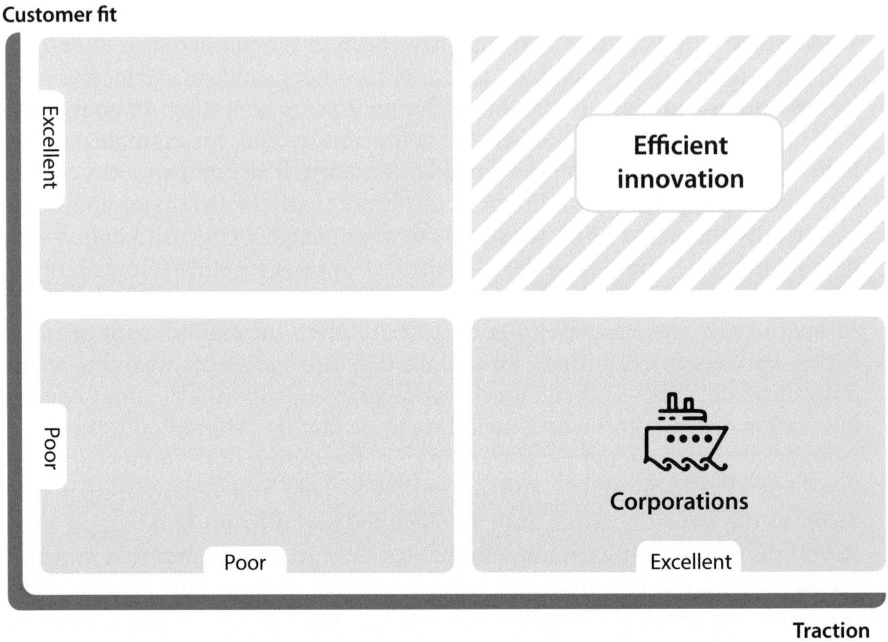

Fig. 1.4 Innovation in large companies: poor customer fit, excellent traction (author's own figure)

and customer and market access as well as optimised structures and processes which can be exploited for innovations. They therefore possess the maximum number of success factors for excellent traction (see Fig. 1.4).

The reply which, for example, the managing director of UPS Germany, Frank Sportolari, gave to the question of whether UPS feels threatened by the wide range of logistics start-ups was in this vein. 'That is not a threat for us. We're in a highly competitive market. What we offer is not so easy to replicate, a global system of airlines and ground networks' (Penke, 2017).

Why are established companies still under threat from disruptive start-ups? Just like UPS, most established companies ultimately know what their core competencies are and also that these are precisely their competitive advantages.

The problem with this is that **companies do not manage to use these strengths to establish disruptive innovations either and thus achieve excellent customer fit**. According to Christensen, it is simply impossible even to develop disruptive innovations inside the company (Christensen, 1997). The above traction factors form the company's brownfields which are hence diametrically opposed to greenfields where customer-centric ideas and disruptive innovations are intended to be developed using today's methods.

But it is precisely this brownfield—the package of existing resources plus the skills to use them productively—which also represents the best opportunity for corporates to win the innovation battle against disruptive start-ups in the long term. It is really incomprehensible then that it is precisely these success factors with

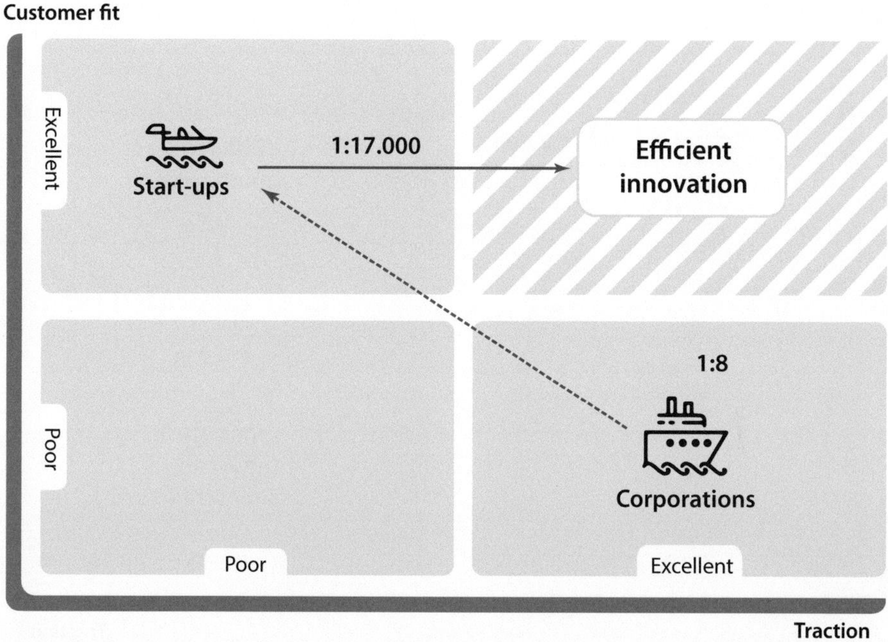

Fig. 1.5 Detour via outsourcing innovation to separate units, such as innovation hubs (author's own figure)

start-up methods and in innovation hubs which are largely ignored, making the chances of success just as poor here as they are with start-ups (see Fig. 1.5). We believe this is exactly the right place to start.

To win the innovation battle against disruptive start-ups, corporates must learn to combine innovation with their existing implementation strengths, and do so before start-ups learn to develop their own implementation strengths (Viki, 2017). If it is possible to develop customer-centric innovations by building on the company's existing strengths, then the traction of the core business can also be exploited to implement these innovations. **Such 'efficient innovation' is as close to the core business as possible and as disruptive as it needs to be** to exploit the strengths of the core business while also ensuring the necessary customer fit.

This efficient innovation should not be confused with the efficiency innovation described by Christensen. That applies only to incremental improvements, or even efficiency gains. Efficient innovation instead helps to make a direct link between traction factors and customer fit. It is then no longer necessary to make a 'detour' via developing greenfield start-ups, so the success of the innovation can be achieved significantly faster and with less risk.

To this end, though, the company's strengths and implementation criteria must already have been considered during the conception phase. Just as a grandmaster manages to think many moves ahead in chess, the corporate factors which are key for implementation and success must be taken into account before

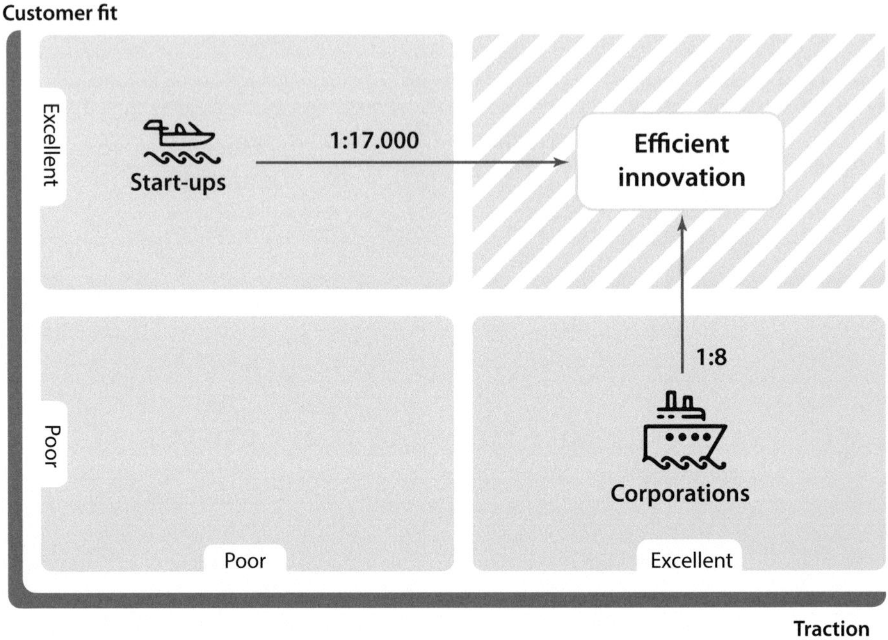

Fig. 1.6 Efficient innovation: excellent customer fit, excellent traction (author's own figure)

the idea is even born—ensuring in this way that disruptive ideas also fit the company.

The advantage is that if this succeeds, corporates will be holding all the trump cards in their hand in terms of driving innovation (Zwilling, 2011). According to the management consulting firm Bain & Company, the chances of a successful new market ultimately increase to 1:8 when the strengths of the core business can be exploited (Zook, 2016). In contrast to the former 1:500 or 1:17,000 chance for start-ups, this represents a clear advantage for such success (see Fig. 1.6).

So the great challenge is to conceive innovations which ensure customer fit *and* traction. Traditional innovation methods concentrate primarily on incremental innovation (they use *traction*) and ignore customer fit. Current methods conversely focus on *customer fit* and prevent *traction* through their greenfield approach. And so, because of a lack of alternatives, incremental innovations continue to be developed in the core business, and disruptive innovations developed in separate innovation hubs, etc. In view of the small chances of success, this cannot represent a long-term solution though. Even the 'inventor' of separate innovation units, Clayton Christensen, notes that this is only a 'backup plan for companies', because 'we have not yet learned how to achieve entrepreneurship internally' (Schwertfeger, 2020).

Summary

Corporates Tomorrow: Efficient Innovation with Customer Fit and Traction

The innovation success of corporates depends on their ability to develop efficient innovations with customer fit and traction. Like this, the company's strengths can be exploited for customer-centric innovations.

- The innovation dilemma is solved successfully by efficient innovations with customer fit *and* traction.
- Start-ups possess excellent customer fit, but poor traction.
- Corporations already possess the best prerequisites for excellent traction due to their existing strengths (e.g. networks, brands, resources, customers, structures).
- Current innovation methods are unable to sufficiently take into account the company's strengths when developing disruptive or customer-centric innovations.
- The dilemma of how to include both the customer's *and* the company's perspective in developing efficient innovations can only be solved by a new innovation methodology.

1.4 Efficient Innovation: From Theory to Practice

Efficient innovations offer corporates the opportunity to win the battle against disruptive start-ups in the long term. They allow companies to exploit the strengths of their core business in new markets or in the face of new threats in existing markets (traction) while at the same time ensuring the necessary degree of disruption (customer fit). Efficient innovation is relevant to any company which wants or needs to take part in the innovation battle, but which also already has an established, successful core business (Charitou & Markides, 2002). Companies, such as General Motors, Nokia, Blackberry, Kodak or Blockbuster, could certainly attest to the need for this. These companies show that disruption has been arriving continuously in every industry for many years and it is therefore a case of keeping the core business profitable while developing new business opportunities (Birkinshaw & Gibson, 2004).

But the challenge lies in the 'how'. **Existing innovation methods are not adequate for working in this area of tension between the core business and disruptive innovation and for systematically developing efficient innovations.** A general rethink is necessary to exploit the core business as an advantage over start-ups (instead of ignoring it as an obstacle) and thus win the battle against disruptive start-ups in the long term (see ◘ Fig. 1.7).

In summary, efficient innovations therefore possess the following basic characteristics:

- They either bring a new technology into an existing business model or a new business model into an existing core business, and/or they combine a new technology with a new business model based on the core business.
- They fit into the restrictions of the core business in order to exploit its resources and skills (traction).

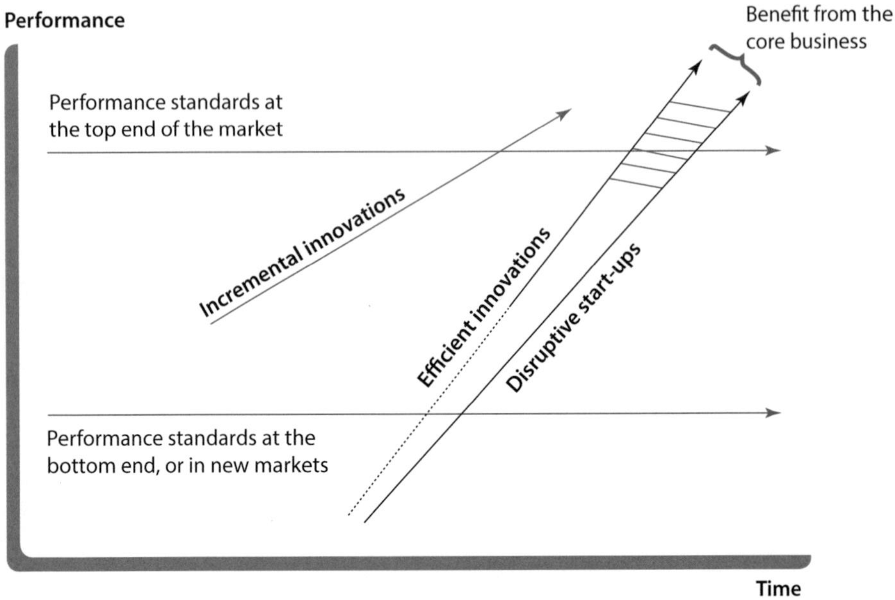

Fig. 1.7 Efficient vs disruptive innovation. (Adapted: Sauberschwarz & Weiss 2017)

- They include customer focus so that they can meet the required degree of disruption (customer fit).
- They are as close to the core business as possible and as disruptive as they need to be to meet the above requirements.

Some selected examples of efficient innovation in large enterprises are able to illustrate these characteristics nicely:

Apple's App Store Apple's App Store has disrupted the market for mobile phones and software applications and provided the best possible customer fit with hundreds of thousands of new apps and opportunities. The innovation is consequently *as disruptive as it needs to be*. At the same time, it relies on the existing iPhone hardware (and its customers) and limits the use of the apps to its Apple ecosystem. In this way, the innovation is also *as close as possible to the core business* while at the same time shielding it from disruption. This is the world largest app store today, and Apple is the most profitable smartphone manufacturer. This innovation would hardly have been possible for a start-up, because it required access to thousands of app developers which Apple already had from its core business and was able to expand further.

Amazon Kindle As a company which was already established, Amazon created a new market for e-books with its Kindle. This digitised the reading process while still providing the most natural reading experience possible using electronic ink. It was therefore *as disruptive as it needed to be* and prioritised customer needs. At the same time, the innovation relied on Amazon's access to publishers and content as well as its existing distribution platform and access to millions of readers, thus enabling Amazon to continue selling books in the digital age. This means that the innovation was *as close as possible to the core business* which made Amazon the driver of innovation in the e-book market. A start-up, on the other hand, would have had to build up contacts with publishers and convince them about e-books, produce the devices themselves (or have them produced) while at the same time communicating to readers that books now have a battery status indicator. They would probably have failed.

Many other examples can be used to illustrate the concept and the success of efficient innovation. With its African M-Pesa digital payment system, *Vodafone* was able to build up a completely new market with a new target group, building on the existing merchant and communications network gained from its SIM card core business. *Amazon* secured its core business which needed a strong IT infrastructure and, at the same time, made the resources available for others. The service now contributes 67% to its annual profits. Less well known though are companies, like *Hilti* or *Kärcher*, which have made entirely new business models possible through sensors in their equipment and digital fleet management (such as automated equipment leasing) based on their core business of equipment manufacture.

Management theory, too, has already dealt extensively with the balance between the core business and the disruptive innovation. **The phenomenon is usually dealt with here under the terms 'dualism' and 'ambidexterity'.** By definition, it concerns 'functioning efficiently today while at the same time, innovating successfully for the future' (Paap & Katz, 2004b). Birkinshaw & Gibson (2004) describe the problem as follows, pointing out that in recent years managers have recognised how important it is to react agilely to new opportunities and market changes although often also forgetting to take the core business 'with them'. Their research shows that successful companies are 'not only agile, innovative and proactive, but they can also exploit the strengths of their proprietary resources, roll out new business models quickly and minimise costs in existing processes'. Besides agility (or exploration) for innovations, they thus also possess the ability of alignment (or exploitation), i.e. a sense of how activities must be coordinated to achieve a positive value added in the core business (see ◘ Fig. 1.8).

For a long-term positive growth, we need to balance these two factors. If we succeed, we will have created a *more ambidextrous organisation*. Normally though, companies are either efficient and achieve large profits through optimisation ('success trap') or they are innovative and achieve large revenues in new markets with small or negative margins ('failure trap').

Sarkees & Hulland (2009) show in their study that companies which are able to link efficiency (profitable core business) and innovation (experimental new business) have clear advantages over their competitors. They can achieve greater revenues, profits and customer satisfaction plus a larger number of new product launches.

The need for this linking of the core business and radical innovation, i.e. efficient innovation, has also been identified in various studies. With Bain's research, (Zook, 2016) not only puts the chances for innovations that succeed in exploiting the strengths of the core business at 1:8. In his book, *Moving Beyond the Core*, he also describes that this tactic should be implemented in 'adjacency moves' in order

1

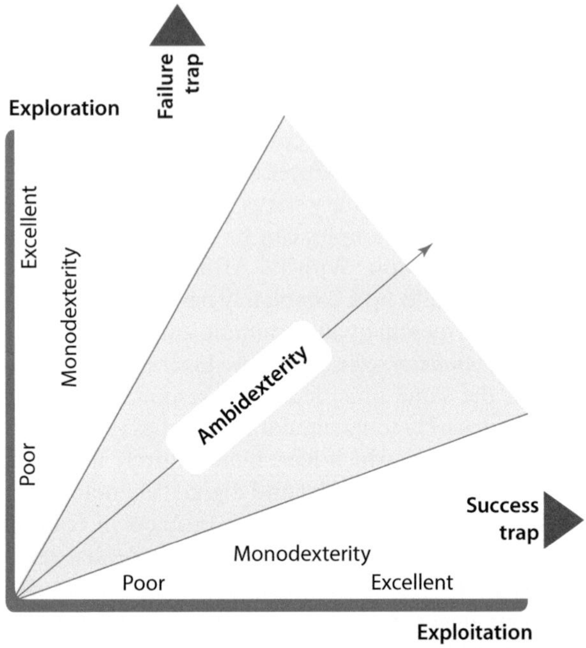

Fig. 1.8 Ambidexterity. (Adapted: Güttel et al. 2011)

to identify and exploit growth areas adjacent to the core business. However, these must always be built on a strong foundation, the core business, to be precise (Zook, 2004). Greenfield start-ups would fizzle out accordingly and would not have a significant effect on the overall company. Innovation researcher and consultant (Mootee, 2011) also established in his study of strategic innovations that 'innovation [is] only strategically [relevant] when all related activities are geared towards revitalising the core business or linking the core business with future business opportunities'. Other innovation paths would be 'very likely lead to failure'. Furthermore, researcher (Kostopoulos, 2002) argues that a company's capacity for innovation depends crucially on its resources and skills. Resources must be recombined with the existing skills and, if necessary, changed to create new competitive advantages, and thus innovations.

In extreme cases, efficient innovations can even replace this in the long term through a suitable link to the core business. This is the way that Netflix (as an 'established start-up') exploited its existing customer base and film studio contacts obtained from its DVD rental business to expand its streaming business. IBM innovated into the services sector based on its large number of business customers and its expertise in the IT sector and eventually mostly replaced its hardware business with IT services. This only works though, because the new services are, in fact, on the one hand, geared to trends and future customer needs (on-demand streaming, IT outsourcing), while, on the other, they were developed on the basis of the current strengths of the core business (subscribers and content or IT expertise and business customer contacts) (Allen et al., 2017). Only efficient innovations can achieve an effect like this—and not small start-up speedboats intended to develop completely new greenfield markets.

These examples show that **a tanker can be faster than a speedboat**. As M. H. Meyer also described in his article 'Disruptive Innovation: But Is It?', corporates must exploit and expand the strengths of their core business and transfer them to new applications, markets and target groups using customer-centric innovations (King & Baatartogtokh, 2015). This is how established companies can manage the interaction between disruptive innovation and gaining the edge over new competitors on the strength of their existing resources, customers and skills (Berglund et al., 2014). Instead of being a sluggish tanker overtaken by a speedboat, this efficient innovation gives tankers new jet propellers which they can use to overtake speedboats.

An example taken from General Electric (GE) also shows how this can succeed. Innovation guru, (Govindarajan, 2016), Professor at the Tuck School of Business at Dartmouth College, describes this as follows: although the company is developing new skills 'separately' for their company with its GE digital unit, it has been closely linked to the core business and can thus have a very considerable impact. Suitable big data analytics services can be developed for customers with the data gathered from thousands of sensors. If, on the basis of such analytics services, a train operator can increase its average speed by 1 mile an hour, this can lead to an increase in annual profits of USD 250 million for the company. Govindarajan therefore concludes that corporates possess all of 'the assets, resources and skills to build sources of innovation'. He maintains that, in the best scenario, start-ups are equipped with a lot of venture capital, but that is still far less than what a corporation would have to offer.

Even a study of innovation hubs paradoxically shows the sense in linking the core business with the innovation. O'Hare (2008) establishes that innovation hubs are more successful the closer they are to the core business—even though they were actually created for the opposite reason. Innovation hubs which are closely linked to the core business are more aligned to the strategy of the company as a whole and have fewer problems actually commercialising their ideas, that is, achieving traction. The basic idea of an innovation hub being as separate as possible now becomes absurd as a result.

Consequently, the challenge remains the systematic development of efficient innovations. Even with the above best practices, a glance at the innovation landscape reveals the enormous challenge of achieving this balance between an efficient core business and a disruptive innovation on a long-term and systematic basis.

If companies concentrate too much on alignment or on their core business, they run the risk of missing out on innovations and becoming disrupted. Yet if they concentrate too much on disruptive innovations, the advantages of the core business are wasted and, under some circumstances, put at risk.

So, what should they do? The solutions to this problem described in theory currently are similar to Christensen's approach. Employees work in separate units or independently either for the core business *or* for innovations. In the first scenario, *structural ambidexterity*, the separate units are anchored in the organisation. The decision here comes down hierarchically from top management which is trying to find the balance between *agility* (the exploration of new opportunities) and *alignment* (the exhaustion of existing activities). In the second scenario, *contextual ambidexterity*, this is, in principle, assigned to individual employees. Everyone in the company is encouraged to spend their time independently between activities for agility or innovation and aligning or improving the core business. In this scenario, decisions about the balance of activities are always made at grassroots level as needed with top management only creating the underlying conditions for it. Employees must therefore also possess the general skills to be able to reproduce the various requirements of agility and alignment (Birkinshaw & Gibson, 2014).

All of these approaches have the same problem though. They see the balance as an 'either/or'. *Either* disruptive innovations are developed, *or* the core business is being managed and improved (even if this happens at the same time, preferably), without the two being clearly connected. According to the concept of efficient innovation and the logic of positive case studies, both must be combined in the innovation process in order to combine it into a solution and thus really create new competitive advantages.

The systematic development of such efficient innovation therefore requires processual ambidexterity. In this process, top management can set the strategy, and employees can then develop efficient innovations within a set process which take into account the strengths and restrictions of the core business as well as the requirements of the (future) market, thus ensuring customer centricity. Such processual ambidexterity equates to the definition of 'dynamic capabilities' noted by Teece et al. (1997): *clear skills, process steps, procedures, organisational structures and decision-making rules*.

These dynamic capabilities would enable an organisation to identify threats and opportunities and to address them by configuring and reconfiguring organisational resources and competencies. If this is made possible, we can achieve traction as well as customer fit for successful, efficient innovation.

Building up the skills required for efficient innovation described above is a complex undertaking. Innovations which are geared to both customer needs and future trends and which also exploit the strengths of existing resources and processes by taking these into account unfortunately do not occur as the result of a flash of genius, but on the strength of sheer hard work. The greenfield ideas needed cannot therefore occur randomly, but must be planned so that they can become a successful innovation. Fortunately, this is possible, because ideas do not occur randomly, but follow a—usually subconscious—development process. If we can unlock this, it can be institutionalised, managed and focused to develop ideas which provide an excellent fit.

If ideas do not occur randomly, they can be developed systematically. In his book (and TED Talk) *Where Good Ideas Come From*, American author (Johnson, 2010) describes the story of the sudden flash of genius as a myth which hardly ever occurs in reality. Instead, it is always a transparent path which leads to an idea and an innovation. Darwin, for example, had been collecting all of the information for his theory of evolution for a long time before he 'suddenly' thought of it. On this basis, Johnson states that the best path to an idea cannot therefore be to challenge the 'flash of genius' or to retreat to a mountain hut to be creative or even philosophise about blue-sky and out-of-the-box thinking. Instead, the basis for new opportunities must be systematically expanded using as much information and inspiration as possible. If this information and inspiration is set in a focused way in advance, the idea-finding process (ideation) can be steered to find the most disruptive ideas within the implementable framework.

We have collected together all of these and many other requirements over the years in our 5C process and systematised them for efficient innovations. This methodology thus exactly illustrates the skills and methods required to enable efficient innovations to be developed, and is explained in detail in the following sections. We will subsequently show how such a process can be implemented in a large company specifically.

Summary

Efficient Innovation: From Theory to Practice

Balancing between today's core business with tomorrow's opportunities (ambidexterity) using the 5C process for efficient innovations provides the key for corporates in the innovation battle.

- Corporates can win the innovation battle with efficient innovations.
- Efficient innovations link the existing core business with future customer needs by staying as close to the core business as possible and as disruptive as necessary.
- The balance between exploiting today's successful core business and researching future opportunities is termed ambidexterity.
- When ambidexterity succeeds, corporations have a significantly better chance of success with innovations than start-ups.
- Processual ambidexterity in the innovation process links the existing business with future opportunities and makes efficient innovations possible.
- The systematic 5C process makes procedural ambidexterity possible by taking the customer as well as the company into account throughout.

Additional material can be downloaded by visiting ▸ www.the-corporates-strike-back.com.

References

Allen, J., Root, J., Schwedel, A. (2017). *The firm of the future*, Bain & Company, January 17, 2017, Online.

Anthony, S. (2012). The new corporate garage. *Harvard Business Review*, September 2012 Issue.

Barney, J. (1991). Firm resources and sustained competitive advantage. *Journal of Management, 17*(1), 99–120.

Beige, O. (2017). Eine kurze Geschichte der Innovation, Gründerszene, 31. January 2017, Online.

Berengian, A. (2017). It's time to ditch your innovation lab, VentureBeat, March 22, 2017, Online.

Berglund, H., Magnusson, M., & Sandström, C. (2014). Symmetric assumptions in the theory of disruptive innovation. *Creativity and Innovation Management, 23*(4), 472–483.

Birkinshaw, J., & Gibson, C. (2004). *Building ambidexterity into an organization*, Researchgate, June 2004.

Birkinshaw, J., & Gibson, C. (2014). *Building ambidexterity into an organization*, Researchgate, June 2014.

Blank, S. (2014). Why corporate skunk works need to die, Forbes.com, November 10, 2014, Online.

Bry, N. (2014). Open innovation is the new normal, December 2014, Online: https://nbry.wordpress.com/2015/12/14/open-innovation-is-the-new-normal-with-hannes-erler-at-swarovski/

Charitou, C. D., & Markides, C. (2002). Responses to disruptive strategic innovation. *MIT Sloan Management Review, 44*(2), 55–64.

Christensen, C. M. (1997). The Innovator's dilemma: When new technologies cause great firms to fail. *Harvard Business School Press.*

Christensen, C. M. (2013). The innovators solution. *Harvard Business Review Press*, November 2013 (Revised).

Dr. Gackstatter, S. (2015). PWC breakthrough innovation study, PWC, January 2015, Online.

Gans, J. (2016). Keep calm and manage disruption, MIT Sloan management Review, 57, 3, 2016, p. 83 ff.

George, P. (2016). The scary truth about Corporate Survival. *Harvard Business Review*, December 2016 Issue.

Gothelb, J. (2017). Intrapreneurship is a lie, Medium.com, March 8, 2017, Online.

Govindarajan, V. (2016). Stop saying big companies can't innovate, *Harvard Business Review*, June 6, 2016, Online.

Govindarajan, V. (2017). Strategy when creative destruction accelerates, Tuck School of Business Working Paper No. 2836135, September 2016.

Adapted from: Güttel, W. H. et al. (2011). Different ambidextrous learning architectures and the role of HRM systems, Researchgate, January 2011.

Hoffmann, A. (2017). Was hat der Lufthansa Innovation Hub in zwei Jahren erreicht?, Gründerszene, January 25, 2017, Online.

Iansiti, M., McFarlan, F. W., & Westerman, G. (2003). Leveraging the incumbent's advantage. *MIT Sloan Management Review, 44*(4), 58–65.

Johnson, S. (2010). Eureka moments are very, very rare, Guardian, 19. Oktober 2010, Online.

King, A. A., & Baatartogtokh, B. (2015). How useful is the theory of disruptive innovation? *MIT Sloan Management Review, 57*(1), 77.

Kleske, J. (2016). Warum die Tempel der Digitalisierung oft scheitern, Whitepaper, 10/ 2016.

Kohler, T. (2016). Corporate accelerators: Building bridges between corporations and Start-ups. *Business Horizons, 59*(3), 347–357.

Kostopoulos, K. C. (2002). The resource – Based view of the firm and innovation: Identification of critical linkages, European Academy of Management Conference, Stockholm, Sweden, 2002.

Kotter, J. (2016). Ein völlig neues Spiel, Haufe Online, June 23, 2016, Online.

KPMG. (2016). Now or never, global CEO outlook, KPMG, 2016, Online.

Kreimeier, N. (2017). Deutschlands beste Digilabs, June 22, 2017, Capital Magazin.

Meck, G., & Weiguny, B. (2015). Disruption. *Baby, Disruption, Frankfurter Allgemeine, Online, December, 27*, 2015.

Mootee, I. (2011). Strategic innovation and the fuzzy front end, Ivey Business Journal, March/April 2011, Online.

Moules, J. (2016). Start-ups struggle to nurture rapid growth, report warns, Financial Times, April 25, 2016, Online.

News, F. (2016). The coolest cooler fails to deliver, backers call foul play, Fox News Online, April 19, 2016.

O'Hare, J. (2008). Innovation hubs: Why do these innovation superstars often die young?, DS 48: Proceedings DESIGN 2008, the 10th international design conference, Dubrovnik, Croatia.

Paap, J., & Katz, R. (2004a). Anticipating disruptive innovation. *Research-Technology Management, 47*(5), 13–22.

Paap, J., & Katz, R. (2004b). Anticipating disruptive innovation. *Research-Technology Management, 47*(5), 13–22; Markides (2013): Business Model Innovation: What can the ambidexterity literature teach us? *The Academy of Management Perspectives, 27*(4), 313–323.

Penke, M. (2017). Uber ist keine neue Idee, Gründerszene, March 23, 2017, Online.

Rettig, D. (2017a). Tod durch Digitalisierung: So sichern Unternehmen Ihr Überleben, Wirtschaftswoche, 01/ 2017.

Rettig, D. (2017b). Tod durch Digitalisierung, Wirtschaftswoche, January 25, 2017.

Eric Ries (2011): The lean start-up. *Crown Business*, September 2011.
Sarkees, M., & Hulland, J. (2009). Innovation and efficiency: Is it possible to have it all. *Business Horizons, 52*(1), 45–55.
Adapted from Sauberschwarz, L. & Weiss, L. (2017). How corporates can win the race against disruptive start-ups. In C. Linnhoff-Popien, R. Schneider, & M. Zaddach (Eds.), *Digital marketplaces unleashed.* Springer.
Schumpeter, J. (2006). Theorie der wirtschaftlichen Entwicklung, Duncker & Humblot, 2006 (Reprint of 1st edition).
Schwerdtfeger, B. (December 7, 2016). Innovations management: Christensen über disruptive innovation, Haufe Online, , Online.
Schwertfeger, B. (2020). Management-Experte Clayton Christensen ist verstorben, Haufe, Online, January 24, 2020.
Spector, L. (2016). The IBM personal computer's 25th anniversary, PC World, August 11, 2016, Online; Tom Foremski (2006): IBM researchers predicted PC disruption, ZDNET, July 31, 2006, Online.
Surowiecki, J. (2016). Essay: Im Hightech-Bereich gewinnt Goliath. *Technology Review*, December 28, 2016, Online.
Teece et al. (1997) In: O'Reilly/Tushman (2008) Ambidexterity as a dynamic capability: Resolving the innovator's dilemma. *Research in Organizational Behavior Journal*, *28*, 185–206.
Viki, T. (2017). Large companies will be the biggest beneficiaries of the lean start-up movement, Forbes, February 22, 2017.
Wadhwa, W. (2015). What the legendary Clayton Christensen gets wrong about Uber, Tesla and disruptive innovation, Washington Post, November 23, 2015, Online.
Wikipedia. (2017). Pebble (Smartwatch), Online: https://de.wikipedia.org/wiki/ Pebble_(Smartwatch).
Wolfangel, E. (2016). Hundert Ideen, damit eine fliegt, Zeit Online, December 1, 2016.
Zook, C. (2004). Moving beyond the core. *Harvard Business Review Press*.
Zook, C. (2016). When large companies are better at entrepreneurship than start-ups. *Harvard Business Review Online*, December 27, 2016.
Zwilling, M. (2011). Innovation is about execution, despite the myths, Forbes, October 24, 2011, Online.

Efficient Innovation with the 5C Process

Contents

L. Sauberschwarz, L. Weiss, *The Corporates Strike Back*,
https://doi.org/10.1007/978-3-030-79114-8_2

Hardly any company will still deny that innovation is a key topic strategically. In an innovation survey of 500 US companies conducted by (Accenture, 2015), 84% of top managers agreed that their long-term success depends on innovation. **Innovation has hence become one of the most important factors strategically for the future of companies**—and one of its greatest challenges as we have already described at length in the first section.

Successful or 'efficient' innovation requires two factors to be combined which cannot be achieved satisfactorily using the current approaches to innovation. These are *customer fit* and *traction*. On the contrary, the better the customer fit, the poorer the traction and vice versa.

Still, it is possible to combine customer fit and traction—using the 5C process (*Configuration, Customisation, Compilation, Construction and Conversion*) for efficient innovation. The following sections are intended to provide a detailed examination of the individual steps of our tried-and-tested 5C process, delivering fresh approaches and a new impetus for handling innovation successfully in your own company. Before we do so, we should explain briefly why companies are not capable of efficient innovation using the current innovation approaches. And why the current strategies of large companies will not solve this either.

The direct path to efficient innovation usually remains closed to companies when applying the current approaches to innovation. As can be seen in ◘ Fig. 2.1, the simplest (and most promising) way for a corporate to achieve efficient innovation is straight up. This means that when established companies manage to develop innovations where they are, in fact, building on their existing strengths from the core business (excellent traction) but also optimally satisfying the needs of their

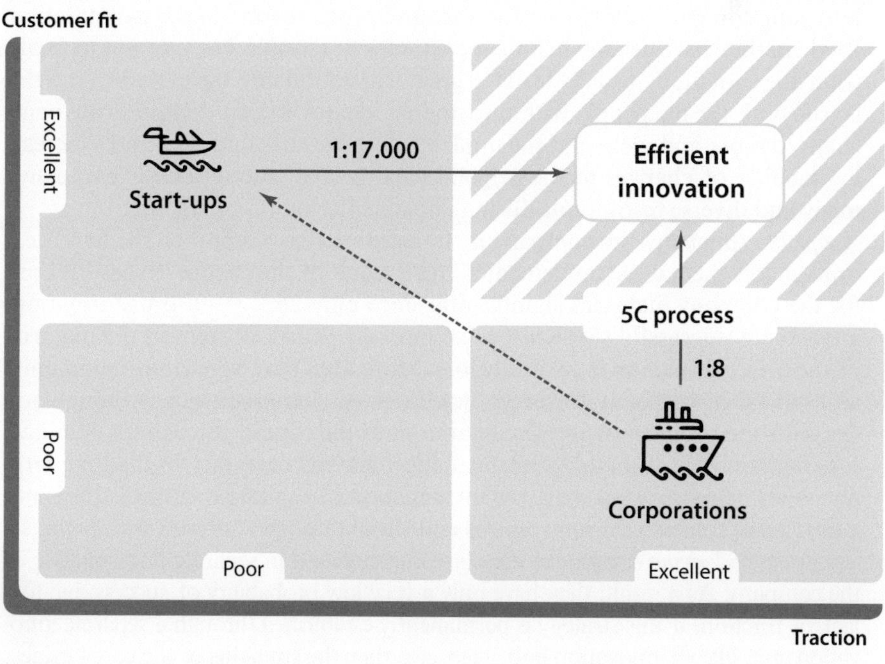

◘ **Fig. 2.1** 5C process as a direct path to efficient innovation. (Author's own figure)

customers (excellent customer fit), the chances of achieving efficient innovation—i.e. achieving a significant value added for the company (see ▶ Sect. 1.3)—are greatest.

Yet **conventional approaches to innovation avoid this way**. If innovation is achieved in an area with excellent traction through, e.g. idea management, stage-gate processes or research departments, this normally results in incremental innovations, i.e. evolutionary improvements to existing offers. Despite or even because of the ongoing improvements, these always run the risk that they will no longer satisfy current and future customer needs at all and will ignore new ways of satisfying them. Thus, the customer fit is continually worsening despite the continuous improvements, because development is occurring 'over the heads of the customer'. Companies run the exact same risk which (Christensen, 1997) described that they will be overtaken at some point by companies with new innovative offers with a better customer fit (see ▶ Sect. 1.2).

If, on the other hand, customer-centric innovation methods, such as design thinking or lean start-up, are used to innovate in an area with excellent customer fit, this can only occur on a greenfield. Implementation in the company's brownfield is similarly problematic as is, consequently, the innovation traction too. That is because these methods do not take sufficient account of the company's traction space or implementation restrictions. Ultimately, the focus should be on the customer's needs (see ▶ Sect. 1.2).

To solve this 'innovation dilemma' which occurs when using existing innovation approaches, companies currently usually use one of the following three approaches to a solution:

1. *Adapt the ideas:* ideas are adapted during their implementation until they fit into your company's existing structures and processes and hence gain traction. By then, they have usually lost their customer fit though. The attempt to 'make what does not fit, fit' usually leads to great frustration into the bargain. And this is true both for the people with the original ideas who find that these are being changed more and more and the implementers who are forced to make increasing number of changes to the original idea to take account of the company's many and diverse restrictions during implementation (Gibbins, 2015).
2. *Adapt the company:* the company is 'transformed' to adapt it to the new ideas or to enable them to be implemented. As a result of the change, the overall risk for the company increases significantly since only 26% of all transformations are actually successful (McKinsey & Company, 2015). Moreover, the majority of the original traction is generally lost. More than that, you cannot reorganise an established company for every new idea. As a consequence, although you can shift the problem of implementation into the future, you cannot eliminate it permanently. Although a transformation may be necessary in the long term due to strategic decisions (e.g. the introduction of digital processes), this is not a long-term solution for innovations and should not be confused with being so.
3. *Adapt the underlying conditions:* ideas are implemented in separate units outside of the company. As a result, they have only a very low probability of success due to a lack of traction. If this strategy is permanently established through a separate innovation unit, like an innovation hub, a lab, etc., then the strengths of the core business will also be ignored in the long run. So these separate units need to hold their own in

open competition with other start-ups. Most of these units either fail or they fail to achieve the required value added for corporates, however (see ► Sect. 1.3).

Therefore, none of the current solution strategies are suitable for systematically developing efficient innovations with customer fit *and* traction. Of course, an idea may randomly achieve customer fit *and* traction straight away. But what is the probability of that happening? Not large enough for companies to rely on this random event. The aim should instead be to use an innovation approach, whereby both the company's perspective in terms of ensuring traction and the customer's perspective in terms of customer fit are taken into account in equal measure throughout the entire innovation process. If this occurs, it achieves the required processual ambidexterity, enabling the large company to innovate *as closely as possible to the core business* and *as disruptively as it needs to for the customer* (see ► Sect. 1.4). The company is then equipped to produce successful or efficient innovations systematically.

The classical innovation process is unsuitable for developing efficient innovations. This applies both to the 'traditional' variant, which particularly works from the company perspective, and to the adaptation of this variant. This is often used today for iterative, 'customer-centric' innovation where ideas are primarily derived from the perspective of the customer rather than that of the company.

The traditional innovation process normally begins when there is either a problem or an opportunity. Depending on the process variant, it then follows a linear (traditional) or an iterative (customer-centric) path, although the building blocks remain similar (Fichter, 2005). That is why it is sufficient for us to consider the linear process here. The individual building blocks differ in their detail, but are fundamentally the following:

1. *Problem*: in customer-centric innovation, the problem or opportunity (usually within a broad spectrum of opportunities) arises either from specific customer needs/requests or from more general consumer trends ('pull'). In company-orientated innovation, on the other hand, the starting point ('push') is new market opportunities, results from research and development or new technologies and processes. These two perspectives are not normally combined at this point so that the greatest potential to be gained can be identified from the perspective of the company *and* the customer.
2. *Ideas*: to solve the customer's problem or to exploit the company's opportunity, creative methods are used to generate as many ideas as possible or are gathered, e.g. from employees or crowdsourced from outside the company. The ideas are therefore always based on *either* the customer's *or* the company's perspective and are derived from the problem in question. On top of that, individual ideas are already being developed iteratively during this phase and tested with the customer, which further strengthens the customer's perspective, but ignores the company's traction.
3. *Assessment*: the ideas generated are assessed (after iteration with the customer) according to particular corporate and market criteria. Thus, a chance would exist here to consider both customer fit and traction. But the problem is that due to the previous focus either just on the customer *or* on the company, it is now a purely random event whether, and the extent to which, the best ideas for the customer also fit the requirements of the company or vice versa. Often the innovation pro-

cess also begins directly with an employee's idea so that no further selection really takes place. Instead, the idea moves straight to the subsequent implementation.
4. *Implementation*: selected ideas are developed (if all goes well) and implemented where possible. Implementation can take place inside or outside of the company. Customer-centric ideas often fail here (or have to be changed considerably) since implementation is now heavily dependent on the company's requirements which have not been taken into account. On the other hand, ideas driven by the company have lower chances to survive in the market (or do not disrupt it), because they lack a strong customer fit.
5. *Innovation*: if the idea has been implemented and launched in the market, it is now an innovation. As outlined in the previous section, only a very few ideas achieve this, because they either fail due to the company's restrictions in their implementation or because they lack relevance for the customer.

So with the traditional (or customer-centric) innovation process used currently, it hardly seems possible to develop innovations which have *both* an excellent customer fit *and* excellent traction, because this requires processual ambidexterity, i.e. simultaneous consideration of the customer's *and* the company's perspective from the outset.

The 5C process ensures this processual ambidexterity (see ▶ Sect. 1.4) and thus enables the systematic development of efficient innovations with an excellent customer fit *and* excellent traction. The 5C process takes you in five successive steps from the company's objectives to efficient innovation (see ◘ Fig. 2.2). By its very nature, in combining the customer's and the company's perspective throughout all five of the steps, the 5C process breaks with some of the habits derived from the familiar approaches to innovation. For this reason, we can obtain a more precise understanding of each individual step, and it is also important to consider the mindset required as well as the relevant methodology and tools. **The five steps (and mind-sets) of the 5C process are as follows**:

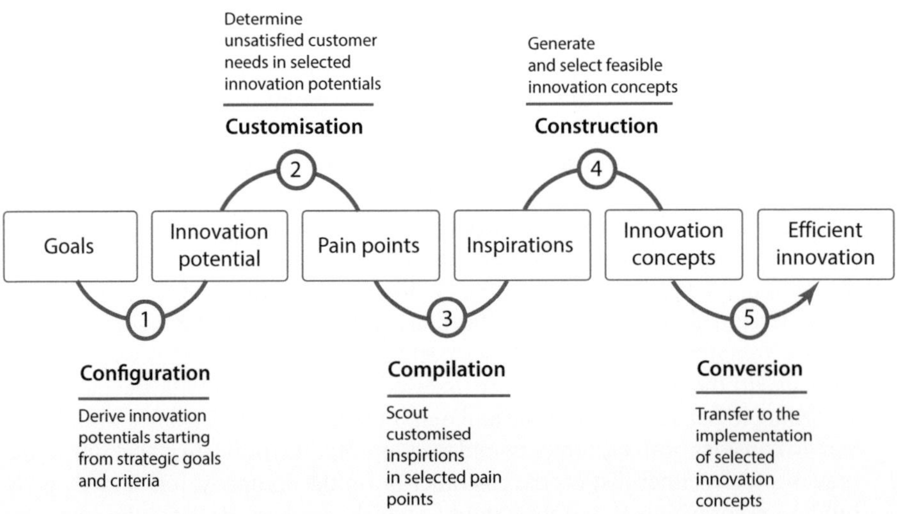

◘ **Fig. 2.2** Overview of the 5C process. (Author's own figure)

1. **Configuration: do not think freely**

   'Think freely' is the start of many customer-centric innovation methods when restrictions are initially ignored, and we give free rein to creativity. Although restrictions can perhaps be ignored in the imagination, in reality they remain and eventually bring about the downfall of the ideas developed freely. Instead, the recommendation for innovation processes in corporates should therefore be 'do *not* think freely'. After all, ideas which have been developed should also be capable of being implemented later on.

   The first step in the 5C process, *configuration*, is based on prioritised goals and criteria in order to then systematically identify the most relevant innovation potential on this basis from both the customer's and the company's perspective. To start with, once the goals and criteria have determined the innovation space with the best fit, then the most relevant opportunity spaces can be derived from the company's internal 'traction factors' and the market's external 'customer factors'. From these, specific innovation potentials are identified from the customer's perspective and prioritised from the company's perspective. This ensures that innovations have both excellent traction and excellent customer fit—and thus a high probability of success.

2. **Customisation: no problem mean no solution either**

   Every efficient innovation should address a clear customer problem or 'pain point' (Ulwick, 2005). This ensures an excellent customer fit to the innovation. But remember, in contrast to any customer-centric methods already used, customer insights are not determined on the basis of greenfields, but within the framework of the previously defined innovation potential (i.e. the outcome of the *configuration phase*). This is because the only problems which are relevant are those which the company is also able to solve. After all, the best solution in the world is no help to the customer if the company cannot implement it.

   In the *customisation* phase, targeted market research methods are used to identify relevant pain points within the innovation potential. The more precisely the customer's problems are understood in this step, the greater the future chances of success are for the innovation in the market. The pain points are then assessed from both the company's and the customer's perspective to identify the greatest opportunities with customer fit *and* traction.

3. **Compilation: if you want to reap, you must first sow**

   There may be geniuses whose best ideas fall into their lap, but generally there are no new ideas without new inspirations. Inspirations broaden your horizons and enable new associations to be made in your brain which trigger new ideas. To move forward as goal-orientated as possible, we search for inspirations (and later, ideas too) within the context of a defined pain point (or several pain points) rather than on greenfields. The focus is on solution directions which did not exist previously ('white spots'). The innovativeness of ideas within the strictly limited pain point is increased through inspirations drawn from your own industry as well as similar markets and 'the future', thus ensuring the innovative power of later ideas.

   In the *compilation* phase, suitable inspirations based on pain points are developed to support subsequent idea development.

4. **Construction: think inside the box**
   'Think outside the box' is the traditional phrase used in every brainstorming session, but to ensure customer fit *and* traction, ideas for efficient innovations must fit 'in the box'. Unfortunately, conventional creative techniques are only suitable for this purpose to a limited extent as they cannot take sufficient account of inside-the-box restrictions—and simple brainstorming sessions are not enough. As part of the first process steps, the 'box' for the ideation has already been specifically defined in the sense of the selected innovation potential or the pain point which is an excellent fit.
   In the *construction* phase, a multidimensional ideation firstly occurs in order to develop solutions which are an excellent fit to customer problems. These are then gradually transformed into innovation concepts.
5. **Conversion: where there is a way, there is also a will**
   If the path to implementation of the innovation concept is clear and is an optimal fit to the implementers' requirements, their will to implement also grows. The good thing is that with our 5C process, the traction factors for implementation are taken into account from the very outset, making this all the easier now. Nevertheless, idea ownership, i.e. personal identification with the idea, must be 'transferred' to the implementers, and then the best possible way of implementation must be tested and implemented.
   The *conversion* phase transfers the innovation concepts into implementation and ensures their success by using methods to transfer the ideas ownership, as well as quick implementation tests.
   In the following sections, these basic modules will be explained in detail, supplemented by specific methods, tools and case studies. It is not possible to describe every step down to the last detail. However, new inspirations and practical tips can always be incorporated into the company's everyday innovation. In addition, an understanding of the logic and the basic structure of an innovation process can be created for efficient innovations.

Summary

Efficient Innovation with the 5C Process

In comparison to the innovation processes used currently, the 5C process combines both customer fit and traction to make efficient innovations possible in corporations.

- For corporations, innovation is a critical success factor—and a huge challenge.
- Efficient innovation can be the solution to corporations' innovation challenges.
- Conventional methods do not map a direct path from the traction of the corporation to efficient innovation.
- The reason for this is that innovation processes always deal with just the customer *or* the company, but are unable to combine both throughout all of the steps.
- The 5C process combines both perspectives and results in five steps from the company's goals through to efficient innovation: *Configuration*, *Customisation*, *Compilation*, *Construction* and *Conversion*.
- The process is described in detail below.

2.1 Configuration: Do Not Think Freely

'Let us now imagine a greenfield.' Many innovation processes for the free generation of ideas (unfortunately) begin with these words. Greenfields do not exist in corporates though. Instead, their reality is more similar to a brownfield where there is no more green to be seen (Hargadon, 2012). Although the many restrictions which a large company brings with it can be '*thought* away' in the greenfield approach—they have not *really* vanished. And so it is precisely these 'thought away' restrictions which bring about the downfall of greenfield ideas at the time they are implemented at the latest.

To develop implementable ideas, you will inevitably have to examine your own company's brownfield. It is only when you know the specific corporate goals, restrictions and strengths that you can take these into consideration when conceiving efficient innovations, and use them proactively. It should also mean that the potential does not fall short from the customer's perspective and that it must be compared to the strengths of the company.

The disadvantage here is that this considerably increases the effort in comparison with the greenfield innovation process. The advantage is that it significantly increases the probability of success of innovations developed in this way.

So the configuration phase deals with the process which starts with the company's goals and continues through to identifying the specific innovation potential from the company's and the customer's perspective (see ◘ Fig. 2.3).

This first process step contains the following three steps:

1. **The destination is the journey** describes the starting point of an efficient innovation process, namely, identifying the most relevant innovation space based on the company's goals and criteria.
2. **Better a step in the right direction than a leap into the unknown** is concerned with determining the most relevant opportunity space in the selected innovation space. This results from the company's internal traction factors (strengths and weaknesses) which are relevant to the innovation space, as well as from the external customer factors (risks and opportunities) of the market. The integration of internal (and any external) stakeholders plays a particularly important role in this.
3. **No risk, more fun** shows how specific innovation potentials can be identified and prioritised within the defined opportunity space using specific customer factors.

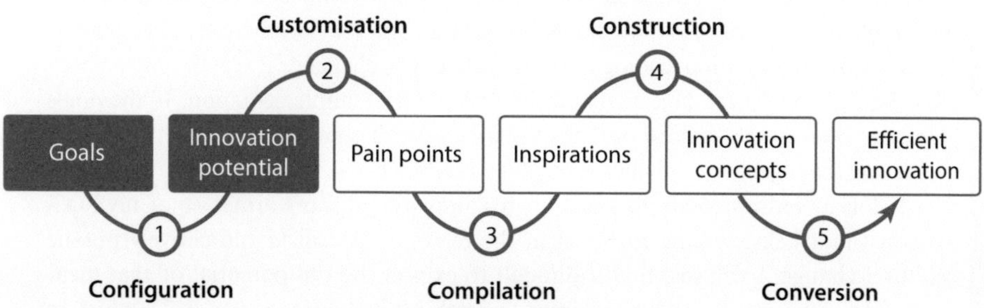

◘ **Fig. 2.3** 5C process – configuration (author's own figure)

We can already lay the foundations for efficient innovations with excellent customer fit and excellent traction at an early stage with the steps described in detail below. An overview table can be found at the end of this section.

2.1.1 The Destination is the Journey

Confucius once said, 'The journey is the destination.' But even if this is all true in many areas of life, it is exactly the opposite in the context of companies. It is the strategic goals (the 'Destination') which determine the path (the 'journey'), and projects are measured against these.

Innovation projects often seem to be the exception, however. In line with Confucius' teachings, 'disruptive business models', 'new services using artificial intelligence' or 'ideas for digital transformation' are worked on freely. Although these types of projects characterise one possible way forward, they are generally not based—or only based to a limited extent—on specific strategic goals, such as revenue, profit, market share, long-term competitive advantage, etc. Is that because this is not so easy with innovation projects? Or because goals already set limitations which block the greenfield idea generation process?

An innovation process without objectives cannot lead to systematic success though. In PWC's Global Innovation Benchmark, 69% of top managers name 'revenue growth' as their innovation goal. However, 65% of all companies which invest more than 15% of their revenue in innovations have problems transferring this to their business strategy (PWC, 2017). In reality, it is often only after a long period of development and testing that a company realizes that the planned innovation measure has no great chance of success or implementation, because the relevant corporate goals cannot be achieved. What happens next? The innovation project is discontinued after a lot of time (and money) has already been invested in it. As a long-term systematic strategy, this sort of approach does not serve anyone well.

Guest Commentary: Nicolas Biagosch, Managing Director, Digitalhafen, former CEO, Simyo, former Executive Board member, E-Plus

"From my role as CEO of an agile company like (telecommunications provider) Simyo GmbH and also from management positions in larger corporates, such as E-Plus and later Telefonica, I have a detailed knowledge of the innovation challenges in these very different environments. As different as the environment may be, there are always alternative paths to a solution leading to the objective. The challenge is identifying the path that best combines the objective and the likelihood of implementation. If the goals have not been clearly defined or if the fixed framework conditions have not been met, achieving the objectives will always rely on a random event.

If I as an entrepreneur pursue a far-reaching digital transformation of my business without being willing to invest in the relevant specialists and actively pursue cultural change, I will just find it difficult to exploit the full potential of that measure. The same applies to any attempt to establish agile procedures in IT which is still organised along traditional lines. You cannot usually make a silk purse out of a sow's ear although obviously both are unique."

Goals must be set at the beginning of the innovation process instead. The first step in this direction should be to analyse and prioritise the relevant goals of all of the stakeholders, i.e. all of the people and units concerned. This is the only way to ensure that these very objectives are taken into consideration as the innovation process progresses. Sue Siegel, Innovation Officer at General Electric, for example, noticed this (PWC, 2017): 'New technologies have a strong impact, but what we need to find out is which sustainable business model we can use within our organisation or in combination so we can drive growth. This can be a great challenge for companies though'. To do this, you need to, 'look at the company horizontally, across the various units'.

In contrast, ideas created randomly in employees' free time which are not linked strategically will rarely produce successful innovations. Innovation is therefore not an end in itself, but must follow clear, strategic goals so that it also leads to strategic successes.

An innovation study from 2013 which Bain & Company conducted with 450 large companies worldwide also shows the importance of goals. It examined the most important factors for successful innovations. In first place came clear innovation goals and strategies (Almquist, 2013). By contrast, idea generation was not a major factor influencing the success of the innovation. It was hence established that innovation is a complex process which must be managed in the same way as other complex processes.

So why do we avoid setting clear and measurable goals when it comes to innovation? The answer is simple. With specific goals, innovation becomes a complex process instead of a creative exercise for which there are hardly any suitable prescribed methods currently. Yet our journey must take us on this challenging path otherwise, there will be a 'rude awakening' at its (non-)implementation stage. The realisation that goals are the most important starting point in the innovation process is the first vital step. It is just as important to make sure that goals are also really measurable and strategically relevant for the company.

So what do potential goals for innovation projects look like? They are practically the same goals as for other strategic projects (but they might have a different priority). These are usually 'SMART' goals: specific, measurable, achievable, realistic and timely. There are plenty of examples of this—increasing revenues, securing competitive edge, increasing market share, reducing costs, increasing employee satisfaction, etc. (see ◘ Fig. 2.4).

In contrast to this, there are 'goals' which see innovation as an end in itself. In PWC's Innovation Benchmark, 40% of companies cited the 'number of ideas' as the primary measure of the success of innovation activities. Often, however, there

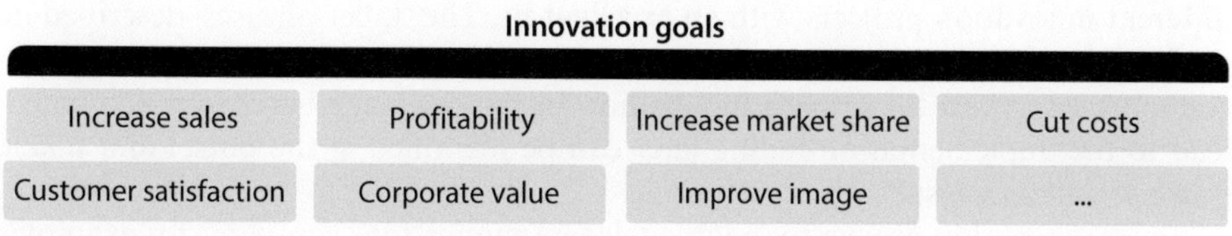

◘ **Fig. 2.4** Innovation goals. (Author's own figure)

are also more unspecific goals, such as developing 'the next big thing' or 'disruptive business models'. In particular, finding 'disruptions' or 'destroying' the current business model in order to openly anticipate other disruptive companies true to the old saying, 'disrupt or be disrupted'—the goal which is currently popular—is completely unsuitable as an innovation goal. Of course, specific disruption risks must be averted, but the company's goals should always remain in the foreground.

The example of Kodak—which is often used in the context of disruption—illustrates the problem of acting without a goal in mind. It is usually claimed that Kodak only incrementally improved its analogue cameras and printers and so missed out completely on digital photography. But the opposite is the case. Kodak developed and patented the world's first digital camera, paving the way for technology which subsequently disrupted its own core business. Millions were invested in developing digital cameras and printing stations. Various design thinking workshops were held with experts from IDEO (Segal, 2017). Kodak even bought a social photo-sharing site long before Instagram existed—but it did not recognise its potential. So ultimately, its error was not missing out on the disruptive technology or the lack of innovation suitability, but instead, the lack of a business model to be able to also profit from this and take its core business with those new developments. Kodak had great success with disrupting itself and the photographic industry—but failed to generate business in the process (Anthony, 2016).

This shows how fatal the wrong or missing goals can be and that 'disruption' is not a suitable goal for innovation measures. Even Christensen had to clarify during the current hype surrounding disruption that 'established firms [should] react to disruptions when they occur—but not overreact by giving up their profitable business' (Schwerdtfeger, 2016). Otherwise, companies may soon feel like a major German energy supplier which set itself the innovation goal of developing an 'Uber for energy'—although hardly anyone could imagine what that might mean. Eventually, specific areas were defined to make the tasks clearer and the success measurable.

Disruption should consequently be understood as a potential way forward—rather than as a goal for innovation measures. You can then decide how radical an innovation must actually be to achieve the targeted goal based on the company's stated goals. Instead of be 'as disruptive as *possible*' in efficient innovation, it should read be 'as disruptive as *necessary*'.

Besides goals, **strategic criteria must also be taken into account** to ensure the success of innovation measures. Similar to the approach for goals, these should be set or prioritised at the very beginning of the innovation process in so far as that is possible. Not every innovation project is realistic in every scenario. Differences in criteria, such as costs, time, target group or use of resources, can lead to completely different innovation projects with an excellent fit. The 'killer phrases' described in the introduction, like 'no budget', 'no resources' or 'no time', make it clear why it is important to test the criteria in advance. In this way, any barriers which could lead to the implementation failing later can be identified at the outset and taken into account as a result.

In an innovation project for a large telecommunications company, for example, it was already decided at the beginning that 'no or hardly any budget was available

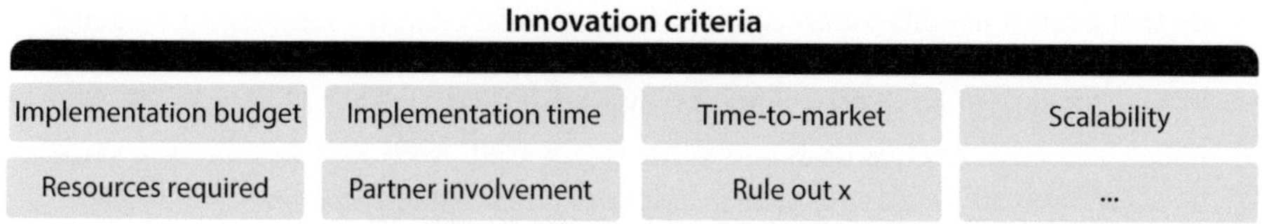

Fig. 2.5 Innovation criteria. (Author's own figure)

for implementing the innovation measures to be developed'. This may seem counterproductive at first. However, in the context of the specific project where they were pursuing the goal of achieving a significant increase in revenue in their store network, imposing a tight limit on the implementation budget was very sensible. In this way, it was possible to ensure right from the start of the innovation work that subsequent innovation measures could be implemented easily and immediately in every branch. So 'no budget' was suddenly no longer a killer phrase. It just changed the kind of ideas people were searching for. Instead, for example, of developing entirely new store concepts, the innovation process focused on 'simple' sales mechanisms and campaigns that could be implemented either without or with only a minimal budget, but which nevertheless met the goal of achieving a significant increase in revenue.

Incidentally, armed with that knowledge about the goals and criteria, it is also quickly clear whether innovations really do need to be 'disruptive' or not—instead of racking your brains about the degree of disruption of greenfield ideas. Disruption is therefore no longer a goal. Instead, it is a possible consequence of the specific goals and criteria set (Fig. 2.5).

The importance of criteria in practical innovation is also underlined by the company HYPE which has focused on innovation management software. Innovation projects which lack clearly defined goals and criteria usually result in a lot of ideas, but few innovations (because their implementation fails) and hence correspondingly huge frustration. What is the recommendation? 'By structuring the start of the innovation project using strategic search spaces and clear problem definitions, you will be able to achieve a better quality and relevance for the ideas which follow' (HYPE, 2017a).

Guest Commentary: Olivier Krüger, Chief Executive Officer, Lufthansa Systems

"As an IT service provider, Lufthansa Systems is one of the innovation drivers in the aviation industry and provides digital solutions for a large number of airlines and aircraft. It is therefore important to be able to proactively offer airlines new, relevant solutions through targeted, systematic innovation development. One example is the development of our BoardConnect wireless in-flight entertainment system.

Here, the starting point in the search for new innovation opportunities was the objective of cost savings as an important goal for airlines. Due to high fuel costs, this can be achieved by reducing weight in particular. Typical levers here are new materials, or the design of seats and other aircraft parts, which, however, have been optimized by aircraft manufacturers for decades. So what could Lufthansa Systems do that aircraft manufacturers cannot? The provision of technology and IT systems! Cabling in particular is a major weight-bearing factor here, and initial installation and maintenance costs are additional. One opportunity therefore stood out: simplified and cost-effective on-board systems, especially with mobile solutions, since 'loose equipment' is not subject to a complex certification procedure.

In the search for concrete potentials for this opportunity, it was initially helpful to take a look inside the company: Lufthansa Systems already offered a wireless, WiFi-based entertainment system for cruise ships. The potential to introduce this for aircraft was subsequently further explored with airline customers. Virgin Australia, in particular, was very receptive. The airline had just found out that for 85% of passengers, in-flight entertainment is the most important factor on flights and that in the age of tablets and notebooks, they are usually dissatisfied with the permanently installed devices on offer—if they exist at all on short and medium distances. With this additional customer factor in mind, the innovation potential became clear: a wireless in-flight entertainment system.

Starting in 2008, this innovation potential was implemented as 'BoardConnect' for the aircraft industry based on the existing system for cruise ships. Herewith, video and audio content can be streamed to your own or borrowed mobile devices. This not only leads to significant weight savings but also to higher customer satisfaction. Thanks to Lufthansa Systems' existing expertise in in-flight entertainment and IT, the system could already be presented at a trade show in 2011. In 2012, it won the 'Crystal Award for Passenger Comfort', and in 2013, it was rolled out across the entire fleet of Virgin Australia, which significantly increased its market share to over 20% in the following years. Thanks in part to Lufthansa Systems' existing customer network, BoardConnect is now (in 2020) installed at over 15 airlines in more than 800 aircrafts. In 2019, it was awarded the 'World Travel Award' as 'Best Portable Inflight Entertainment System' for the third time in a row and is continuously being developed into a complete in-flight experience platform. According to forecasts, the corresponding market is expected to grow to over USD 3 billion in 2025. Thanks to efficient innovation, the future is already a reality for Lufthansa Systems' customers.

Note: changes due to the Corona crisis are not included in this commentary as of 01/2020.

The example of a large insurance corporate similarly shows the importance of taking an early decision about goals as well as the relevant criteria in the context of innovations. The task was initially formulated as developing product innovations for a younger target group, a sensible consideration since the goal was to generate a revenue increase with this specific target group. However, there was also one key implementation criterion. The goal was to be achieved in the course of the following year. But product innovations in the insurance industry often take 2–3 years to develop due to the regulations they must comply with. Even new product bundles cannot simply be implemented from 1 year to the next. This means that any idea for the original task (i.e. the development of product innovations) would end up failing, because it could not be implemented next year—no matter how strong its impact on sales might have been. And that also meant that to ensure innovation measures were successful in a specific scenario, the task definition needed to be changed completely. Further analysis showed that the greatest potential did not lie in new products (apart from the fact that these were incapable of being implemented by next year anyway), but in new ways of selling and marketing the existing product portfolio to younger customers. Measures in this area could also be implemented at short notice, ensuring that the time criterion for this changed task definition could also be met.

But who sets the goals and criteria for an innovation project? So that these are actually of value for the innovation project, it is important to let them be tested and assessed by all of those stakeholders who will also be deciding on the implementation of ideas later, and do so before selecting or starting a specific innovation project. This may seem obvious, but in many companies, it is handled the other way around. Innovations are developed there 'in secret' for as long as possible—bypassing the official processes and budgets—to then present decision-makers with a 'done deed'.

It makes no sense to smuggle innovations past decision-makers or existing structures and processes, as (Blank, 2014), Stanford's professor and co-founder of the lean start-up method, also describes. He notes that innovation must be an important part of every company today and requires the support of decision-makers. It is the only way to anchor innovation in the company in the long term. Many of the separate innovation units intended to take care of innovations—which operate separately from the company—are hence intended to be viewed in a similarly critical light. This separation reinforces the feeling that innovation does not belong to the actual company. Mark Ridley of ► Reed.com maintains that 'Labs whose goal is "innovation" are completely wrong. Companies should not create innovations separately. Instead, there must be a business strategy which sets the goals and tasks for innovation' (Samuels, 2016).

As opposed to the traditional innovation process, with the development of efficient innovations, the starting point is not the customer's needs or an employee's idea. Instead, the strategic goals and implementation criteria of the relevant stakeholders set the direction for linking innovation into the overall strategy in a meaningful way. We must therefore unequivocally disagree with Confucius who we mentioned at the start. It is not the journey which determines the destination, but the destination which determines the journey, at least in the context of innovations in large companies.

But what does the journey determined by the destination look like? **Innovation spaces set the direction for this** (see the following excursus) (Doblins, 2017). In this way, we can see that there are many different ways to arrive at a goal. Besides traditional product innovations, the focus might also be, for example, on sales innovations, innovative monetisation models, new markets or process innovations which require different ideas in the follow-up process.

Excursus: Overview of Possible Innovation Spaces

The following innovation spaces can each serve as the basis of an innovation project and are assessed and selected on the basis of the company's goals and criteria. Selected examples for each innovation space are intended to improve understanding.

Markets

Market innovations include new offerings aimed at penetrating other existing markets (red oceans) or creating new markets (blue oceans). Vertical or horizontal business expansions, brand extensions, collaborations, licensing, mergers and acquisitions and similar forms can be chosen in order to realise new market innovations. The basic goals are often either to increase corporate value and/or revenue or even to secure competitive edge through diversification.

- Amazon offers cloud storage for other companies with its Amazon Web Services.
- REWE supermarket chain offers package holidays via its existing online and offline channels with REWE Reisen.
- Apple also sells media content in addition to products like the iPhone and iPad with iTunes.

Processes

Process and operational innovations include improvements to operational processes (e.g. production) or business processes (e.g. sales). They are often used in the later phases of a product life cycle to maintain competitive edge, but can also form the basis of a completely new offer. Typically, process innovations serve to increase productivity (and thus profitability) or to achieve cost savings.

- IKEA offers its furniture at a lower price as a result of the customer assembling their own products.
- Dell uses its built-to-spec program to assemble computers only after purchase.
- Adidas produces customised shoes straightaway in its stores using 3D printing.

Human Resources and Culture

Human resources innovations include innovative measures for optimising internal organisational structures, culture and personnel processes. These enable the company to achieve, for example, sales and cost targets (increases in performance), growth targets (recruitment) and quality targets (increases in expertise). Human resource innovations are also relevant as regards integrating new generations of employees (Generations Y and Z, Millennials) to maintain the basic functionality of the company.

- P&G hands out a Failure Award for employees at regular intervals to support a learning culture.
- Google offers its employees free choice of new projects and ideas to work on 20% of their time.
- At the Kameha Grand Zurich hotel, each employee has a budget of CHF 2000 per customer for any service needs.

Customer Experience

Customer experience innovations include special brand experiences for customers. These can take place at different touch points (e.g. online, offline) for different groups (premium customers, at random, non-customers, families, women, etc.) using different mechanisms and technologies (e.g. virtual reality, competitions, gifts, surprises, etc.). Customer experience innovations primarily serve to improve the corporate image which indirectly leads to increases in revenue and profitability.

- Coca-Cola offers customers Google Cardboard VR glasses integrated into their packaging.
- Marriott hotels offer virtual reality travel with teleporter booths.
- True Religion uses smartwatches to customise its customers' in-store shopping experience.

Products and Services

Product and service innovations are the best known and most popular innovation space. Products can either be redeveloped from scratch (e.g. on the basis of new technologies, materials, ingredients, production processes or designs) or optimised (e.g. in terms of performance, taste, speed, quality, price, etc.). New and improved products and services may result in significant revenue and profitability increases. In addition, special products and services can also improve brand image.

- LEGO offers its Serious Play bricks explicitly for workshops with adults.
- Rügenwalder Mühle (originally a sausage and ham producer) now has a significant share of its revenue from meat-free products.
- Snapchat helps you to send money thanks to a collaboration with Square.

Customer Service

Customer service innovations include innovative assistance for the customer at all of the relevant touch points, e.g. for searches, advice, purchases or after-sales. Depending on the design, innovations can contribute to an improvement in customer satisfaction and brand image or even to revenue increases, e.g. by selling additional products and services or by minimising cancelled sales orders.

- IKEA offers a lifetime return policy in some countries.
- Bosch offers a global network of service partners by certifying workshops.
- Amazon ships selected items within 1 hour in cities.

Monetisation Models

Monetisation models include redeveloping or rejuvenating the value added of a company or an individual division, product or service. They make use of new mechanisms, such as subscriptions, leasing, freemium, open source, etc., so new monetisation models are not only particularly suitable for attaining revenue, profitability and cost objectives but also for increasing market share or corporate value in the long term.

- HILTI offers a constantly updated fleet of equipment for business customers with its equipment leasing.
- Apple offers the opportunity to obtain music via a monthly subscription with Apple Music.
- BMW offers the opportunity to rent vehicles by the minute with ShareNow.

Sales and Channels

Innovations in sales and channels are focused on innovative sales mechanisms and channels and are used to sell existing (or new) products or services to new target groups or, increasingly, to existing target groups. This also enables companies to achieve increases in revenue and market share in the short term.

2

- Lufthansa sells premium economy flights via Airbnb as a special sales campaign.
- Tesla offers reservations for new models with an order fee so that it can plan demand.
- Amazon offers a paid customer club with an increasing number of advantages through its Amazon Prime service.

Brands and Marketing
Brand innovations anchor the brand with customer in the long term, e.g. through partnerships, PR, positioning, charity work, viral content, etc. Brand innovations pay particular attention to corporate image and can therefore lead to a secondary increase in revenue through increased market share or profitability. In addition, companies can also obtain a positive effect for the recruitment of new employees.

- Red Bull's stratospheric skydive broke the record for the number of live viewers on YouTube.
- Jägermeister achieved a new image as a party drink through its party promotion teams.
- TOMS helps children in need with every pair of shoes bought.

The potential offered by the many innovation spaces is precisely what companies often misjudge. This is because many companies generally focus on traditional product and service innovations. The 2015 PWC Breakthrough Innovation Study shows that 40% of German companies' innovation projects were exclusively focused on product innovations (PWC, 2013). By contrast, only 10% of the companies surveyed had carried out innovation using the monetisation model—notwithstanding that this could deliver significantly greater potential, depending on the goals set. And even if companies (sometimes very consciously) innovate in very varied innovation spaces, the innovation space is not usually selected on the basis of specific goals and criteria.

Innovation spaces with the best fit can be prioritised and selected depending on the goals and criteria prioritised previously. Based on intuitive assessment, benchmarking and the experience gained from previous projects, it is easy to assess the innovation space which is best suited to fulfilling the specific innovation goals and criteria (see ◘ Fig. 2.6). So, for example, a product innovation is generally better suited to achieving revenue goals than a process innovation whereas a process innovation is particularly well suited to cost reduction goals. A new market is not usually a good idea either when time or resources are limited although an innovation in sales and channels can just be right then.

Innovation spaces must therefore be assessed according to their potential in relation to the chosen goals and criteria, and an appropriate selection made on this basis. Instead of taking the very first path, you can take the right path.

The selected innovation space now sets the direction for the innovation project. This does not mean, for example, that an innovation project in the 'monetisation model' innovation space is not also able to contain thinking about new processes, sales or products. It shows, though, where the focus, and thus the starting point, for the innovation process should be (in this case, on the new opportunities for

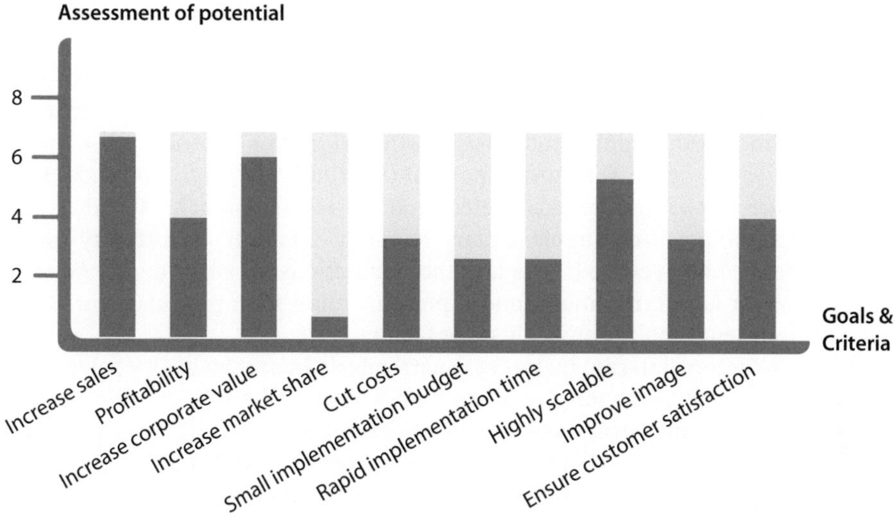

Fig. 2.6 Example of the assessment of an innovation space ('monetisation models'). (Author's own figure)

monetisation, such as subscription models, services, open source, freemium, etc.). This focus makes it possible to subsequently identify the most relevant innovation potentials (for the company and the customer) and to thus create the basis for the subsequent search for ideas and the development of specific innovations which can make the optimal contribution to the company's goals and criteria. The following two *configuration* steps show how we can take this journey to our destination.

2.1.2 Better a Step in the Right Direction Than a Leap Into the Unknown

With greenfield innovation projects, the start is often like a leap into the unknown. In response to a trigger, such as a customer insight (i.e. discovering a customer need), a research result or a new technology, the company rushes into the search for the most exciting ideas possible on the strength of this new knowledge. Companies rarely ask whether they can also address the question about the issue they have 'discovered' in a meaningful way. After all, the first step should be to think as freely as possible to ensure they do not rule out anything which might lead to the million-dollar idea later. But how is that supposed to succeed 'later' if the ideas do not fit the company and cannot therefore be implemented at all? And how successful will an implementation be if market trends or significant customer needs are not, or are not fully, taken into account?

Instead of leaping blindly into the unknown, it is better to make progress with systematic steps—along the right path. Even if an innovation space with an excellent fit has been selected on the basis of goals and criteria, this does not yet represent an adequate direction for the subsequent innovation process.

Accordingly, the first step in the right direction is to **identify the opportunity spaces within the selected innovation space**. An opportunity space is made up of the innovation space supplemented by an external and/or internal factor. In the chosen innovation space, the most important (internal) *traction factors* and (external) *customer factors* are firstly collected in an iterative approach—together with the key stakeholders and supplementary research—and any opportunity spaces are then derived and selected. This lays the foundations for ensuring *traction* and *customer fit* for later innovations, and it prevents innovation projects from failing during implementation for precisely these factors.

Traction factors (internal factors) are particularly important at this point. They include, for example, personnel or IT resources, existing brands, existing customers or even established structures and processes (see ▶ Sect. 1.3). Together, these form the company's internal strengths and weaknesses in relation to the selected innovation space. Collecting these traction factors is initially like preparing a sort of specifications sheet. You need to identify all of the significant factors when implementing your ideas. If a specific factor of the company can be exploited as a strength when implementing ideas, that represents a *positive traction factor*. This factor can increase the traction of an innovation. If, on the other hand, a factor must be taken into account as a restriction when implementing ideas, this should be noted as a *negative traction factor*. If it is ignored, this is a factor which can diminish the traction or even completely prevent the implementation of an idea. The fact that factors can therefore be positive or negative results in a 'traction space' (see ◘ Fig. 2.7) in which the strengths of the company are to be exploited and weaknesses avoided as far as possible. Thus, the traction factors ensure that the selected opportunity spaces possess excellent potential traction. If you pursue this system, internal corporate factors will no longer represent a barrier to innovation later on, but, on the contrary, can even inspire innovation.

The definition of such a **traction space** may appear surprising at first, because it significantly limits any innovation space and thus makes the subsequent generation of ideas (*ideation*) more difficult. But this step pays off as the largest innovation process problems are usually to be found in the implementation. 'We have enough ideas; implementation is the problem' is a sentence which has probably been said hundreds of times in every company. And this sentence precisely illustrates the misinterpretation of the problem. If generating ideas is easy and implementing them is difficult, this does not usually mean a lack of implementation skills. Instead, it reveals a lack of the *right* ideas. In this case, many ideas are simply many wrong or unsuitable ideas. With these ideas, implementation problems occur as there is friction with the existing organisation that has not been taken into consideration beforehand (Govindarajan, 2010).

Was Kodak unable to build digital cameras? Could Air Berlin not see the process changes which Ryanair could introduce to offer cheap flights? In each of these cases, it was not the implementation which was the problem as such. It was more that these disruptive ideas did not fit their own company. However,

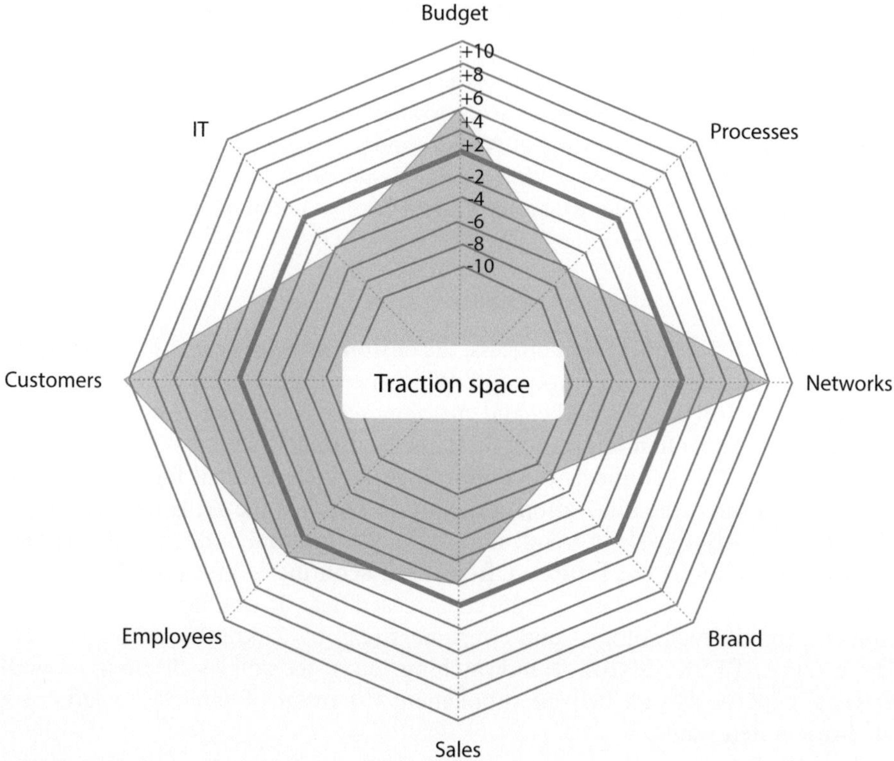

Fig. 2.7 Traction space (simplified). (Author's own figure)

if Kodak had systematically developed innovations for digital photography which had fitted its own core business or if Air Berlin had changed its business model based on its own structures and processes, the market position of these companies might perhaps look different today. As (Zwilling, 2011) remarked in *Forbes Magazine*, 'Innovations should never be isolated from the existing business. Virtually every significant innovation must exploit the company's existing resources and skills'. This required combination ensures the exact definition of the traction space.

Once you have identified the traction space, **you need to identify the most relevant customer factors**. The customer factors ensure the relevance of the opportunity spaces from the perspective of the customer or the market—and hence, the *customer fit*. They are based on external changes, such as new trends and technologies, amended regulations or market trends. In contrast to traction factors, they therefore describe external opportunities (and risks). Similar to traction factors, customer factors are also collected starting from the innovation space and the industry—by both internal and external experts in the company as well as using supplementary research and analysis, for example, trend reports, forecasts, market reports, studies, etc.

Guest Commentary: Luke Mansfield, Vice President Innovation, PepsiCo Beverages

"Many large companies see their size as an obstacle to innovation, but I don't see it like that. If you gave entrepreneurs access to all of our resources, imagine what they would do. This is how we view it at PepsiCo, and we exploit our resources, size and power as our competitive edge. We stock brands and products which have been giving people pleasure for more than 100 years. That does not simply disappear and it is a strong basis for innovation."

At this point of the innovation process, the customer factors can still be very general. Which megatrends are important? Which new technologies could play a role in the future? How are the market and customer needs changing? Answers to questions like this give a first impression of suitable customer factors.

Rohrbeck (2014) confirms the importance of such external factors. 'To beat the competition in the innovation competition requires the skills to innovate on the basis of early signals in trends and to involve internal and external partners in discussions about the future'. Often trend scouting is already taking place, such as a 'trend radar' whose results can be used here. If not, numerous publications on trends, technologies and consumers (e.g. by Zukunftsinstitut, Gartner Hype Cycle, PFSK, Stylus, Trendwatching, etc.), as well as discussions with external experts, can all help to supplement the input of internal experts in a goal-orientated way.

Stakeholder management is very important for collecting traction factors and customer factors. Those stakeholders who are key to deciding and implementing ideas are involved as internal experts in gathering together the factors. In contrast to skunkworks which people use in an attempt to bypass decision-makers and employees, in this approach stakeholders are involved at an early stage. Partly, this ensures that no factors are overlooked. Partly though, it is so that stakeholders are on board at an early stage and will not reject the ideas later when they see that their ideas have already been taken into consideration (◘ Fig. 2.8).

Conversely, this means that successful implementation will be unlikely if it is not possible to gather in the relevant decision-makers and persons concerned at an early stage through their input (and actually take it into account later). In that case,

Technologies	Megatrends	Consumer trends	Market trends	Regulatory
Artificial intelligence	Urbanisation	On-demand	Category growth	Data protection
Blockchain	Globalisation	Cashless	New needs	Regulations
Machine learning	Demogrphics	Customised	New competition	Standards
Robotics	Customisation	Price war	New target groups	Bans
Internet of Things	Migration	As-a-Service	Consolidation	Guidelines
Industry 4.0	Climate change	Experience	Convergence	Government premiums
Wireless	Digitisation	Online	Decreasing margins	Sanctions
...	...	...	...	...

◘ **Fig. 2.8** Example of customer factors. (Author's own figure)

ideas will be repelled as if by an immune system when companies try to implement them. Then, employees and processes seem to be antibodies which are not allowing any new ideas. For these employees, new ideas seem like diseases threatening the stability of their current core business which they need to protect.

Best (2012), Innovation Leader at PWC in the USA, describes how the most important corporate antibodies can be included in planning a company-wide innovation project. 'It wasn't hard to identify the most powerful corporate antibodies. They were the people whose job it is to worry about risks to the ongoing organization—legal, finance, IT and the brand team. To make them into allies, we held a series of highly personalized meetings in which we asked each person to use his or her core area of expertise to help us plan out the details of our PowerPitch [innovation] initiative. […] We collaborated with our CFO to think through the budget and prize strategy. We engaged our brand team to help us increase the impact of the project through our newly launched visual identity'.

Stakeholder involvement like this ensures that they buy in when it comes to investments and resources for the implementation later on—provided that the traction and customer factors they report are actually taken into consideration in the ideas (HYPE, 2017b). Like this, employees can be involved in the innovation process without having to deliver specific ideas or solutions. Even though they will often know best what will work and what will not—or what customers do and do not want—they can experience difficulty in finding really new potentials and ideas in their area. Whereas small improvements are the responsibility of every employee, employees usually do not have the opportunities or the interest to develop strategic innovations in addition to their day-to-day tasks (Zwilling, 2011). With the methodology described above, it is now possible to involve employees from the bottom up in strategic top-down innovations, thus ensuring the success of strategic innovations at an early stage.

A similar approach is also recommended for involving external stakeholders, such as potential partner companies, suppliers or customers. Like integrating internal stakeholders, they should act as input providers rather than idea generators. The development of ideas requires specific skills and should therefore be left to specialists (see ► Sects. 2.7.1 and ► 3.2) to make it possible to plan ideas systematically.

On top of that, if external stakeholders 'only' have to provide input for innovation projects, the advantages of co-creation, crowdsourcing and other popular open innovation methods can be exploited without also having to accept their disadvantages or risks. And there are numerous advantages to this like acquiring an external perspective and thoughts, early feedback and thus better acceptance in the market, leveraging of synergies, establishing of potential partnerships, increasing customer satisfaction through involvement, etc. However, if you rely too heavily on external stakeholders as idea generators, then you can no longer plan innovations systematically, while at the same time you are under a huge pressure of expectations from the participating external idea generators.

In comparison with other, more successful companies, the example of Yahoo! shows why it is important to involve external stakeholders as input providers rather than idea generators. Although Yahoo! was the first mover in the online search engine industry, its share price fell from USD 100 to USD 50 per share between 2010 and 2017, whereas Google climbed from USD 300 to USD 1000 per share over the same period. As Jens Martin Skibsted described in his article for the 'Fast Company' journal, one reason for that could be the wrong innovation strategy (Skribsted, 2014). In terms of open innovation, 'Yahoo! listened to everyone too much, and bought companies here, there and everywhere based on customer feedback. Open innovation is more likely to be the reason for Yahoo!'s problems rather than the solution to them.' Yahoo! was too focused on external factors and ideas and did not look closely enough at its own strengths and weaknesses.

By contrast, companies like Google and Apple are particularly successful because of their strong focus (on context-based advertising and selected hardware and software). As one Apple employee remarked, 'At Apple, we don't waste our time asking the user [about every little thing], we build great products people will love.' Other successful brands do not rely on their customers or other external stakeholders to be idea generators either, but set the direction themselves. At IKEA, the unspoken philosophy is 'we show people the way' (Skibsted, 2014).

These examples make it clear that companies should not rely on receiving ideas from external stakeholders for successful strategic innovations. However, this does not apply to their input generally. Through early dialogue with the relevant stakeholders, it becomes clear what is actually possible and what is wanted during implementation, and also what is not. This provides the traction space and potential opportunity spaces for a successful implementation with excellent customer fit and excellent traction.

The traction and customer factors you collect can then be analysed and assessed to derive the potential opportunity spaces. Each of these illustrates, on the one hand, where innovation is useful overall from an external perspective and, on the other, where the company's existing strengths can be optimally exploited in the implementation of ideas (see ◘ Fig. 2.9). The following applies as a result:

$$\text{Opportunity space} = \text{innovation space} + \text{general customer factor}$$
$$(+\text{any traction facto, if applicable})$$

Which trends play a role exactly? Which regulations will be key in future? Which processes have to be taken into consideration and which resources are available? Customer factors and traction factors are able to yield specific new innovation opportunities as answers to such questions (and also add to the opportunity spaces

Markets	Products and services	Sales and channels	Monetisation models	...
Digital offers	On-demand services with a branch / store link	Artificial intelligence consultants	Software-as-a-Service models	...
Collaborations on healthcare offers for senior citizens	Internet of Things products	OTC via online channels	Pay-as-you-go offers	...

Opportunity space = innovation space + general customer factor (+ any traction factor)

◘ **Fig. 2.9** Example of opportunity spaces in innovation spaces. (Author's own figure)

identified previously). As a result, the selected innovation space can be filled with suitable opportunity spaces, making it possible to achieve a potentially excellent customer fit *and* excellent traction.

At the end, a **final assessment and prioritisation of the opportunity spaces developed is carried out**. These opportunity spaces are initially assessed based on their potential to meet the goals and criteria defined at the start. Afterwards, it is better to double-check the traction capabilities using the traction factors identified along the way. Each opportunity space can be impacted positively or negatively by the traction factors. In particular, an opportunity space based substantially on one customer factor would otherwise run the risk that it might lie outside the traction space. After this, the final opportunity spaces must then be transferred to a prioritised list or roadmap depending on the outcome. Opportunity spaces can also be sorted according to their short-term and long-term relevance, if necessary, and grouped in clusters.

It makes sense to carry out or review the assessment with the relevant stakeholders. What is the result? It is the prioritised opportunity spaces in the most relevant innovation space based on the most important goals and criteria, plus traction and customer factors (see ◘ Fig. 2.10).

One or more opportunity spaces can be selected for further processing depending on the resources. In the second scenario, the process described below must be carried out several times (in parallel). The task now is to identify the greatest innovation potential in the selected opportunity space(s). This innovation potential already has one thing in common with the approach described in this section, customer fit and traction, which is a good start for a systematic innovation project.

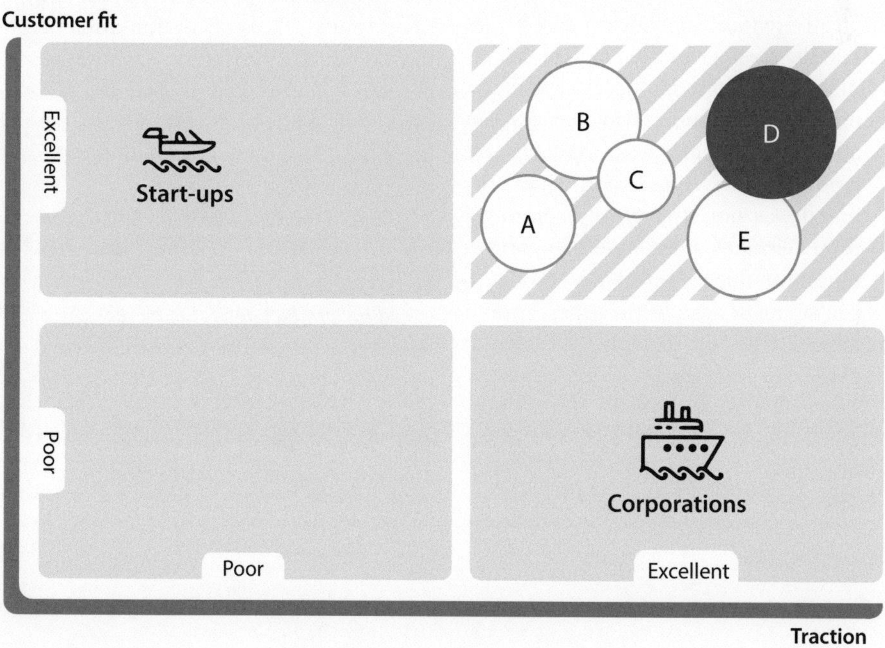

◘ **Fig. 2.10** 'Efficient' opportunity spaces. (Author's own figure)

2

Case Study: Estée Lauder Companies

Development of a 3-Year Growth Strategy for the Lab Series Brand

Lab Series is a skin care brand from the Estée Lauder Companies' portfolio which has dedicated itself entirely to the individual needs of men's skin care. In Germany, the brand is distributed exclusively through selected perfumeries. To strengthen the brand's premium image, the number of distribution partners in Germany was reduced by about two-thirds shortly before the start of the project, while at the same time, new, challenging growth targets were set for the brand.

Configuration

At the beginning of the *configuration phase*, the goal was first set, namely, to achieve large, double-digit growth of the brand over the next 3 years. Since the number of perfumeries had been greatly reduced previously, this meant that the revenue for each individual perfumery needed to multiply. Key criteria for implementation also existed. No additional budget was available for innovation measures, and since the brand was not strategically controlled from Germany, there were no opportunities to influence future new products, packaging designs or the general brand image. Due to strongly sales-driven goals, the *innovation space 'products'* was was selected in view of the enormous significance of a few selected sales points in addition to the *innovation space 'sales and channels'*.

No product innovation was possible with the analysis to develop the relevant *opportunity spaces* in the '*product*' segment—due to the criterion given—however there was great potential concealed in an *optimisation of the overall brand portfolio*. Ultimately, about 50% of the brand's revenue was generated by less than a fifth of its products. It also became apparent that, in particular, the *product launches* planned (by the international marketing team) for the next 3 years could lead to significant revenue increases—when enriched with innovative mechanisms by the German team. In terms of '*sales and channels*', analysis showed that the perfumery sales staff were still too *uncertain about Lab Series products* compared to their main competitor Biotherm Homme, so customers were usually advised about the competitor's products. Hence, the opportunity spaces of 'optimisation of the product portfolio', 'innovative product launches' and 'optimisation of sales staff's advisory certainty at the point of sale' were identified for the remainder of the processing.

During the remainder of the 5C process, a number of different innovative measures were developed which optimised the product portfolio, increased the repurchase rate, improved the efficiency of employees at the POS and, in particular, fuelled the launch of a new product, Pro LS. Over the next 3 years, the brand even exceeded its ambitious growth targets.

2.1.3 No Risk, More Fun

Although most innovation projects fail, little is done in advance to minimise their risks. It seems that people continue to believe innovation projects must be risky by definition. More risk, more return ("fun"). Yet compared to financial products, 'more risk, more fun' does not apply to innovations. On the contrary, a corporation's management board may be more likely to welcome it if the innovation project can generate as high a return as possible (excellent customer fit) with as low an implementation risk (or excellent traction) as possible. So when it comes to innovation, the saying is 'No risk, more fun'. Yet how can we achieve the best possible traction and customer fit to minimise an innovation project's risk?

From the outset, by working **on the most relevant innovation potential as determined by the customer perspective (customer fit) which the company is also able to address (traction)**. We have already taken the first step towards reducing an innovation project's risk by identifying the opportunity spaces based on the traction factors and customer factors. In doing so, the innovation project is automatically within the right framework. Customer fit must now be maximised within this framework to ensure the best possible chance of success for the innovations. (Note: since the selected opportunity space has already been identified based on the traction space, the traction factors do not need to be actively included again although you should keep them in the back of your mind.)

To maximise customer fit, the best innovation potential within the selected opportunity space is specified. These are the areas which contain the best potential for new solutions, particularly from the customer's perspective. To this end, the customer factors researched normally in the previous process step must be broken down from a general level to a specific level. Mootee (2011) also emphasises the importance of such a step in his explanation about the development of strategic innovations. He sees the focus for idea development in the acquisition and synthesis of *contextually relevant information* in order to recognise and detail potential.

Where exactly should we start to search for this innovation potential though? Finding 'contextually relevant information' or, in our case, 'specific customer factors' is no easy task. Although there are many different sources which can include customer factors (e.g. consumer trends, customer surveys, studies or market data), it is hardly possible to search for these in a goal-orientated way without a suitable system. Just as archaeologists cannot simply start digging anywhere when they are looking for ancient artefacts; you cannot search in an unstructured way for specific customer factors either. Instead, the search area (in our case, the opportunity space) should be divided up as systematically as possible so that you can 'dig' in depth for specific customer factors.

The morphological box developed by Fritz Zwicky in 1966 offers a **structured approach for systematically dividing up the opportunity space** (Zwicky & Wilson,

1967). This methodology is normally used to solve non-quantifiable problems where the logical and non-logical connections to these parameters become clear by showing all of the possible parameters rather than by reducing the number of variables. The concept has already been adapted to various methods. Warfield used it for his options field/options profile approach, Michael Michalko describes it as a creative methodology in his book *Thinkertoys*, and Dym and Little use a morphological chart in their book *Engineering Design*.

When adapting this methodology to an innovation project, it is sufficient to use the system in its basic way. Firstly, as many relevant parameters as possible are collected for the selected opportunity space. In this way, potentials with an excellent fit are identified faster and more efficiently than as a result of random, ad hoc brainstorming.

Basic questions are a good place to start: *who* (target groups), *where* (touch points, locations), *how* (mechanisms, models), *what* (added value, offers) and *why* (needs). For further examples, see ◘ Fig. 2.11. These parameters thus form individual sub-areas in the opportunity space where you can search for specific customer factors.

To this end, the various parameters are enriched with their possible variants. For example, for the touch point parameter, we can determine the variants: 'point of sale', 'at home', 'on the road', 'at work', etc. (to fit the relevant opportunity space).

The variants result in an overview of possible potentials within the opportunity space which can then be confirmed, supplemented or rejected by a targeted search for specific customer factors within these parameters or variants. In this way, we can identify specific customer factors with the best chances of success (and hence, the lowest risk).

Parameters	Variants					
Who (target group)	Core customers	New customers	Friends	Pensioners	Alone	...
Where (location)	At POS	Website	Shopping mall	In the car	At the beach	...
How (mechanisms)	Pay as you go	Subscription	Take-away	As a gift	Over-the-air	...
Why (need)	Saving	5 minutes of fame	Reward	Freedom	Security	...
What (added value)	Product	Service	Packaging	Gift	Acceleration	...
Business model	Freemium	Software-as-a-Service	In-app purchase	Direct purchase	Kick-back	...
Feeling	Anxiety	Grief	Joy	Rage	Fun	...
Technology use	Smartwatch tracker	Smartphone tracker	TV	Smart home	...	...
...	...	...	...	...	...	...

◘ **Fig. 2.11** Example of a morphological box. (Author's own figure)

Digital offers	On-demand services	Artificial intelligence advisers	Software-as-a-Service models	...
Digital offers for young travellers	On-demand women's fashion service with a store link	Artificial intelligence advisers for new customers abroad	Software-as-a-Service models for mobility service suppliers	...
Digital offers for single senior citizens	On-demand transport services for senior citizens with a branch link	Artificial intelligence advice for WhatsApp users	Software-as-a-service for hospitals	...

Customer insight = New customer need discovered (pain point = unsatisfied customer insight)

Fig. 2.12 Example of innovation potentials in opportunity spaces. (Author's own figure)

Ultimately, it is now a question of deriving the most relevant innovation potentials. An innovation potential is always an excellent fit for a specific customer factor (including target groups) found in the opportunity space. Since the opportunity space consists of an innovation space + general customer factor (+ any traction factor), the following applies:

$$\begin{aligned} \text{Innovation potential} &= \begin{pmatrix} \text{innovation space} + \text{general customer factor} \\ (+\ \text{any traction factor}) \end{pmatrix} \\ &\quad + \text{specific customer factor}\left(\text{incl. target group}\right)\text{, in short,} \\ \text{Innovation potential} &= \text{opportunity space} + \text{specific customer factor} \end{aligned}$$

This sounds more complicated than it is, as the following examples (based on selecting the previous opportunity spaces in the examples) show (see Fig. 2.12).

To simplify matters, it is advisable to firstly group the list of specific customer factors researched on the basis of the morphological box (e.g. using the selected parameters) in order to aggregate any similar customer factors and then formulate them as a possible innovation potential in the opportunity space.

These innovation potentials are then assessed using the goals and criteria to identify the most relevant innovation potential for the company. As with opportunity spaces, it is better to carry out this assessment together with the key stakeholders or have them review it.

Since each innovation potential lies within the selected opportunity space (see Fig. 2.13), you have essentially already ensured traction, customer fit and relevance to the company (in terms of goals and criteria). You have similarly ensured that the risk to the company is normally low. Selecting the innovation potential with the best fit (i.e. the one with the best assessment) now maximises customer fit and hence the chances of success for the innovation project. Going forward, you have now paved the way for the innovation process—with a lower risk, but a better chance of success (several potentials can be processed in one project, but the following steps are explained using a single innovation potential to simplify matters).

2

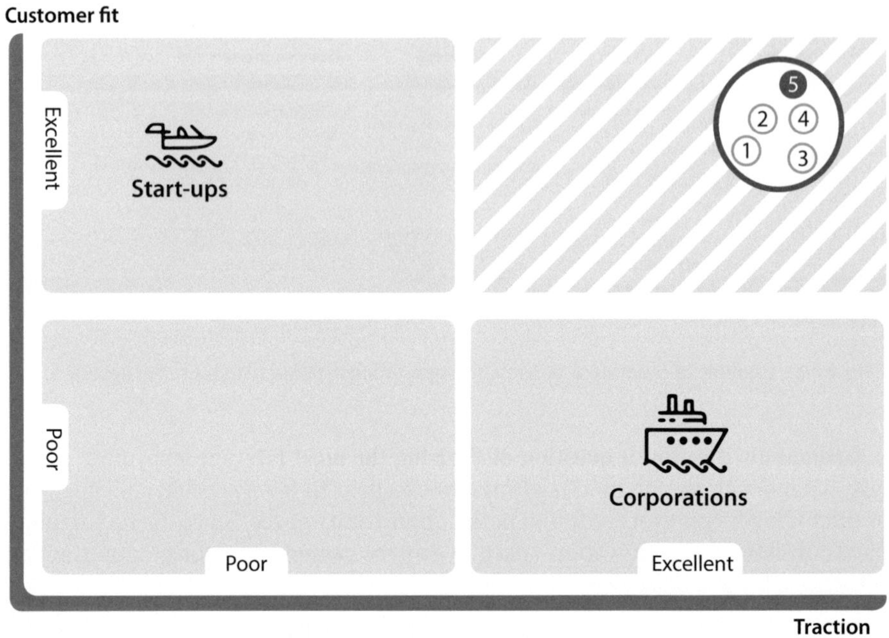

Fig. 2.13 Efficient innovation potentials within the selected opportunity space. (Author's own figure)

Unilever delivers a good example of a relevant innovation potential in the innovation space 'brand'. In a study of 3,200 women, only 2% of the women described themselves as 'beautiful', while 76% wanted to change the basic idea of beauty (HYPE, 2017c). The company was thus able to exploit the potential of 'addressing women who want to change the definition of beauty'. Starting from this innovation potential, the Dove brand was completely repositioned with a specific target group and a clear fit to Unilever (care products) using campaigns, products and services ('campaign for real beauty') to change the view of beauty. So, for example, a variety of 'real' women were used as models in the advertisement, making the brand very successful. This shows how even a single innovation potential can provide a major innovation boost.

What about ideas which do not fit any of the innovation potentials in the opportunity space? Due to the strong limits on the space for the search for ideas, is there not a risk that particularly exciting ideas will be ignored or not found, simply because they lie outside the opportunity space or innovation potential? The answer is yes. Generally exciting ideas are either not taken into consideration or not found. These generally exciting ideas are not the most relevant ideas for that

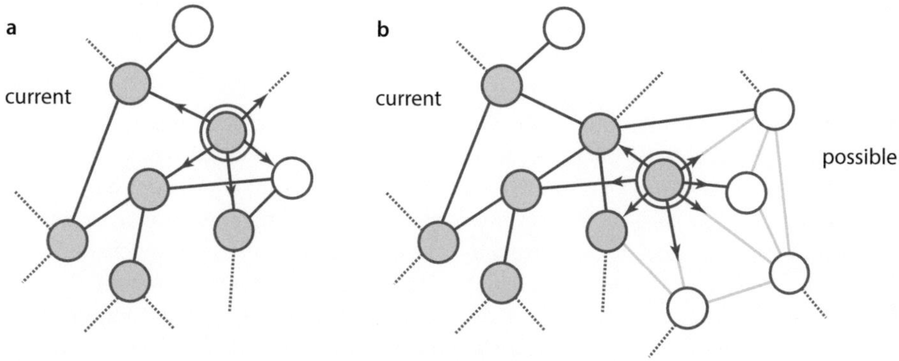

■ **Fig. 2.14** (**a**, **b**)The adjacent possible. (Adapted: Loreto et al. 2017)

specific company though. For example, they would not have an excellent customer fit, they would lie too far outside the company's traction space, or they would not be an optimal fit for its goals and criteria. Identifying and selecting an innovation potential ensures that the ideas which lie within it can be achieved from the company's current position—in this way, minimising the risk. This fits the theory of the adjacent possible which states that new ideas are always located on the edge of the present state of things (see ■ Fig. 2.14a) and are achieved as a result of it (see ■ Fig. 2.14b) (MIT, 2017).

The adjacent possible shows that just as an iPhone could not have been invented without the telephone and a book could not have been invented without writing, companies cannot simply jump to the next, completely disruptive business model either, but have to approach it step by step. Consequently, limitations do not mean that companies should not and cannot change. It is just that this change should follow the greatest potentials, step by step.

The alternative to limiting the search area for innovations is, incidentally, to continuously transform the company which needs to adapt repeatedly to new ideas. This is only possible up to a certain company size though. For corporates, continuous transformation makes little sense because besides innovation, operative excellence is also vital even though that is inconsistent with transformation. Besides, studies show the low success rates of organisational change processes. In the McKinsey Global Survey 2015, for example, only 26% of the board members surveyed reported that transformations had been successful (McKinsey, 2015). And even if there sometimes need to be larger transformation projects due to certain influencing factors (e.g. often during the digitisation of a company), this should not become standard for innovation projects. After all, innovation must function in every company, no matter its size.

2

Case Study: Telekom Innovation Laboratories

Increase in Customer Satisfaction with Connectivity Solutions

Deutsche Telekom's Telekom Innovation Laboratories (T-Labs for short) focus on medium- and long-term innovation topics in the information and communication technology segment. An innovation project was initiated for a specialist product category in the connectivity solution segment with the objective of increasing the customer satisfaction of end customers.

Configuration

In line with the above goals and department-specific criteria, the *innovation space* 'customer experience' was firstly selected as part of the *configuration phase*. On the basis of general customer factors in the selected product category, such as low market maturity, weak market penetration and high barriers for potential consumers, the *opportunity space* 'improve customer experience when acquiring new customers (in the selected product category)' was then defined.

To develop specific *innovation potentials*, all of the relevant parameters and their variants within the opportunity space were identified systematically using the morphological box and then categorised and assessed. The customer journey when initially purchasing the connectivity solutions represented a particularly important parameter. Variants included, for example, information, advice, purchasing, usage, customer service and installation. Other relevant parameters relating to the goal selected included, for example, 'touch points' (with variants, such as branches, shop-in-shops, website, home, events, etc.) or 'transaction' (financing, subscription, freemium, free of charge, etc.).

From an analysis of the most relevant parameters and their variants based on market studies, statistics, surveys, etc., nine innovation potentials were finally derived for the remainder of the innovation process. It turned out, for example, that the 'installation' variant for the customer journey was particularly crucial since the purchase decision was significantly impacted by concerns about excessive complexity during installation and thus represented a relevant hurdle for potential new customers (◘ Figs. 2.15 and 2.16).

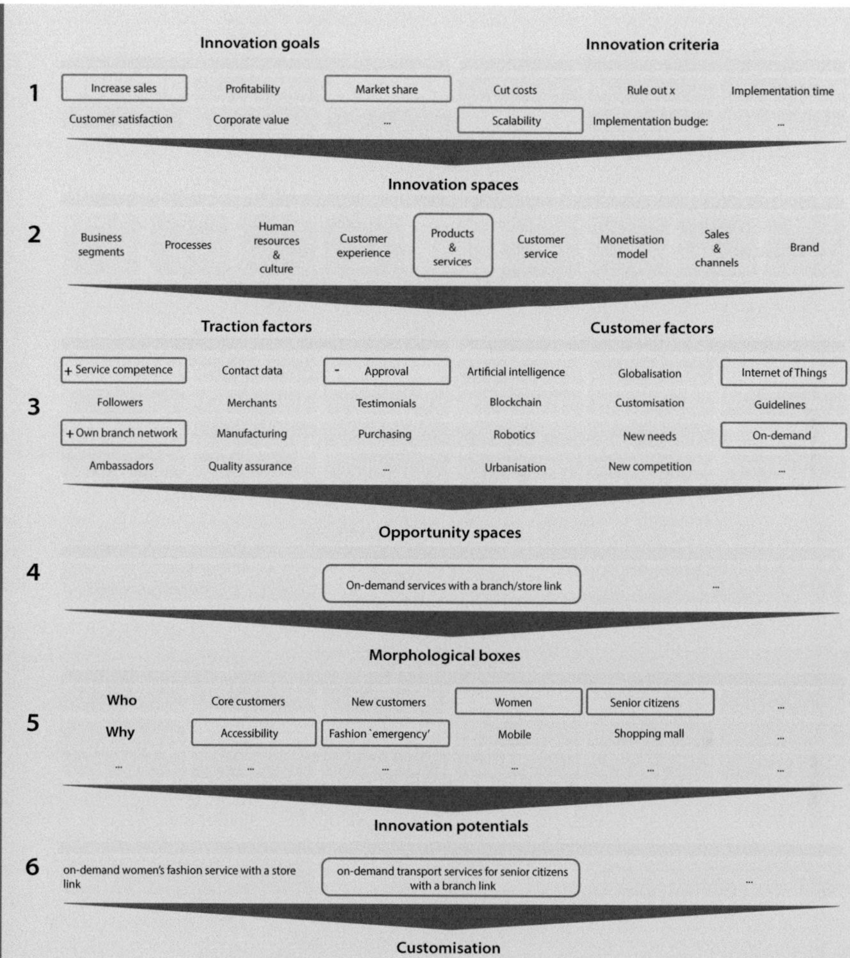

Fig. 2.15 Configuration process workflow. (Author's own figure)

2

Configuration Customisation Compilation Construction Conversion

1 2 3 4 5

Mind-set	**Don't think freely**		
Section	**The destination is the journey**	**Better a step in the right direction than a leap into the unknown**	**No risk, no fun**
Outcome	✓ Innovation space based on goals and criteria	✓ Opportunity space based on traction and customer factors	✓ Prioritised innovation potential
Methodology	1. Collect and weight the goals and criteria of all decision-makers (from 0-3; from irrelevant to highly relevant) 2. Assess innovation spaces against goals and criteria 3. Select the most relevant innovation space	1. Collect traction factors from stakeholders 2. Collect general custmer factors from stakeholders 3. Potentially supplement traction and customer factors (research) 4. Derive opportunity spaces: innovation space + customer factor (+ any traction factor) 5. Assess opportunity spaces according to whether they meet the goals and criteria 6. Select the most relevant opportunity space	1. Rely on morphological boxes for the opportunity space selected (e.g. \`W' questions) 2. Research specific customer factors according to morphological box variants 3. Derive innovation potentials: opportunity space + specific customer factor incl. target group 4. Assess according to goals and criteria 5. Select the most relevant potential
Aid	▫ List potential goals and criteria ▫ Overview of innovation spaces	▫ List potential traction factors ▫ Select current trends and technologies (customer factors) ▫ List goals and criteria (2.1.1)	▫ Morphological boxes ▫ List of goals and criteria (2.1.1) ▫ List of traction factors (2.1.2)

Fig. 2.16 Overview of configuration. (Author's own figure)

2.2 Customisation: No Problem Means No Solution Either

A solution without a problem is not really a solution. So innovation projects which do not solve any customer problems or pain points are simply obsolete. And yet the question of what the customer's actual problem is receives hardly attention in many innovation projects. Oliver Wyman's Car Innovation Study 2015, for example, showed that of the approximately EUR 800 billion research budget in the automotive industry, around 40%, i.e. EUR 320 billion(!), is wasted on the wrong projects. Of the 315 innovations studied, only 10% had the potential to be well received by the customer (Wyman, 2015). A ratio like this can be easily improved by identifying the relevant customer needs even before the idea has been developed.

A specific customer problem is described as a pain point if it represents an unmet or unsatisfied need. A pain point is always based on a specific customer insight, i.e. an insight gained from the target group or the customer. Here, the customer is the person who the innovation project is aimed at. With process innovations, for example, this can even be the employee. Since 'no problem means no solution either', we must therefore identify the most relevant pain points for the innovation project before we can start the search for ideas. So customisation describes the process from the innovation potential to the pain point (see ◘ Fig. 2.17).

Many companies have already internalised the importance of pain points with customer-centric innovation methods, such as design thinking. With the right mindset and with methods and tools which are an excellent fit, the customer is once more the main focus of innovation efforts. Since these companies are already working specifically on the customer fit of ideas, we can easily build on the system for efficient innovations described here.

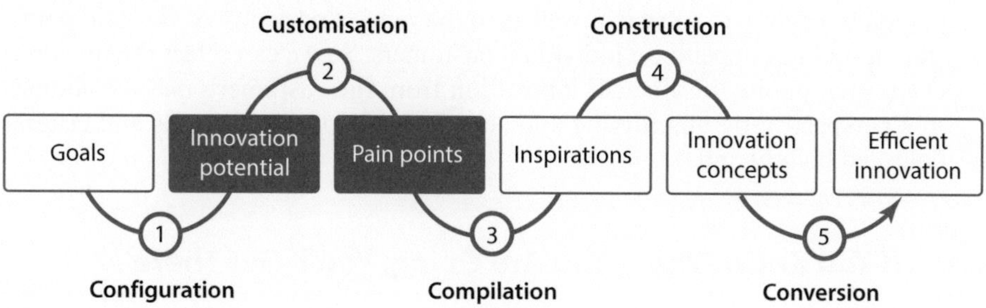

◘ **Fig. 2.17** 5C process-customisation. (Author's own figure)

In contrast to design thinking, however, searching for and selecting relevant pain points follows a much more analytical system. This is so that later on we can identify the exact pain points whose solution not only offers the best customer fit, but the best traction too. The methodology must ensure that the pain points also fit the traction space, that is, we must identify those customer problems which the company can best solve. After all, no customer can profit from solutions which the company is unable to implement (or is unable to implement well), no matter how customer-centrically they were developed.

The following **three steps are key for determining pain points** and are described in more detail below:

1. **If you know where you are going, you'll get there**: customers always have problems, if you only ask them. Consequently, you could be inventing new solutions all over the place if you blindly followed the customer's problems. Yet systematic preparation in advance will allow you to identify the most important pain points for the innovation potential in a goal-orientated way based on customer factors. This will enable you to clearly identify and select search spaces, methods and participants so that you arrive at the key pain points.
2. **If you don't ask, you won't get**: if you do not ask the right questions, you will not get the right answers either. When identifying pain points, it is similarly important to use the right type of questions and the right methods to identify significant pain points in a goal-orientated way. Specific techniques ensure that customers talk about the problems which are relevant to them. This enables us to dig deep enough to get to the real pain points rather than just superficial complaints and aspirations.
3. **The customer is not always king**: because if that were the case, we would not be able to decide which pain point to solve. Since this decision is also linked to the company's ability to solve it as well as to the general relevance of the pain point, this should not depend on individual customers. So we can select the most relevant pain points for efficient innovation from the customer's *and* the company's perspective by quantifying and selecting the company's goals and criteria collected beforehand.

2.2.1 If You Know Where You Are Going, You'll Get There

'If you don't know where you are going, you might wind up someplace else', as the author Mark Twain already remarked. This statement also holds just as true in the innovation process. It is only if you know beforehand which problem you need to solve that you will be able to develop a suitable solution. And it is only if you systematically plan in advance exactly how you can identify the relevant pain points that you will end up identifying the customer problems which can best be solved by the company. The good news is that no matter what innovation potential you choose and how strongly you focus on it in advance, there will usually be enough customer problems to solve. It is therefore crucial to identify the most important ones.

The problem or customer need should always be as specific and sufficiently relevant as possible. The more specific the customer problem is, the more innovative the solution can be for the customer (customer fit). All pain points should lie within the defined innovation potential so that they can also be solved successfully by the company in the end (traction). To achieve this, it is not enough to use learned market research methodology with more or less randomly defined participants. Instead, you must determine the pain points systematically by examining the most relevant target groups in the most important *search spaces* using methods which offer the best fit, depending on the innovation potential.

The first step is to establish the right **framework for determining the pain points**. This depends on the following three questions:

1. *Where should you search?* To determine pain points, you need **search spaces** which set the topic you are to survey the target group about. Normally, companies fall back on a given system to identify possible search spaces. For example, in design thinking we use the 'customer journey' which divides up the entire customer process for a product or service into individual steps and then uses these as search spaces for the pain points (HYPE, 2017c). But we must also question whether the steps in the customer journey are actually always the most relevant search spaces—from both the customer's and the company's perspective, in fact. Are there not perhaps other aspects which are at least just as important, but which do not appear specifically enough in the customer journey? We can thus regard a supermarket purchase as a customer journey, from the empty fridge at home to selecting the products and paying for them to filling the fridge. Yet, what about when there are different target groups, different causes, other channels and touchpoints, media influence and situations with different needs? In the best scenario, factors like that turn up in the customer journey on the fringes. Whether the focus will return to these depends entirely on the customer surveyed though. The customer journey alone is therefore not enough. Instead of using such a rigid system, it is worth selecting the most important search spaces in the selected innovation potentials from a larger pool of customer factors in advance. These spaces can then be filled in a goal-orientated way with customer insights to determine the pain points from them. For the sake of simplicity, it makes sense to select the most relevant customer factors for the innovation potential to be surveyed from the list of parameters assessed previously on the basis of the morphological box (see ▶ Sect. 2.1.5). So the customer journey does not set the search spaces in advance. Rather, these emerge from the most important customer factors within the innovation potential.
2. *Who should you survey?* Identifying suitable participants for a survey is not an easy task. A **clear target group** has not always been identified in the beginning, because discovering new target groups can form part of the innovation process. Design thinking suggests overcoming this problem by creating fictive 'personas' which precisely describe possible customer types. Personas are fictitious characters with specific characteristics, such as a name, age, gender, occupation, consumer habits, income, aspirations, etc. In the best scenario, these multifaceted

stereotypes are based on field and milieu research, but often also simply on empathy and the power of imagination (Jung, 2017). This methodology is hence a further development of traditional target group descriptions—like 'a 40-year-old man with a middle income'—to put yourself in the customer's position and develop differentiated ideas during the search for ideas and development as best you can by condensing and reducing complexity. A solution which would not be used by at least one persona would then drop out of the innovation process. The problem with this comes from generally dividing up target groups in advance—whether that occurs in the traditional way or using personas. Customer insights are then made to depend on more or less randomly selected personas. Yet a targeted search needs you to survey the most relevant target group. In this process, this target group should already have been selected by identifying the innovation potential, because this always follows on from combining the customer factor and the target group (see ► Sect. 2.1.5). However, if the target group is still unclear or insufficiently detailed at this point, then you will need further in-depth research into the customer factors which are key to the innovation potential. Depending on how specifically or generally you can ultimately determine the target group, you also need to select the participants based on customer factors in your market research. Then instead of providing customer types with qualitative (imaginary) characteristics, like we do in design thinking, we determine these by a delving deeper into the key customer factors to collect more details about the innovation potential's target group.

3. *How should you search?* There are many possible methods for identifying pain points—interviews, focus groups, online communities, lead users, ethnography, observations or social experiments—and they all have their advantages and disadvantages (see the following excursus). Often, **market research methodology** is only selected on the basis of the underlying organisational conditions or subjective preferences. People like to conduct simple on-the-street interviews in brief design thinking workshops. Marketing agencies often hold discussions in carefully arranged, representative focus groups, and innovation consultancies extend their surveys to observations or ethnography. Innovation consultancy RED, for example, describes its approach as 'Observing, participating, questioning and being in the same psychological and physical environment as the customer [which] enables us to understand and give an account of their stories' (RED Associates, 2017). The 'lead user analysis', originally devised by Eric von Hippel, is also enjoying increasing popularity. This involves working with customers who are already heavily involved with a product or service and developing new solutions for it. In the 1970s, for example, mountain bikers started building their own bikes from various motorcycle and bicycle parts. A company named Specialized Bicycle Components in California, USA, noticed this use of their bicycle parts and began to manufacture their own mountain bikes. Today, mountain bikes account for 60% of the market for specialist bicycles (Phillips, 2009). So this methodology can be very successful. In particular, companies with 'enthusiast products', such as LEGO, rely on such lead users. LEGO hence works with experts from BrickFest, the annual LEGO customer conference, to develop the next generation of its Mindstorms series (Lund, 2014).

All of these methods always lead, of course, to *a few* customer insights and pain points, and sometimes even to new ideas. Although whether those are even the most relevant pain points and solutions for the innovation potential remains a random event. To make it possible to plan for success here, we should also select the methods to identify the pain points to fit the innovation potentials and search spaces (customer factors). This system can determine which methods are able to best process which search spaces. So while it may be helpful to ask customers for their opinion about a price, if the most interesting parameter is, for example, the commissioning a device process step, observations about that may be more meaningful. Similarly, lead user analysis can help when product features are a relevant search space, whereas feelings may be best discovered through ethnography or technological tests, etc. The same is true for innovation potentials themselves. If, for example, the subject is incontinence, it can be difficult to put together a focus group on that, whereas using incontinence pads yourself will identify many pain points. So it is important to know the different methods and their possible areas of application—and then to select one which fits the search space and the target group.

Excursus: Overview of Selected Market Research Methods

The following methods enable market information and customer insights to be included for assessing or validating innovation projects.

Focus Groups

A focus group usually refers to a moderated group discussion which is usually based on guidelines containing open questions. The goal of the research method—which you could also describe as a partially standardised interview—is to find out participants' relevance system. They can express their personal views via broad questions. The influence of the group in open discussions is welcomed and regarded as part of the dynamics.

Surveys

When collecting data in the form of a survey, respondents are asked a series of questions drafted in advance. This survey may be spoken or written, online or real. It is characteristic that the possible answers are set in advance, and closed questions are asked to generate quantitative data material. The person being surveyed assigns a score to a particular question or statement depending on their degree of agreement or selects an appropriate preset answer option.

Ethnography

This methodology uses unfiltered research into people's behaviour patterns to establish the relevant behaviours, rituals and problems or opportunities. One classic application is participatory observation in which the researcher involves themselves in real problems and application scenarios alongside the target group. The person being observed is left to themselves and is not controlled by anyone running the experiment. Another variant is making a video recording of the customer during the interaction which is being investigated.

2

Censuses

Censuses are a direct form of collecting information in addition to observations. Here, the goal of the study is defined and measured quantitatively. It is used for visitor flows or traffic surveys in particular.

Online Tracking

With tracking, the movement of the subject to be observed is tracked so that their time-space behaviour can be studied. These days, it is happening increasingly online. It can, for example, establish how long a user lingers on a certain webpage and observes which links they click and other user behaviour (such as cursor movements).

Lead Users

The lead user method focuses on trend leaders who are actively interested in meeting their own needs in an innovative way. Lead users enjoy a certain expert status due to their intensive examination of the topic in question. To involve lead users in the market research and development process, joint workshops are particularly suitable for developing new application spaces or solution approaches or for jointly validating or optimising new solutions developed.

Once you have systematically selected and prepared your search spaces, participants and methods based on the previous analysis, you can generate customer insights in a goal-orientated way in the next step. In this way, you will end up where you wanted to go—at the pain points with the greatest relevance for your company and your customers.

2.2.2 If You Don't Ask, You Won't Get

'If I had asked people what they wanted, they would have said "faster horses".' This famous quotation by Henry Ford does *not* show that you should not ask the customer, only that you cannot expect them to present you with an instant solution to a problem. The customer survey step should therefore not be used to discover from the customer what they want, but to understand what their problems are (customer insights) and what their hidden and as yet unsatisfied needs are (pain points).

In the Henry Ford example, the question 'What should be improved about the carriage?' would probably have led to the answer 'The horses should be faster'. With this answer, you can at best develop incremental innovations, such as better feed or training for the horses—but not the car. That problem still exists even today. Companies usually ask their customers what they want. They then reply in product or service terms, that is, they want 'faster horses', 'a video telephone' or 'to buy food online'. When these requests have been granted in the form of products and services, customers do not buy them at all, because their real needs have not been recognised. This problem is exacerbated by companies often only looking at trends or big data and then deducing customer needs from those. As these have already been considered in the 5C process as general customer factors in the previous steps and covered under focus, we now need to drill down deeper to identify the specific pain points and hence the actual unsatisfied needs underlying the generic customer factors.

Lindstrom (2016) describes this phenomenon in his book *Small Data*. Using the company LEGO as an example, he points out that it is important to discover the real problems of real people and to see them in their natural environment. In 2002, LEGO was in crisis. The problem was quickly identified. Video games tied the children to the television and resulted in quick gratification and correspondingly low attention spans. This enabled them to identify the suspected pain point. LEGO then reacted with larger bricks to offer success in minutes rather than hours. However, its revenues continued to fall, only even more so.

It became clear that the real pain point had not yet been found. Children seemed to have other needs which LEGO had not yet been able to recognise or serve. LEGO employees then visited the room of an 11-year-old boy in search of small data and asked him what his most valuable possession was. Surprisingly, he pointed to his worn trainers. These were the proof that the boy was the best skater in the city, because the soles showed all the traces of his tricks and slides. From this, LEGO learnt that despite toys which provide immediate gratification, children could also spend hundreds of hours with their passion when it was the focus of their attention. So LEGO developed products to fit this, such as smaller blocks and more complex builds as well as a storytelling tailored to this (e.g. *The LEGO Movie*).

Real pain points and trends can hence be derived from small customer insights and served by solutions—provided these are identified correctly. A simple question about what kind of LEGO product the boy wanted would probably not have led him to realise that he primarily wanted to be able to show off something proudly and feel like the centre of 'his' LEGO world.

An assessment of customer needs using simple, superficial or direct questions is therefore wrong on several accounts. It runs the great risk that you will not find the best solution at all, because it has not been considered by the customer and so is not included in the selection. Furthermore, customers are not necessarily able to make the link between (technological) products and services and their personal needs.

Surveys must instead find out **which function or job a product or service does for people** and how a company can design them better or cheaper. Henry Ford would then have found out that the horses did not really matter. People just wanted to get from A to B as quickly as possible, take their own individual route, be sheltered from the weather or that horses were expensive to maintain, etc. Many of these fundamental problems were solved with the car. And LEGO has just found out that playing should make children proud and must put them at the heart of the story.

This process is described in more detail in models, such as outcome-driven innovation or the jobs-to-be-done approach (Chatterjee, 1998). Anthony Ulwick (2002a) from the innovation consultancy Strategyn tells how, for example, customers should not be expected to produce solutions, because they are not experts and are therefore not sufficiently well enough informed for this part of the innovation process. Instead, customers should only be asked about outcomes which describe what a new innovation should do for them. Instead of 'video telephone', they might perhaps have received the answer that customers wanted to be more connected to the people they are talking to on the phone, and instead of 'to buy food online', it might have been spending less time shopping. It should be the company rather than the customer deciding what the solutions to these pain points look like.

Clayton M. Christensen (2016) describes in an example how the specialist glass manufacturer Corning Inc. repeatedly focused on the 'job to be done'. The company is strongly technology-driven. When premium prices can no longer be achieved in a sector as a result of technological advances, the company therefore relies on innovations. For example, Corning was a market leader in CRT displays. Instead of just asking their customers what could be improved so it could continue achieving high prices with the technology, the company focused on the job to be done, manufacturing the best possible displays. Logically, Corning realised that LCD technology would have many advantages for this job in future, and so it developed LCD products and left the CRT market altogether in the end.

This example shows that companies win in the market if they produce innovations which enable customers to achieve the outcomes they want faster, cheaper or better than with the existing solutions. To find these innovations, we need to identify and assess not just solutions and ideas, but customer insights and the pain points derived from them.

A **good customer insight addresses the three 'Ws'. What does the customer do? (subject), Why does the customer do it? (job to be done), and Does it have the Wow factor? (wow, nobody knew that before)**. An insight is therefore always *focused* on a specific subject, or in our case, customer factor. It is *real* in relation to a specific need or a job to be done, and it is *new* if this is an unprecedented insight (see ◘ Fig. 2.18). If no suitable solution exists for such an insight (i.e. there is just the 'pain', but no solution to alleviate it), a potential pain point exists. This then has the potential to trigger innovations with an excellent customer fit.

A good example of a relevant customer insight is the repositioning of the Persil brand for washing powder. In an observational study with mothers and children for its Persil brand in the United Kingdom, parent company Unilever discovered that 'dirt' had positive associations for many of the mothers. They saw

Digital offers for young travellers	On-demand women's fashion service with a store link	Artificial intelligence advice for WhatsApp users	Software-as-a-Service for hospitals	...
Want to travel alone, not confident enough	Want to spend less on clothing	Want personal contact	Find software too complicated	...
Want time out from their mobile	All felt the same brands	Want to bypass the waiting time	Don't want to worry about anything	...

Customer insight = new customer need discovered (pain point = unsatisfied customer insight)

◘ **Fig. 2.18** Example of customer insights in innovation potentials. (Author's own figure)

dirt as a learning experience for their children who were playing outside or were creative inside and acquiring new experiences—and they were proud of their children. This customer insight was also a pain point as it had not yet been resolved. In their brand message and positioning, detergents (naturally) all focused on describing dirt as a negative and promised clinical cleanliness. On the strength of this pain point, (Persil, 2017) was transformed into a much more emotional and friendly brand with a new message ('dirt is good') and new products and services. These included not only that slogan but also, for example, a focus on introducing children to more outdoor activities. The brand thus achieved double-digit growth for many years.

But how specifically do you find the key customer insights? They are mostly hidden under layers of superficial answers, assumptions and ambiguities. Like an onion where you can peel away all of the layers, you therefore need to remove layer after layer using the right—and always in-depth—questions or experiences until you find the most revealing customer insights in the search space. Depending on the methodology you use, your type of question or experience is crucial. Open questions can help to open up the space to obtain possible answers. Repeated 'why' questions help to get to the heart of interesting customer insights. Your own experiences (ethnography) or 'why' questions combined with observations may also reveal deeper insights.

At the same time, the researchers themselves are also important. This questioner (for interviews), moderator (for focus groups) or observer must be able to enter into a real dialogue with the customer, listen intelligently so they can understand what was said and which questions they need to ask to find out where potential might lie. They must therefore be able to lead without asking any leading questions and understand without being told everything. It needs a researcher who can work their way through the layers of vague statements, anecdotes or irrelevant comments. Statements must be clarified, detailed and validated while at the same time ensuring all of the key aspects are taken into account—making previously unconsidered directions within the search space possible (Ulwick, 2002b).

In an example, the customer satisfaction for a smaller bank was evaluated. The company was convinced that satisfaction depended on its client advisors as these were the very people who formed the core of the bank's offer. Detailed questions which went beyond the mere bank advisor showed that, in fact, it was the call centres which were causing the greatest dissatisfaction as they limited access to the customer advisors and had no access to the relevant customer data (Lawrence Somerset Ltd, 2017).

The exact pain points which are based on the customer insights for the innovation potential now need to be identified. Trained market researchers or anthropologists can help to identify the most relevant outcomes, patterns and opportunities using content analysis and discussions with business experts, designers, marketers and other specialists and transfer these across to potential pain points. A pain point is always an unmet need based on at least one specific customer insight or pattern. Further details on a process also termed coding can be found in the social science literature, in particular.

It is only if you know which are the most relevant pain points within the innovation potential that you can develop solutions with the best possible customer fit. To ensure that pain points have not actually been resolved and to identify which pain points offer the greatest potential, you still need to quantify them formally and prioritise them from the customer's perspective (customer fit). You must also assess and prioritise them from the company's perspective to ensure an optimal fit with the company's goals and criteria (traction). The next section describes the specific approach to this.

2.2.3 The Customer Is Not Always King

'The customer is king' is the motto of customer-centric innovation—and fundamentally, that is the way it should be. But this does not mean that every pain point which is important for a customer should be blindly incorporated into the innovation process as the basis for the search for ideas. When selecting the most relevant pain point, the customer is not always king. Instead, both customer fit and overall traction must be maximised to achieve efficient innovation.

To maximise customer fit, pain points should be quantified and prioritised in a statistically significant customer survey. This ensures that the small data insights really have far-reaching relevance too. To maximise traction potential, the most important pain points are then re-assessed against the company's objectives and criteria which were stated at the outset. Even if all of the pain points tend to lie in the innovation potential and thus in the traction space of the company, this then ensures that the customer's problems *and* the company's skills *and* the will to solve them are in proportion to each other to the maximum possible extent—and it is not the customers who are driving the company forward without it having a recognisable strategy. The customer really feels like a king, especially when they are not only asked what they want, but their problems are then solved in the best possible way.

The most successful companies lead the customer rather than the other way around (Skribsted, 2014). Take Amazon, for example. If the company had selected random pain points for its book customers, it might have developed a reading lamp, a bookmark or online book exchange. However, by specifically identifying the most relevant pain points in terms of their innovation potential—the consumption of e-books—before there was even a market for them, the Kindle could be developed as a separate device with a special e-ink screen and a long battery life and set off on its march of triumph, armed with Amazon's strengths in the content business.

Similarly, Apple did not prioritise every little thing which was bothering users about mobile phones. Instead, they looked at why users were not yet using the Internet and digital media sufficiently on their mobiles—because for Apple, that was the most relevant potential. Rather than manufacturing a mobile phone with a faster Internet connection and a longer battery life, the iPhone was developed with native apps and a large touch screen which disrupted the mobile phone market.

In order to maximize the customer fit, the pain points should be quantified and prioritized in a statistically significant customer survey with the target group. This is because the customer insights from the previous primary research are mostly based on the statements of individual customers ('small data'). On that basis alone, it is not yet certain whether a problem also has general significance. Quantitative methods, such as surveys, censuses or experimental notes using as representative a sample as possible, are able to help here. From practical experience, we particularly recommend using an online survey which enables you to assess whether the potential pain points for a target group are statistically significant based on a larger number of cases. In the *Harvard Business Review*, Anthony Ulwick (2002b) proposes an assessment based on two criteria. Each pain point is initially assessed on a scale of 1–10 according to its importance and then its current satisfaction. The questions are therefore as follows:

1. *Meaning: How important is the pain point/problem XYZ for you? (1 = unimportant, 10 = important)*
2. *Satisfaction: To what extent has pain point/problem XYZ already been solved? (1 = not at all, 10 = completely)*

If you insert the quantitative answers into a mathematical formula, you can then estimate the relevance of the respective pain point or level of customer fit. The formula is very simple:

$$\text{Meaning} + (\text{meaning} - \text{satisfaction}) = \text{relevance}.$$

If a problem is very important to the customer, but has already been addressed, it will have a lower score than an important problem that has not yet been addressed: $10 + (10 - 10) = 10 < 10 + (10 - 1) = 19$. Like this, you can create an initial ranking of the most relevant pain points from the customer's perspective.

To maximise the traction potential as well, the second step is to assess the most relevant pain points from the company's perspective. This ensures that you process the needs with the greatest potential for customer fit *and* traction. It now makes sense to assess the pain points with the highest ranking from the customer's perspective in terms of the innovation project's goals and criteria collected previously, e.g. from 1 (poor potential) to 10 (great potential).

You can then **simply select the most relevant pain point**. The pain point (or several pain points, depending on the resources) which ranked the highest in this two-step logic (customer fit and traction) can be used as the starting point or 'task definition' for work on the selected innovation potential in the next steps. Decision-makers should double-check everything latest at this point. In this context, you can present and discuss the pain points which have been determined and how they have been derived. The more easily stakeholders understand how the pain point has been selected, the more confidence they will have in the innovation project in the future. For this reason, a further round of assessments should also be carried out with the decision-makers so that you actively take them with you and optimally determine their needs for the subsequent steps, allowing these to flow into the assessment. To this end, the key stakeholders can assess the various pain points according to their potential to achieve the goals and criteria—as may have already happened when selecting the opportunity space and the innovation potential.

2

With this insight-based pain point which has been confirmed by customers and all of the key stakeholders and derived from the *customisation*, we now move into the preparation of idea development in advance, termed *compilation*. Here, we describe how we can meet the relevant pain points with the relevant inspiration and the information required to find solutions.

Case Study: A Container Shipping Company

Differentiation Strategy for Selling Maritime Services to Third Parties

When the global financial and economic crisis broke out in 2008, the shipping industry was hit hard. Constant pressure on the income of shipping companies worldwide triggered momentous losses for investors. As part of this development, this particular container shipping company was forced to sell some of its own ships. At the same time, it was decided that the resulting personnel overcapacity would be offered to third party shipowners in the form of 'maritime services'.

Configuration

The most important goal for this container shipping company was to increase or stabilise revenue over the long term. At the same time, a quick solution had to be found for the existing personnel overcapacities as these produced costs, but no revenues if they were not used by third parties. The *innovation space* sales and channels was therefore selected.

On the basis of an analysis of the market situation, it became clear that banks and private equity funds were a particularly relevant target group for maritime services, and so the *opportunity space* of 'marketing maritime services to banks and private equity funds' was consequently identified.

There is enormous competitive pressure in the maritime services sector. Globally, more than a thousand companies offer similar services. However, initial benchmarking among the main competitors revealed that there was hardly any differentiation between the offers, and that the target group of banks and private equity funds had not yet been precisely addressed with specific offers. Consequently, 'developing a differentiation strategy for marketing maritime services to banks and private equity funds' was set as an *innovation potential* for the remainder of the process.

Customisation

As part of the *customisation phase*, various insights were obtained using quantitative surveys and qualitative individual interviews with people from the target group of banks and private equity fund (which own container ships). The most important *pain point* was identified, namely, existing offers by maritime service providers were not yet focusing on the *profitability* of the investment (i.e. the ship). This precise factor was the (only) essential one of interest to the banks and private equity funds. This is in stark contrast to usual shipowners who, for example, want to know exactly where the ship is, how many crew members are on board of the ship, how much fuel or load the ship is carrying, etc.

Based on the pain point identified, differentiation features were developed for the maritime services of this container shipping company during the remainder of the 5C process and were translated into a sales strategy targeted at banks and private equity funds. Using this new strategy, the personnel overcapacities could not only be eliminated, but a new maritime services division was substantially built up within just 6 months (◘ Fig.. 2.19).

Configuration (1) – **Customisation (2)** – Compilation (3) – Construction (4) – Conversion (5)

Mind-set	**No problems mean no solutions either**		
Section	**If you know where you are going, you'll get there**	**If you don't ask, you won't get**	**The customer is not always king**
Outcome	✓ Framework for market research	✓ Customer insights and pain points	✓ Pain points validated and prioritised
Methodology	1. Identify the search spaces using the parameters/variants from the compilation phase 2. Review and potentially specify the target group and participants 3. Identify the market research methodology (ies) using the innovation potential and relevant search spaces (parameters)	1. Prepare suitable questions/studies for the search space (depending on the methodology) 2 Gain customer insights using the selected methodology 3 Analyse the customer insights (coding) to derive the relevant pain points	1. Validate the pain points using a quantitative customer survey ***(How relevant/how unsatisfied is the pain point?)*** 2. Analyse the customer survey to determine the most relevant pain points (quantitatively) 3. Assess the pain points based on goals and criteria from 2.1.1 (with the critical stakeholders) 4. Select one or more pain points to be processed
Aid	▫ Overview of market research methods ▫ Morphological boxes (2.1.3)	▫ Search spaces (2.2.1) ▫ Overview of questioning techniques	▫ Survey tool ▫ Goals and criteria (2.1.1)

◘ **Fig. 2.19** Overview of customisation. (Author's own figure)

2.3 Compilation: If You Want to Reap, You Must First Sow

What applies to working in the fields applies equally to ideas. Without the right seeds, you cannot reap the desired crop. Even Newton would not have had the infamous apple fall on his head making him reflect on the idea of gravity if someone had not planted an apple tree beforehand.

Experience shows that it is difficult to find targeted solutions for a specific pain point if you can only use your existing knowledge. The search for ideas then degenerates into a game of chance, especially when these new ideas need to be unique worldwide. The rule for a systematic innovation process should therefore be *no new ideas without new inspiration*.

Inspiration is new information which can be used as the impetus for new ideas, like a kind of 'springboard for creativity' (Kaufman, 2011). They always precede the actual idea. Oleynick/Trash (2014) refer to the inspiration phase resulting from a stimulus (i.e. new information) as *evocation*, and the subsequent transformation of inspiration into a new idea as *transcendence*. Creativity expert Dave Birss describes the phase of collecting inspiration as 'dot collecting' where 'dots' stand for individual pieces of information. He explains that the brain can only work with what it receives in input. He therefore recommends collecting as many and varied dots as possible to obtain a wide diversity of input, and consequently, as large a number of different ideas as possible for a particular task definition (McGowan, 2016). New external information hence expands your horizons. It forms the basis of finding a sufficiently large number of new ideas.

If you search for inspiration at precisely the pain point you have selected previously (and thus also at the innovation potential in the traction space), it can be used to innovate as closely as possible to the core business and as disruptively as needed. You can thus ensure traction *and* customer fit systematically. Compilation describes the process undertaken from the selected pain point (or several pain points) through to the relevant inspiration (see ◘ Fig. 2.20).

A foray into neuroscience also shows why inspirations are so important. Ideas can be regarded here as manifestations of a complex network of neurons which fire in the brain. *New* ideas are always possible in this network when *new* connec-

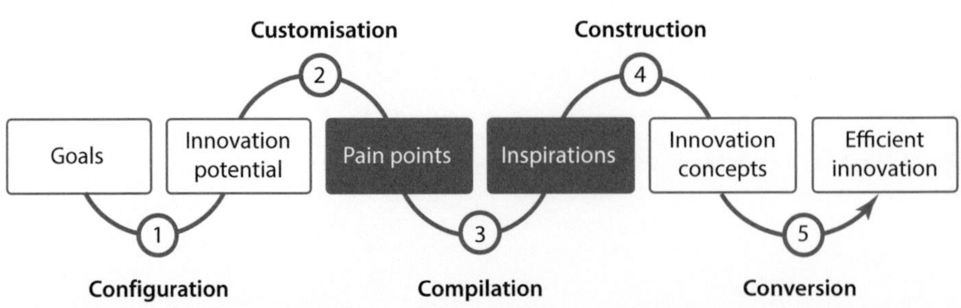

◘ **Fig. 2.20** 5C process: compilation. (Author's own figure)

tions are made—which usually happens when *new* information meets the existing knowledge base (we recommend the TED talk on the subject: Where good ideas come from by Steven Johnson).

This was also shown in an experiment by neuroscientist Charlan Nemeth. Two groups were supposed to produce associations with certain colours. The first group was only shown different colours. In the second group, however, people who had received prior instructions from the researchers were integrated into the group. Occasionally they claimed to see different colours—and thus added new information to that shown. While the first group produced rather obvious associations (e.g. 'sky' for the colour blue), the second group was much more creative. The additional information provided by the 'mistakes' obviously inspired the participants to consider a larger number of opportunities (Lehrer, 2012).

Research from sources of inspiration contradicts many of the current innovation methods which support quick brainstorming and testing. However, our experience has repeatedly shown that it is worthwhile developing a good basis for inspiration and information before (or for) generating ideas. If this does not happen, there is a probability that companies will process exactly the same ideas and solutions as their competitors. This is because companies in the same industry usually work on the basis of similar information or a similar wealth of experience, and thus come up with similar or even identical solutions when searching for ideas. This is a phenomenon which the relevant actors are often unaware of. If the competition launches an almost identical solution in the market a few months before or after their own product innovation, players tend to assume that it was an unfortunate random event or even industrial espionage. They fail to recognise what is obvious, namely, that there is systemic error in their own innovation process. This is because their process is obviously not adequate enough to ensure that really new solutions are found. This is exactly what is key though if you are to achieve competitive advantages in the long run. And so it is worth distinguishing between 'norm ideas' and 'ideas outside the norm', that is, ideas which are particularly likely (norm ideas) in stark contrast to ideas which go beyond the previous limits of our experience (ideally, that of the entire industry) thanks to a solid basis of inspiration (ideas outside the norm). It is only the latter category of ideas which systematically ensures that a company's own innovations generate competitive advantages over their competition.

In one project for a snack manufacturer, we had an opportunity to examine the phenomenon of norm ideas in detail. During the first step of the innovation project, we had already noted down ideas which occurred along the way without further inspiration. After some time, we were presented with a list of ideas from an agency which had already brainstormed the same topic for the snack manufacturer a year earlier. It was a huge shock. Of the 20 ideas on the agency's list, 18 of the ideas were almost identical to those we had already developed along the way without sources of inspiration. By contrast, after ideation supported by inspiration, we ended up developing more than 70 feasible innovative concepts which had not appeared on any previous list.

Since then, we have been excluding norm ideas from the very start of the ideation. We ensure that really new solutions are found not only by collecting targeted inspiration and information. We even start every innovation project with a brainstorming session to exclude the ideas generated during this brainstorming from playing any further part in the process. The logic behind this is that if we generate new ideas built on a similar knowledge base (ours and that of our customer), these ideas are likely to match the ideas which are already being developed in other companies. Once these norm ideas have been identified, we can exclude them from the possible solutions in the innovation process going forward. In this way, we can systematically increase the probability that our own later innovations will actually generate new, competitive advantages in the long run.

The following three steps help with the targeted identification of suitable sources of inspiration:

1. **Seek and you will find**: we have already outlined above that the search for inspiration is key for the wider innovation process. However, it is also important that this is a goal-orientated search. Ultimately, you should ensure that you do not find just any old sources of inspiration, but only the 'right' *ones*, i.e. sources of inspiration which can actually contribute to solving the problem. Benchmarking can be used to determine best practices in terms of existing innovations for solving pain points in the domestic and international market. This will simultaneously enable you to identify white spots for which there have so far been no obvious solution approaches (best practices) to the problem identified—and for which the subsequent search for inspiration is particularly worthwhile.
2. **Good artists copy; great artists steal**: on the basis of the white spots and other search parameters you have identified, you need to think outside your own enterprise and market from now on. You must identify solutions to similar problems in other industries. These similar examples can then be adapted in the ideation and made to fit your own problem and the implementation which is needed.
3. **Put off until tomorrow what you cannot do today**: it is not always the case that problems have already been solved in other industries or markets. White spots will therefore stay white initially. All the better, because this shows that the potential is all the greater. And what cannot be solved today might be solved tomorrow. You can find inspiration for this by looking into the future. Whether this is technologies, concepts, research results or patents—often, solutions and insights which have not yet been implemented can provide the crucial inspiration.

2.3.1 Seek and You Will Find

The search for sources of inspiration seems by definition to be random and chaotic—you are always hoping that any associations will randomly lead to a brilliant idea. In fact, it is exactly the other way around. The most helpful sources of inspiration are those which can be used as specifically as possible to provide the exact solution to the problem. So you must look for the most relevant information and sources of inspiration to increase the quality and accuracy of the ideas generated on this basis. If you seek inspiration in a targeted way, this also increases the probability that you will find the ideas with the best fit.

But where should this targeted search begin? Since we are to process solutions for one (or more) specific pain point(s), it is these very pain points which also represent the starting point for the search which follows. We will search for any solutions and approaches to solutions to the customer's problem in various stages to generate an initial source of inspiration for the following idea phase. For example, just as a chef who has been awarded stars and is inspired by Asian cuisine can combine this with his existing knowledge to create something completely new, best practices drawn from the market can lead to new ideas. In the first step, it is crucial to search in your own industry so that you understand which solutions exist already—and which do not. Even for a single pain point, there can be different solution directions as well as approaches (e.g. expensive, inexpensive, digital, analogue, centralised, decentralised, etc.), making benchmarking worthwhile.

The search for **best practices**—i.e. success stories in your industry—forms the **basis for collecting sources of inspiration**. It is now a good idea to first draw up a **list of the most important competitors currently** and to start there with your analysis. The basic questions (who is offered what and at what price) can establish a structure here, as can the most relevant parameters and variants in the morphological box (see ► Sect. 2.1.5).

In addition, we recommend including important **start-ups in your benchmarking process**. Start-up databases, such as Crunchbase, offer a good starting point for this with their topic-specific search options. One exciting side effect is that you can also identify possible start-ups for a potential acquisition or investment in a goal-orientated way like this. A certain fit accuracy is already systematically built in with start-ups identified in this way, because their business should at least fit certain objectives, criteria and the opportunity space. So the M&A activities of large companies can also benefit from this step in the innovation process if external acquisitions are also an option in addition to developing their own innovations.

Furthermore, it is worth extending the search area to international markets. You can achieve this using Internet research and/or local specialists. Trade fair visits at home and abroad which focus specifically on the pain point you are looking for can complement your search for best practices while at the same time expanding your existing contact network.

Energy drink manufacturer Red Bull provides a particularly prominent and simple example. The owner discovered the energy drink in Thailand and realised that a drink like this did not yet exist in most other countries. By licensing the drink for the rest of the world (and by innovative marketing), Red Bull was able to develop into a very successful international company.

The **search for best practices** also reveals another important piece of information, **white spots**. A white spot (often also called a 'white space') is a potential solution area for a certain pain point where no solutions so far exist. This may arise on the basis of a gap in the existing offers or represent an area without competition or even offer potential for a completely new market. It must be noted here that a wide range of definitions exist for this (Johnson, 2010). In our definition, white spots are *market opportunities based on a pain point which could be better served by a solution that does not yet exist.*

If it becomes apparent after a detailed examination that such a white spot for a certain pain point actually exists, a particularly large potential for the further innovation process may be identified successfully. Ultimately, this reveals a customer need which has not yet been met with a solution which is an excellent fit.

Incidentally, this does not mean that successful innovation is impossible in spaces where solutions already exist. The potential for innovations in white spots is particularly great though. For this very reason, some innovation methods, such as the blue ocean method, rely almost exclusively on identifying and processing such white spots (cf. excursus).

Excursus

Blue Ocean Strategy

Blue ocean is a method derived from strategic management for developing long-term, profitable business models. The basic idea is that a lasting competitive edge can be achieved by creating new markets.

In this context, the term 'ocean' refers to a market or a branch of industry. A distinction is made between untouched markets (blue oceans) and established markets full of competitors (red oceans). The idea behind this concept is that only market leaders or cost leaders can survive in red oceans in the long term. Successful companies should therefore not orientate themselves towards their competition, but should instead create their own blue oceans. As a result, they will be exposed to little or no competition for a long time. They benefit from higher margins and can retain customers more consistently. Innovations which create access to blue oceans are rarely based on technical innovations, but in most cases on a new form of offer. They are often based on redefining the market or refocusing on customer needs.

The goal is to offer existing and potential customers a truly differentiated and relevant benefit. One example of a successful blue ocean strategy was provided by the low-cost airline Southwest Airlines which in terms of domestic flights within the USA regarded itself as competing with the car—rather than with other flight providers. With an adapted business model which has been designed for reduced prices, faster check-in times and a higher departure frequency, customers could be offered greater travel speeds at lower prices comparable to those achieved with a car. The offer, in this case, was adapted to the needs of the ordinary traveller rather than focused on holiday or business travellers.

In a simple example, a specific healthcare problem might only currently be solved as a result of *expensive* medical treatment. Now if a significantly *cheaper*—but similarly effective—alternative could be found as a result of using new technologies or alternative treatment approaches, its potential for success would certainly be very great. In this case, the white spot would be a *cheaper* treatment for that healthcare problem.

By definition, white spots require new solutions which are not covered by the company's current offer. However, since the corresponding pain point already lies within the selected innovation potential because of the previous process steps—and is thus based on the company's traction factors, goals and criteria—you have hence ensured that the white spots are in an area which can be addressed by the company with new solutions. To develop these very solutions, we must now especially focus the following research into sources of inspiration on the white spots we have identified. This does not as such mean that other solution areas (apart from white spots) are excluded from further research though. After all, solutions may even be found here later which exceed the added value of previous solutions for the customer and thus lead to goals being achieved.

2.3.2 Good Artists Copy, Great Artists Steal

Are there really any new ideas? Studies show that new innovations are usually made up of existing ideas. So it is important to be inspired just by what exists, but to adapt it in such a way that you create something new. You could even sum this up with *good artists copy, great artists steal*, a saying (allegedly) by Picasso. In art, it is completely normal to be inspired by other artists. It is only then that epochs and phases emerge which are characterised by similar styles. The best artists, however, manage not only to copy other works, but to 'steal' them—that is, to develop their very own interpretations and to make what exists their own. Even when you are searching for ideas within the framework of the innovation process, you do not need to reinvent the wheel every time. Here, too, existing solutions can (and should) be used as a source of inspiration—especially when they come from other industries and hence do not yet exist in their own market. Ultimately, these can be adapted to their own market context as part of the subsequent ideation, or else their value proposition, function and/or use can be changed (even when this concerns solutions taken from the existing market).

Guest Commentary: Nicolai Andersen, EMEA Lead Innovation and Head of Deloitte Garage, Deloitte

"Using inspirations from other markets, industries and areas of life as part of your own innovation process could also be described as 'stealing'. In the context of innovation, this term has positive connotations, because the goal of 'stealing' is to develop innovations which better meet existing customer needs and so create new value for the company. But it is crucial to not only 'steal' inspirations, but to actually turn them into innovations for specific needs in your own market or your own industry.

Nowadays, you particularly find 'stealing' in digital business models which are often transferred from one country to another. Think of Zalando and Zappos, for example. And even if this may look at first glance like crass copying, the most successful ones in the end are the 'copiers' who manage to optimally adapt the business model they have copied to local preferences and infrastructures in terms of brand, look and feel, product selection, pricing, communications, logistics, etc. These adjustments become all the more relevant when business ideas are transferred not only across national borders but industry borders too. For example, Amazon's cross-selling and up-selling mechanisms can also be used in other B2C industries like financial services, travel or food—although changes are necessary in accordance with the specific pain points.

One example of success for me is the development of Tesla. In comparison to other barely differentiated cars, a tablet—long established in other areas—has been installed in the Tesla's interior as a control panel. By combining two existing subcomponents, this has resulted in a groundbreaking innovation for ease of use. BMW also made use of an existing solution. Here, a joystick which was common in video games was used to manage the user interface with as few buttons as possible. Whether it is a question of whole business ideas or individual components, these examples show that 'stealing' can be worth it—if done right."

This **thinking outside your own company's and market's limits happens in the innovation process with the help of analogue examples**. These are solutions to similar problems in other industries or even completely different areas of life, such as art. It is therefore crucial to identify problems and their solutions in other areas which either have direct or structural similarities with your own market or with the pain point or white spot to be investigated.

Famous examples of ideas which have been born of similar analogue examples include the Internet and the book press. The World Wide Web was initially a network used for exchanging research results between universities before it was adapted to be used in online shopping, pornography and payment processing, for example. Gutenberg, conversely, produced the first book press based on a 1,000-year-old invention, the wine press. The mechanism of the wine press—which had long been used to press juice from grapes—could actually be adapted so that it could be used for letterpress printing.

You can observe examples like this time and again even on a small scale. Especially when there are many restrictions, anything which exists must be used creatively for new purposes. This 'frugal innovation', as it has been termed, can be observed especially in developing countries. In India, for example, the ChotuKool refrigerator was developed. It functioned similarly to a computer's cooling system and could also be operated with simple car batteries (Wipo, 2013).

Such 'analogous thinking' does not occur randomly. It requires a systematic approach. Like in the search for best practice in the existing market, you must ensure you do not find just any old analogue examples. It needs to be specifically the ones which can be used in the subsequent ideation to develop new solutions for the corresponding pain points.

The prerequisite for this is that you formulate a problem as clearly as possible. That should already be given by the chosen pain point. Next **you need to abstract the problem** so that it is applicable universally enough to allow you to search for more unrelated solutions. In the example of the innovation project for Hymer (see the case study "Case Study: Hymer"), we abstracted the problem of 'product innovations for camper vans for two solo travellers', for example, to the problem of 'dividing the space between two people (or couples) when space is limited'. We were subsequently able to study this using, for example, cruise ships, yachts, aeroplanes, spaceships or space stations, micro-apartments, etc.

Based on the abstract problem, the **search for similarities** can begin. Which similar solutions (depending on the innovation space, e.g. products, services, processes, mechanisms, etc.) already exist and could be used differently? To answer this question, it is a good idea to first identify comparable industries which are relevant to the chosen pain point so that you can then search for suitable solutions in these.

For this, we recommend that you work in concentric circles, i.e. you gradually move away from very closely related similar contexts. For example, if we are talking about a new road system, one obvious similarity would be a rail system. You could then move increasingly further away to airport transport systems and warehousing systems and on to blood circulatory systems in biology.

The further away the analogies are, the more difficult it is to identify them—and the better cognitive abstraction skills are required. Here too, the parameters and variants of the morphological box can help to identify and investigate the structural similarities.

What is the outcome of this search? Examples or solutions which are similar to the selected pain point can eventually lead to innovations by adapting existing solutions from a particular industry to a new use in a different industry using creative ways and means. Studies show that analogies contribute significantly to the development of very novel innovations, because combining unrelated information requires more creativity. At the same time, innovations based on similarities minimise the risk of uncertainty as implementation capability and customer fit have already been proven in a similar example (Zeschky & Gassmann, 2013).

Ski manufacturer Fischer also knew how to exploit this. It identified the pain point that skis were especially difficult to control at a certain speed. While analysing the problem, the company uncovered that the skis vibrated after a certain velocity because they were in a resonant frequency >1800 Hz. The resulting white spot (as existing solutions did not exist at that time) was damping or eliminating the vibration through a corresponding product innovation. With the abstract problem description 'damping a vibration >1800 Hz', the company searched for similar examples. Research showed that this frequency range was particularly relevant in acoustics. A suitable solution already existed in that industry for the problem identified. It had been developed in the context of damping unwanted vibrations in stringed instruments by Stradivari. Fischer transferred this vibration harmonisation to skis by inserting an additional layer into the skis which was similar to the solution used for string instruments in terms of its structure and materials. This frequency tuning can be found in almost every ski today.

There may be other innovative solutions which have not yet been implemented beyond similar examples even. The following section deals with how precisely you can determine these approaches to solutions with a view to looking into the future and then using them to search for ideas.

2.3.3 Put Off Until Tomorrow What You Cannot Do Today

'Do not put off until tomorrow what you can do today', goes the saying. But what if something cannot be obtained today? Satisfactory solutions to every pain point do not always exist, either in your own market or an analogue one. The relevant examples then fail to appear as inspiration—and the white spots remain white.

On the one hand, this is the perfect starting position, because if a white spot has not been solved yet anywhere, the innovation and earnings potential is usually all the greater. You can virtually create a completely new market. On the other hand though, this is also a particularly big challenge. Finding a new solution to a problem which has never been solved before is a difficult undertaking. So it is all the more important that inspiration assists the search for ideas there too. Since best practices and analogous examples are no help in this scenario, it is worth **looking into the future** instead. What you cannot solve today, you can solve tomorrow.

By the way, this is also advisable if 'enough' approaches to solutions have already been found through best practices and analogue examples, i.e. if there is no pure white spot at all. In this scenario, inspiration from the future also helps to find completely new approaches to solutions which may provide a significantly better customer fit than existing solutions.

Looking into the future, there are different **sources of inspiration for this**. These range from very specific solutions which have not been implemented yet through to research results whose insights might be used to develop new solutions in the future. In the light of this, here again, we advise using a step-by-step approach—in this case from the near, to the distant future.

(a) **Patent research**: patents offer innumerable approaches to solutions which have often not (yet) been implemented, but can still provide inspiration—and hence are practically a map of ideas and potential innovations which can be used for (re) development. For example, new patents by Apple are the source of constant discussion as they provide a glimpse into the possible future of iPhones and iPads.

    Since patent databases are freely accessible, they can be very useful for a targeted search of (yet unimplemented) solution approaches to the pain point identified. Due to the large number of patents and their demanding content, assessment is not easy even in a small area, however. If the relevant competence does not already exist within the company or with its partners, a technical solution may even be used. Here, Fraunhofer Institute for Industrial Engineering IAO offers, for example, a text mining solution which allows you to automatically study patents for the problems and solutions they contain. The results of such patent research then provide a relevant basis for a relevant inspiration. Or they again confirm the white spot which has been identified (through the lack of results).

(b) **Concept studies**: concept and design studies allow you to look to the future too. They ultimately reveal a variety of new ideas and approaches by companies, consultants, agencies, designers, programmers, etc. The best known of these are certainly the concept vehicles produced by car manufacturers. The equivalent studies can also be found in many other areas though. Design and consulting firms, such as IDEO, for example, regularly develop new concepts in various areas. Databases like Behance or GitHub collect concepts from different designers and developers. Designs and ideas are regularly shared on various blogs and social networks. Idea competitions and awards often showcase promising concepts being developed too. Crowdfunding platforms, like Kickstarter, also exhibit countless ideas awaiting funding. It is now important to identify the appropriate community and suitable sources by topic so that you can be inspired there.

(c) **Thought leadership**: thought leadership encompasses all contents where individuals or companies are thinking in new directions. Reading their literature can be similarly worthwhile for looking into the future. Depending on your budget and the time available, you can either use the complete reports published by management consultancies, think tanks or trend companies, such as Z.Punkt, PSFK or the Zukunftsinstitut, or you can search them yourselves. Searching like this through blogs, articles and whitepapers written by experts and start-ups is time-consuming, of course. But it offers you a better opportunity to find inspiration and approaches to solutions which your competitors have not yet found.

(d) **Technology scouting**: even if any patent research has already uncovered some new technologies, a specific search by experts for new technologies or technological processes and desk research can sensibly complement these. Often there are even new, open innovation partners who you can work with later on a specific implementation. Wearable manufacturer Misfit, for example, worked on the pain point that smartwatches or fitness trackers need to be charged frequently which discourages many potential new customers from buying them. Crystal cutting company Swarovski—which cuts crystals using its specialist technologies to concentrate sunlight in a particularly effective way—finally found a solution. On this basis, Swarovski and Misfit jointly developed the wearable Shine which can be charged with 15 minutes of daylight a day using its violet crystal. Besides traditional desk research, it is also worth activating and expanding your own network to find technologies and processes like this. If no distinctive, open innovation resources yet exist in your own company, open innovation databases, such as iDEX, may be suitable or even publicly available networks, such as LinkedIn. Alternatively, you can ask innovation brokers, like NineSigma or Presans, as well as management consultants to search in their network.

(e) **Research**: universities, institutes and often even the company's own research department carry out foundational and applied research. The results of this can lead to exciting new solutions. Often this is also about technologies, but the social sciences, for example, can also provide inspiring insights. The simplest path to these results is to assess the scientific publications. Databases like SCOPUS or Google Scholar enable you to do this very easily. However, identification by academic experts in the subject area and recourse to research institutions' corporate contacts can also represent worthwhile options. Often, researchers themselves are even looking for a partner for testing and validation in practice, which can be an advantage later on when you are refining your ideas.

Ultimately, you need to **select the most relevant sources of inspiration and prepare them to be used in the search for ideas**. Sources of inspiration are selected on the basis of the pain point. Which of the best practices you have collected, or similar examples and future inspirations, are particularly well-suited to solving the pain point during the search for ideas which follows? This selection should then be processed visually. This can easily be done in a presentation using pictures and descriptions. Depending on whether one or more innovation potentials and pain points have been processed, this kind of visualisation can also be interactive so that you can select goal-orientated sources of inspiration for different pain points. Moreover, it is often possible to even order inspiring products so that you can experience them in real life on your premises.

Guest Commentary: Dr. Klaus Suwelack, Senior Manager New Business Development and Innovation Management, Janssen Deutschland, Johnson & Johnson

"In the pharmaceuticals industry, even large companies reach their limits when it comes to developing new solutions for patients. The complexity of health issues and the sheer number of pain points (in the truest sense of the word) can often not be solved by one company alone. With this in mind, Johnson & Johnson (J&J) has established its own, global innovation network. This is designed to take in and process new research results and solutions from the scientific community and industry quickly. It focuses on clear innovation potentials to find solutions which are as specific as possible and can—even in partnerships—be brought to the patient using Johnson & Johnson's excellent traction.

Three sectors have been identified for this scouting: pharmaceuticals, medical devices and consumer, each of which contains about 10–20 main focus areas. In these sectors, dedicated teams focus on the search for new solutions by all possible partners, such as the scientific community, start-ups or established companies. Scouting is worthwhile in several respects. On the one hand, it brings new solutions into the company which can then be further developed and implemented as rapidly as possible. On the other hand, it helps to identify the most relevant potential partners for future collaboration. It is crucial to focus as much as possible on the needs of patients and the company so that the results actually create benefits in the end. At Johnson & Johnson, this strategy has already been used for many years to find groundbreaking new solutions jointly with partners and to introduce these successfully into patient care."

We recommend that you double-check with the relevant stakeholders after the *compilation*. The *compilation* results do not necessarily need to be shared with your stakeholders, though, since the sources of inspiration are particularly relevant to the search for ideas which follows. Nevertheless, we recommend giving a presentation at this point. There are several reasons for this. Firstly, the results of the *compilation* are usually very inspiring for all parties. Secondly, the many possible approaches to a solution increase people's desire to see the outcomes of the next steps even further. And thirdly, feedback from stakeholders on the findings you presented can give you an initial feeling about which solution directions are particularly well received by the individual actors.

Armed with the relevant sources of inspiration from the *compilation* (and any further feedback from the relevant stakeholders), specific work on suitable ideas can now (finally) begin as part of the following *construction*.

Case Study: Hermes Arzneimittel

Development of Innovative Offers for the Target Group 'New Senior Citizens'

Pharmaceutical company Hermes builds on many years of tradition and competence, especially in the production of over-the-counter (OTC) products, such as effervescent tablets, powders or tablets. These are either manufactured for third parties or distributed independently via *pharmacies with whom a long-term partnership exists. To remain strategically competitive, the company was forced to focus increasingly on potential, new markets for the future.*

Configuration

The goal of the innovation process established during the *configuration phase* was to generate new revenues. An important criterion was specially to ensure the long-term value added of innovations. So 'markets' and 'product and service innovations' were identified as the most relevant *innovation spaces* for the remainder of the process and were summarised as 'new offers'.

Competence in certain manufacturing processes and partnership with pharmacies were identified as the most important traction factors. Out of a total of 12 *opportunity spaces* identified, 'new offers for the target group of new senior citizens' were ultimately selected for the project. This group was categorised as being particularly relevant on the basis of demographic, technological and social trends. Three specific *innovation potentials* were then identified in this opportunity space, namely, innovative offers for new senior citizens for: 1) independent healthcare provision, 2) diagnosis and 3) treatment and healing process.

Customisation

Relevant *pain points* were then researched with the target group as part of the *customisation phase* in the context of the selected innovation potentials, for example, a lack of natural alternatives, dealing with new technology, gathering information for your own use from the Internet or anxiety among single senior citizens about retirement homes. In addition, pharmacies were visited with Hermes sales representatives and interviews were conducted with pharmacists and their employees to be able to include the pharmacies' needs and findings in the remainder of the process.

Compilation

In the *compilation phase*, *best practices*, such as health wearables, were studied along with personalised medicine by Google or smartphone attachments to assist diagnosis in Africa. In *analogous examples*, innovations like the bone broth trend in New York, on-demand platforms like Helpling and Zipjet and cooking boxes like HelloFresh provided valuable inspiration. Many *white spots* also became apparent, especially for the domestic German market, although some of these had already been met internationally. A total of more than 300 best practices, analogous examples and future concepts were recorded, systematically assessed and visualised. Besides being used for the subsequent ideation, a selection was also presented to the stakeholders so that they could directly gain new insights for their business units.

Based on the varied input from the previous process steps, various innovative offers for Hermes were developed during the remainder of the 5C process. Concepts ranged from Nespresso-like herbal infusions (as a 'quick win') and nutrition plan-dependent cooking boxes through to a service platform for single senior citizens where the entire range of objectives was met by innovation potentials and pain points. The needs of the 'new senior citizen' target group were taken into account in the concepts just as much as those of the pharmacists (◘ Fig.. 2.21).

Configuration (1) – Customisation (2) – **Compilation (3)** – Construction (4) – Conversion (5)

Mind-set	**If you want to reap, you must first sow**		
Section	**Seek, and you will find**	**Good artists copy, great artists steal**	**Put off until tomorrow what you cannot do today**
Outcome	✓ International best practices ✓ White spots	✓ Analogous examples	✓ Future inspirations
Methodology	1. Collect the most important competitors 2. Search for relevant start-ups 3. Identify relevant solution dimensions (e.g. `W' questions, morphological box parameters/variants) 4. Benchmarking: search for examples (best practices) in all relevant dimensions for the pain point 5. Collect white spots = solution dimensions without best practice	1. Abstract the issue 2. Identify analogous industries (ranging from `nearby' to `far away') 3. Search for analogous examples for the solution to the abstracted issue within analogous industries 4. Use any different dimensions (from 2.3.1) for the systematic search	1. Determine any relevant sources of inspirtion 2. Use any different dimensions (from 2.3.1) for the systematic search 3. Search for future sources of inspiration (patents, concept studies, thought leadership content, technologies, research results) 4. Select the most relevant inspirations (especially about white spots) from 2.3.1-2.3.3 5. Visualise all of the relevant inspirations from 2.3.1-2.3.3
Aid	▫ Start-up databases ▫ Analyse the competition ▫ Morphological boxes (2.1.3) ▫ Pain point(s) (2.2.3) ▫ Innovation potential (2.1.3)	▫ Collect similar industries ▫ Solution dimensions (2.3.1) ▫ White spots (2.3.1)	▫ Sources/databases ▫ Solution dimensions (2.3.1) ▫ White spots (2.3.1) ▫ Best practices (2.3.1) ▫ Analogous examples (2.3.2)

◘ **Fig. 2.21** Overview of compilation. (Author's own figure)

2.4 Construction: Think Inside the Box

When it comes to searching for ideas, in many workshops the goal is clear very quickly. 'Think *outside* the box!' To ensure this, workshop participants work with creative methods aimed at achieving a huge number and breadth of ideas ('diversity'). What is the problem with this? By definition, *out-of-the-box* ideas cannot be implemented *inside the box*. It is precisely this sort of 'box' (or a similar traction space) that a company operates in after it has reached a certain size. So out-of-the-box ideas can often simply not be implemented in corporates.

The challenge is to find **innovative ideas (*which are as disruptive as they need to be*) but which still fit inside the box (*and thus are as close to the core business as possible*)**. The good news is that this is essentially always possible, because the number of potential solutions in each space is theoretically infinitely large. The bad news is that traditional creative techniques and simple brainstorming sessions are not suited to working in a limited space as they cannot take sufficient account of inside-the-box restrictions. Instead, we need a systematic multidimensional search for ideas ('ideation'). The aim is to bridge the gap between the most specific task definition possible for the ideation and the (nevertheless) greatest possible number of different solutions. This is where the preparatory work in the previous process steps pays off. The narrowed innovation potential from the *configuration phase* and the specific pain point from the *customisation phase* enable you to achieve a precise, goal-orientated definition of the task. The sources of inspiration with a precise fit taken from the *compilation phase* provide the necessary input for extending the solution space for novel idea even inside the box. Supplemented with the right participants and other aids and techniques, the innovative ideas needed can now be generated in the *construction phase* (see ◘ Fig. 2.22).

A few words on a Post-it note are a good start, but certainly do not yet represent an adequate solution. To refine your ideas and simultaneously ensure they can be implemented and will enjoy market success later, the best ideas must be developed step by step into detailed innovation concepts and validated with experts and customers. On this basis, the relevant stakeholders can then carry out a comprehensive assessment and selection of the concepts.

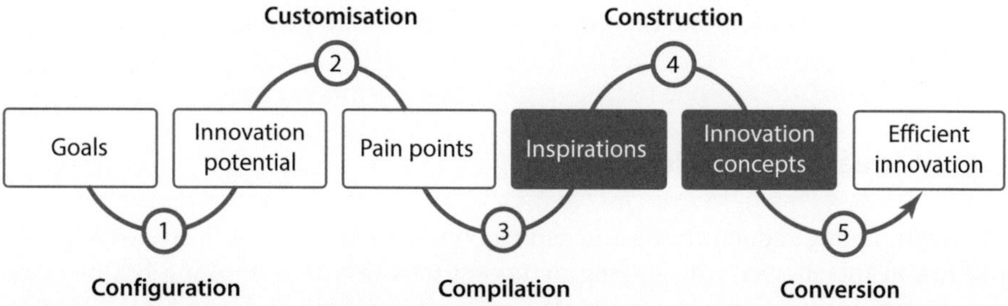

◘ **Fig. 2.22** 5C process: construction. (Author's own figure)

The following three sections show how conceiving inside-the-box innovations is successful:

1. **Ideas are not random**: eureka! Ideas are usually perceived as being random. It is not for nothing that the term *flash of genius* exists for an idea which seems to come to you unexpectedly. Yet, ideas occur as part of a clear, neurobiological process composed of inspiration and solution finding which can be triggered systematically. Existing creative methods have already been attempting this using a wide variety of formats, but always require as open a playing field as possible. Using the right sources of inspiration, perspectives and tools, it is possible, however, to systematically generate innovative ideas even in a limited space—thus separating (implementable) ideas from random events.
2. **No pain, no gain**: as Edison already remarked, 'Genius is one percent inspiration and ninety-nine percent perspiration'. In other words, it is down to pure hard work. The first idea scribbled on a Post-it note is not sufficient to result in a successful efficient innovation. The special (or even impossible) thing about an idea usually only becomes obvious when you look at it in detail. All too often though, the success of an innovation process is judged by the number of Post-it notes on the wall. The hard work involved in actually making this into an innovation concept which fits the customer—as well as the company—is often left to follow later. Like this, ideas either disappear into the drawer or are tested straightaway on the customer without even finding the best possible variant for customer fit and traction beforehand. The best possible variants of these ideas can be found through detailed work on the concepts. This gives rise to a wide range of innovation concepts which provide a clear picture of the potential solutions.
3. **You can also count your chickens before they hatch**: for an idea to become an innovation, it must be implemented. Or to put it another way, 'vision without execution is just hallucination'. Yet it is also possible to assess whether the implementation of an idea or an innovation concept will succeed before you implement it provided you ask the right stakeholders in the company what they think. It is similarly possible to check before implementation whether an idea has the potential to meet the targeted customers' needs in the desired way after its implementation. So what is qualitative and quantitative market research ultimately for? If the innovation concepts are also assessed intuitively by the decision-makers, then you will have adequate data or information available to make the final decision about the implementation of one or more innovation concepts.

2.4.1 Ideas Are Not Random

The myth about sudden flashes of genius continues to cling on bravely. Whether you are in the shower, out jogging or taking part in a free-thinking brainstorming session, inspiration can apparently occur at any time and 'randomly' lead to a great idea. No wonder that the search for ideas is often referred to as the 'fuzzy front end' (where implementation sits at the back end of the innovation process in this scenario). Yet in fact, the infamous flash of genius is the rarest form of inspiration. In an interview about his book *Where Good Ideas Come From*, popular scientist Steven Johnson remarked, 'It's weird, but innovation is one of those cases where the defining image, all the rhetoric and all the assumptions about how it happens, turn out to be completely backward. It is very, very rare to find cases where somebody on their own, working alone, in a moment of sudden clarity has a great breakthrough that changes the world. And yet there seems to be this bizarre desire to tell the story that way' (Burkeman, 2010).

Even ideas, which in retrospect seem like a flash of genius, are not in most cases. Edison is known to have carried out tens of thousands of experiments before the light bulb was invented in its original form. Ironically, it is the symbol for an idea as a sudden enlightenment today. Even Charles Darwin's theory of evolution was not a flash of genius although he always said that the insight about natural selection came to him on 28 September 1838 while reading Thomas Malthus' essay on population. An analysis of his notebooks, though, showed that this theory had already been emerging for more than a year. Presumably then, he merely assembled the prepared information at the moment he described.

So if the way that ideas occur does not depend on one random event, this also means you can systematise the very process of developing ideas. Such systematisation is crucial if we are to develop efficient innovations. After all, you must find ideas for a certain problem within a limited solution space and within a fixed period of time.

Traditional creativity methods do not suit a systematic search for ideas in large companies. To underpin free thinking—and thus make (supposed) eureka moments possible—they normally work on greenfields (see the following excursus). People impose the smallest number of restrictions possible, declare that there are no bad or wrong ideas—and the crazier the solution, the better. Staying true to the saying 'think *outside* the box'. And all of that coupled with the hope that, with a bit of luck, you can find an idea you can implement in your company later. But is this realistic?

Excursus: Overview of Selected Creativity Methods

Brainstorming

Brainstorming is one of the best-known creative methods. It is carried out in a group in which each participant can carry out free association and contribute ideas or suggestions about a particular problem. These are recorded visually for all participants to see so that they can build on other participants' contributions. For the method to be successful, it is important that participants are able to express their ideas without fear of criticism. This increases the inspiration potential for the rest of the group with each contribution.

Brainwriting

Brainwriting is a written form of brainstorming in which participants write down their thoughts and associations without saying them out loud in the group. The advantage of this is that writing can enable several series of associations to exist at the same time. Also, 'quieter' participants can contribute their ideas. This method is particularly useful when groups do not know each other well, and it has not yet been possible to build up sufficient trust among the participants. The disadvantage of brainwriting is that as a rule duplicate ideas emerge when all participants are working on the same issue.

Six Thinking Hats

Six thinking hats is a creative process in which participants each play a different role in a group discussion (represented by different coloured hats). Contributions to a discussion should be valued equally while, simultaneously, as many modes of thinking as possible should be considered. The hats represent different modes of thinking (analytical, emotional, critical, optimistic, creative, moderating). In a discussion, participants should play the role which corresponds to their hat/thinking mode until everyone changes hats at the same time at the request of the moderator.

SCAMPER

SCAMPER provides support for brainstorming and is particularly suitable for developing new products or processes which are derived from those which already exist. It is based on a checklist which enables a set problem to be processed point by point. Participants are requested to substitute, combine, adjust, modify and put to other use what exists and to eliminate and reverse elements in order to stimulate their creativity.

Business Model Navigator

The business model navigator is a tool for realigning business models. More than 90% of all business model innovations are recombinations of the 55 successful business model patterns identified by researchers at the University of St. Gallen in Switzerland. Successful patterns can be recombined like this and applied to your own business model or can serve as inspiration during various phases (initiation, brainstorming, integration and implementation) using specialist techniques.

For an idea to offer potential for efficient innovation, it should ultimately lead to solutions to a specific pain point within the identified innovation potential (taking into account the goals and criteria set initially) and also lie within the company's traction space. Traditional creativity methods have not (yet) coped with these challenges. Moreover, it is precisely that focus on out-of-the-box ideas which often prevents solutions from being implemented inside the box (i.e. within the company's traction space).

Brainstorming—supposedly a success story—is often the death knell for innovation projects. Probably no other methodology is used so often to search for ideas as the brainstorming described by New York advertising guru Alex Osborn in 1939 in which ideas are generated quickly and discussed together in group discussions. In most cases, the four basic rules identified by Osborn are applied as follows:

1. *No criticism of other contributions.*
2. *Quantity over quality—the more ideas, the better.*
3. *The crazier the idea, the better.*
4. *Incorporate other ideas as much as possible and build on other people's contributions.*

The inflationary use of this methodology is understandable. How else could you find ideas quickly? Since brainstorming success is usually measured by the quantity of output (at least, it was by Osborn himself, but has been in many other studies too), the method seems at first to be successful.

By now, brainstorming has almost become a synonym for the search for ideas, wrongly. As a creative methodology, brainstorming alone cannot achieve much. Quite the reverse. It can even harm the search for ideas. Although, whenever the quality of ideas plays a role rather than just the quantity, all of the four of the above fundamental rules are counterproductive as a matter of principle:

1. *No criticism of other contributions:* this principle is indeed helpful in discussions, but it is important—especially at the outset—that the moderator clarifies what kind of ideas they are seeking and what goals and criteria will be used when they are assessed later. If this does not occur, participants are operating in great uncertainty, and they either offer ideas which, in the end, are not needed and cannot be implemented or they do not even mention ideas because they are doubtful or because they cannot assess whether these ideas are relevant or 'right' beforehand. This latter can be observed especially when a variety of levels of the company's hierarchy are present in the brainstorming.
2. *Quantity over quality—the more ideas, the better:* if more ideas means more *wrong* ideas which ultimately fail to meet either customer fit or traction, producing a large number of them achieves nothing. Focusing on the quality of the ideas makes more sense here.
3. *The crazier the idea, the better:* this basic rule is the forerunner of out-of-the-box thinking, so it is unsuitable when it comes to finding ideas which represent an excellent fit. Even if every crazy idea can still inspire a solution, the focus in this process step should now be on the search for ideas which are as good a fit to the task as possible. After all, creative resources should be used efficiently.
4. *Incorporate other ideas and build on them:* this rule at first seems to make sense in coming up with more specific ideas based on initial sources of inspiration, but it also runs the risk that other potential solutions will not even be discussed in the first place. Combining and developing ideas further should therefore only occur after (or at the end of) the initial search for ideas.

The basic setup for brainstorming is also problematic. Some participants exert an influence over the overall direction of the discussion by means of the discussion in the group. This phenomenon known as anchoring occurs when dominant participants monopolise the discussion. Added to that, participants usually interrupt their own search for ideas when other participants are explaining their ideas. Furthermore, hierarchies and competitive thinking often lead—especially in a professional context—to participants feeling inhibited (Coyne et al., 2007).

The fact that brainstorming requires a search space which is as 'free' or as large as possible shows that it is virtually impossible to produce suitable ideas systematically in combination with the above methodological problems and counterproductive fundamental rules (Greenfield, 2014).

This methodology is nevertheless used repeatedly in this, or a similar, form which is due especially to the fact that too much attention is still attached to the quantity of ideas as an indicator of success. This error of judgement goes back to the beginnings of brainstorming, as Osborn maintained when he introduced his methodology. 'It is almost axiomatic that quantity breeds quality in ideation. Logic and mathematics are on the side of the truth that the more ideas we produce, the more likely we are to think up some that are good' (Reinig & Briggs, 2008). But is that really so?

Numerous studies show that more ideas are not more good ideas. Quite the opposite. Contrary to popular belief, the quality of ideas even decreases with a larger number of ideas. A study by (Reinig & Briggs, 2008) illustrates this very clearly. In their test, 14 groups of 5 students each were supposed to generate ideas in 40-minute brainstorming sessions. What was the outcome? In all 14 sessions, the quality of outcomes decreased the larger the number of ideas (see ◘ Fig. 2.23).

So using creativity methods particularly aimed at increasing the quantity of ideas is unsuitable for efficient innovations. Instead, the goal is quantity *and* quality in terms of as many diverse ideas which are a good a fit as possible (Girotra et al., 2010). Is this even possible though if these ideas are also intended to fit the goals and criteria set?

Surprisingly, limitations help to boost the quantity and quality of ideas. At first glance, it may seem sensible, though, to set as few restrictions as possible in the search for ideas. After all, we should not exclude any ideas, and participants should not be limited in their thinking. Anyone who still remembers MacGyver—the hero of the 1980s and 1990s television series—will remember that his surprising and innovative solutions to free him from the most impossible situations always came to him as a result of the existing limitations. Without those limitations, he would not have built a lie detector from a blood pressure monitor, a stethoscope and an

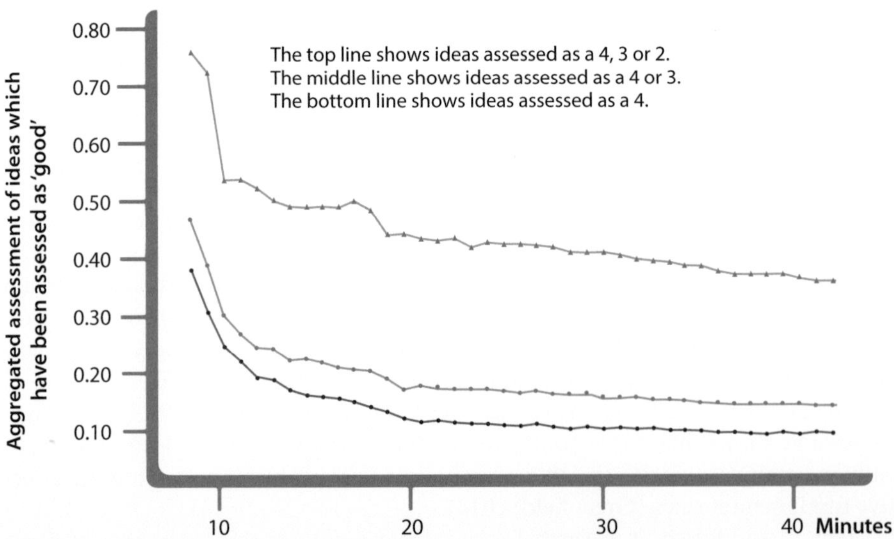

◘ **Fig. 2.23** Quantity vs quality of ideas. (Adapted: Reinig & Briggs 2008)

alarm clock. So is it actually easier to find diverse ideas which are an excellent fit when you are thinking 'freely'? Or is the exact opposite in fact the case? One small exercise can answer this question.

Take five minutes and develop a new business idea.

Finished? How many business ideas did you find? How many of them are actually innovative in your opinion? Now repeat the exercise again, but with the following change to the question.

Develop a new business idea for young tourists in the mountains which you can achieve for less than EUR 1,000.

In the second exercise, you should now have found a larger number of ideas. In any case, they are more innovative than they were before.

The more specific task combined with the given limitation has already provided sources of inspiration and guided your thinking in a specific direction. That is, you are searching inside the box. And this is actually easier—and above all, more productive—than searching for ideas without any limitations.

This was also shown by the results of a research team investigating, for example, how people developed new recipes and products, or repaired toys. If these were limited by a budget, they were significantly more imaginative than without such a limitation (Coyne et al., 2007). This is because it is virtually impossible to generate innovative ideas in an unlimited space. Where should you search? What should you search for? Which directions are good directions and which are bad? Without a specific task and suitable limitations, your brain needs to answer these questions itself first before it can generate ideas. It then selects the simplest way to a solution. Preset restrictions and limitations conversely focus your mental energy directly on finding solutions, thus inspiring more innovative solutions, because you are unable to opt for the easiest way.

Even so, companies often oppose limiting the search space. After all, limiting it like that seems to embody the risk that an insufficient number of ideas are found, hence their concern. Yet working inside the box does not limit the quantitative potential in the search for ideas. Besides a large number of scientific studies, this can also be shown using a simple mathematical formula:

$$0 < x < 1 = 0 < x < \infty.$$

This formula expresses that there are just as many possible solutions between *0 and infinity* as there are between *0 and 1*. And the same applies to ideas. Just as many solutions (which still fit all of the criteria) can be found in limited spaces as in greenfields. The great advantage of this is that these are all potentially implementable and have excellent customer fit.

Systematic ideation with specific tasks in a limited space ('inside the box') is therefore much more promising than a search for out-of-the-box greenfield ideas. If you accept this, you now 'only' need to find the ideas there too.

Creativity alone is not enough to search for inside-the-box ideas. Instead, ideas which fit inside the box need to be triggered systematically. To do this, possible solution directions inside the limited space must be revealed in a targeted way. That means giving ideation participants as many preset limitations as possible to systematically steer their ideas in the right direction. But it also means providing them with as many different sources of inspiration and information as possible so that they can process the problem from many different perspectives or dimensions.

When searching for greenfield ideas, instead of thinking in unlimited breadth, work in-depth, so to speak. In this way, we can ensure quantity *and* quality in the sense of providing as many diverse ideas with an excellent fit as possible. This takes place in **structured ideation workshops** which require clear task setting, suitable aids, a systematic process and the right participants.

An important foundation for these ideation workshops has already been laid in the previous innovation process step. On the one hand, there is a strong focus on content up to the most relevant pain point (through the *configuration phase* and the *customisation* process steps). On the other, a sufficient number of sources of inspiration and information for the targeted processing of the pain point is available (through the *compilation* process step).

We must firstly **specify the task for the ideation participants**. This is derived from the innovation potential, selected pain point and intended target group. In a simple formula this is therefore:

$$\begin{aligned}&\text{Task} = (\text{innovation potential}) + (\text{pain point})\\&+(\text{target group})\,\text{so we hence arrive, for example,}\\&\text{at 'innovative products for simple cooking for single senior citizens'}.\end{aligned}$$

The more specifically you can formulate the set task, the better. If this leaves open too many questions or too much room for interpretation (i.e. if the search space is too large), this quickly leads to insecurity among the participants.

We recommend informing participants about the task a few days in advance of the ideation session to place an appropriate 'primer' or stimulus in their brain at an early stage. Through this priming, participants subconsciously collect sources of inspiration for solving tasks in their day-to-day lives. This is because the primer put in their brain then influences the processing of subsequent primers (Michalko, 2012). The power of subconscious priming has been shown in a large number of psychological tests. If, for example, a word is to be completed, the accompanying images can be used to steer word selection. Consequently, *so_p* is written as *soap* when people are shown pictures of a bathroom, but as *soup* with food pictures. Priming for ideation works in a similar way by subconsciously perceiving things in everyday life in a more targeted way as a result of paying attention to the task.

Depending on the task set, **suitable aids** must then be prepared. Partly, these are the sources of inspiration developed within the context of the *compilation phase*, and partly these are content parameters and their variants. These are also referred to below as auxiliary axes. Both serve to demonstrate as many different solution directions within the task as possible and hence to systematically expand the search for ideas within a limited space. Thus, they ensure that the ideation is multidimensional.

The sources of inspiration collected as part of the *compilation phase* must be adequately prepared—if that has not already happened—for the ideation session in such a way that they can be understood at a quick glance or after a brief explanation provided by the moderator. The individual inspiration categories (best practices, similar examples, the future) should be clearly distinct from each other.

Who (target group)	Pensioners	Teenagers	Neighbouring residents	Groups	Global community	...
Where (location)	At home	On holiday	In the train	At work	Anywhere in the world	...
What would x do	Apple	Amazon	Tesla	Netflix	Alibaba	...
Why (need)	Fame	Fun	Feel-good	Independence	Excitement	...
What (added value)	Add-on	Cost savings	Acceleration	Peace of mind	Functionality	...
Business model	Subscription	Leasing	Financing	Open source	Pay as you go	...
Random event	Red	Sauna	World	Quick	Cheap	...
Lateral	No budget	With €1 million	Can't be bought	Only 1 in the world	No time	...
...	...	...	...	...	...	...

Fig. 2.24 Examples of auxiliary axes. (Author's own figure)

Like the sources of inspiration, the **auxiliary axes must also be prepared or selected to fit with the ideation session**. An auxiliary axis describes a particular *parameter*, while the *variants* of this parameter which fit the task, provide the specific aid (the approach to a solution). The morphological box prepared at the outset of the project can supply the first relevant contents here. As our starting point, basic questions can again serve as the parameters or auxiliary axes. Overall though, the opportunities for inspiring auxiliary axes are almost unlimited (see Fig. 2.24).

To be able to use the auxiliary axes flexibly in the ideation session, it makes sense to note the individual variants on cards and sort them according to their respective parameters. In this way, for example, the set of cards for the 'where' auxiliary axis can contain cards with various touchpoints and locations. Another set of cards could inspire different business model mechanisms or target group segments, etc. by using random words.

An **ideation workshop is a structured process** aimed at systematically producing ideas which fit the formulated problem. Once the participants have gathered for the ideation workshop, they must initially be primed with additional information for the upcoming task. Firstly, it is important to provide them with as good an understanding as possible of the pain point stated in the task set as well as the corresponding innovation potential and intended target group. Secondly, participants need a sufficiently good understanding of the underlying conditions for the task set. To do so, knowledge of the identified goals, criteria and any other important restrictions or traction factors is key for this. This is the only way that participants can always be sure that their ideas are going in the right direction and they need not worry about it during the ideation workshop. Depending on the level of knowledge of the participants, a description of the company or its division as well as its products, services, business model and market can also be helpful. Visual and physical objects, for example, for brands and products, can complement this. Once participants are properly prepared, the actual search for ideas can begin.

In a systematic search for ideas, it is not specific creativity techniques which ensure the best possible quantity *and* quality of solutions with an excellent fit. Rather, these depend on the systematic structuring of the process of searching for ideas in terms of its timing and content. The system for structuring pursues the goal of repeatedly producing new and different ideas during the workshop. For this reason, the individual components of the workshop must be designed to be as diverse as possible. Different variants of the task set are processed by different groups—in conjunction with a variety aids—using different methods every time. In this way, these groups can systematically avoid any subconscious copying which would lead to the same ideas every time.

Specifically, different task-setting variants are processed in several rounds—always in the same sequence (described below), but with varying components (see ◘ Fig. 2.25).

An ideation workshop follows five phases:

I. *Task setting:* in each 'round', a task is supplemented with a specific new focus (parameter), e.g. by adding a specific touchpoint (e.g. in the supermarket, at home, at work), time (e.g. in summer, in the morning, at night), etc. In this way, participants are always working on the selected pain point within the identified innovation potential, but are nevertheless thinking of new directions every time. Where several pain points have been selected for processing, these can be used accordingly as different tasks. To select the focus, we recommend to focus on the morphological box from the *configuration phase* and the white spots from the *compilation phase*.
II. *Best practices:* at the start of each round, the entire circle of participants can be shown suitable best practices for the specific task (from the *compilation phase*) and can discuss them together. This can be used partly to inspire par-

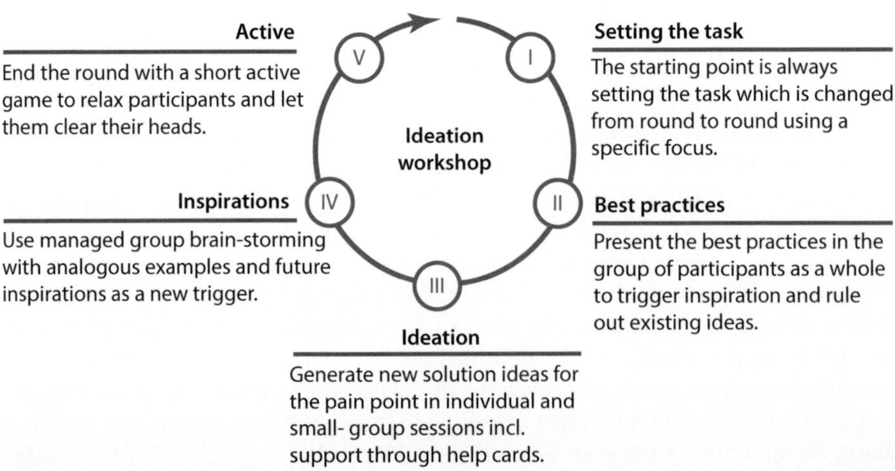

◘ **Fig. 2.25** Ideation workshop. (Author's own figure)

ticipants, because existing solutions can also trigger completely new ideas. Partly though, it ensures that existing solutions and norm ideas are excluded from the following search for ideas.

III. *Searching for ideas:* the aim is for participants to generate as many specific new ideas as possible with the help of the auxiliary axes. To do so, each participant first receives suitable help cards. Ideas are then developed in several successive idea sessions lasting between 10 and 30 minutes each. These short units follow a hybrid structure (Girotra et al., 2010): participants initially start with brainwriting on their own. This gives them the time to (further) develop their own ideas. Next, more ideas are generated in small groups. The group composition should be different in each idea session. A group totalling six people can, for example, keep being divided into different groups of two or three. This is important for maintaining a high level of involvement among the participants, producing more numerous—and more diverse—ideas and limiting the influence of dominant participants. Participants can use their help cards at any time. For this purpose, each help card is identified as an inspiration. Not every card is an excellent fit or inspiring. There is usually a trigger, at the latest after examining several help cards, and this leads to a new idea. Searching for ideas in a small group looks similar to the brainstorming criticised earlier. However, we can eliminate its biggest disadvantages by specifying the task set, using brainwriting as outlined above plus aids, and changing the groups around. Mutual inspiration remains a relevant advantage of this methodology. At the end of the idea sessions, individual ideas which the participants consider to be particularly exciting can be discussed again in the whole group to provide further inspiration.

IV. *Sources of inspiration:* during the search for ideas, participants generated ideas for the given task—from various perspectives using various help cards in a variety of combinations. The potential for ideas is not yet completely exhausted from doing so, however. We will now use the analogue solutions for the pain point which were identified as part of the *compilation* as well as any relevant sources of inspiration drawn from the future. These act as additional, completely new triggers for the participants and can thus often lead to additional, completely new ideas, even after intensive involvement in the task by participants. These inspiration sessions are key especially when you are working in white spots. After all, by definition, in this scenario, there are no best practices available from the existing market.

V. *Action*: at the end of each round, a short interruption—preferably combined with an active game—ensures that participants clear their heads again. This is similar to the famous use of coffee beans when testing different perfumes to clear the nose for a new round. Depending on the group of participants, you can introduce small competitions or games requiring speed or skill (like pictionary or charades). The next round of the ideation workshop then starts from a fresh mind with a new variant of the task set.

If you follow the described process for several rounds, there is a very high probability of generating a large number of diverse solutions with excellent fit. If you also make sure that the individual ideas are noted on a Post-it note as specifically as possible in one clear sentence, then you will achieve sufficient raw material for further steps.

One question remains though. Is ideation still fun and 'sexy' in this sort of structured process? We have found that yes, it is, but in an unusual way for a creative session. The fun does not come from going mad and saying the craziest ideas out loud. Instead, it comes from the feeling of having achieved a huge amount in a comparatively short time—without noticing that you have had to make an effort. The best evidence we have is that participants in our workshops are always surprised when they are paid to take part, because they assume that an experience like this is reward enough.

You can now hold an ideation workshop based on fundamental preparation in advance using this process. All that remains is the question of who you should actually invite.

Participants in ideation sessions are not experts. This may be surprising since it often seems almost impossible to develop ideas and solutions for an area you are unfamiliar with. In almost every project, we hear people say 'Our industry is so specialised that no one outside it will understand it'. Nevertheless, in over 60 projects, we have been able to generate relevant solutions every time using participants from completely outside that industry. Experts or employees in the relevant corporate division can usually develop incremental improvements well, although they are often too caught up in their usual ways of thinking to develop more innovative solutions. It is therefore better to invite as many outside participants to an ideation session as possible. They should at least come from an innovation team within the company, but best of all, from outside the company.

The image of the 'curious, creative generalist' can help to identify participants with the best fit for ideation (see ▶ Sect. 3.2). These are people who do not come from a specific subject area, but instead possess the suitable soft skills. They are interested in a wide range of topics and as a result can always fall back on a variety of different sources of inspiration or 'points' which they link to new ideas. Even if this has already been simulated systematically in the ideation session, participants still require a certain broad training and creative competence to generate ideas from the given sources of inspiration. With a handful of participants like these, ideas can then be processed in the ideation workshop and then developed further into specific solutions in the next step.

2.4.2 No Pain, No Gain

An idea is 1% inspiration and 99% perspiration. In other words, it is down to pure hard work. Edison had already established this, and with over 1000 patents to his name, he knew what he was talking about. He himself once said, 'Most of my ideas belonged to other people who never bothered to develop them'.

This problem of a lack of development can be found again and again in many innovation processes. People look with satisfaction at walls full of Post-it notes after a brainstorming session. Yet the time-consuming (but also worthwhile) work of developing them into the best possible concept either does not happen often, or if it does, then only half-heartedly.

This problem of the lack of development is a widespread one. The first patent claim for a mobile phone dates back to 1906. It hence took 70 years to implement the original idea. It has been shown time and again that it is comparatively easy to find an idea, but the real challenge lies in actually getting it implemented (Agan, 2014). There is no lack of general execution though, as people often assume. Quite the contrary. This is a core area of expertise in large companies. It is more that we simply lack a sufficient number of ideas which are both *suitable* and *mature*.

So the diagnosis of frustrated managers—"We have enough ideas, implementation is the problem'—is usually wrong. That is because our benchmark is often focused exclusively on the *quantity* of available ideas. Although as we explained in detail in the previous sections, it is more a question of their *quality* and sufficient 'degree of maturity' in terms of being a well-thought-out and complete concept.

Even if the brainstorming is followed by further work on the ideas, people often economise on the thinking work in the conception phase. Ultimately, prototypes should be developed and tested on the customer as quickly as possible. Even then, it is only the customer determining exactly how the idea must look. Many aspects which are relevant either for the company or for the actual implementation of the idea are still not taken into consideration.

Before starting customer validation, we therefore recommend that you take Edison's advice and put in some hard work to develop your ideas into innovation concepts. They do not necessarily have to comprise 40,000 pages, like Edison's notes for a light bulb. A few, detailed pages are perfectly adequate.

This *conception phase* forms the basis for later implementation success. Imagine two painters. One of them talks about a superb painting. The other has the same vision and paints the painting. At least the second can call themselves a successful artist. But can the first too? No, because he only had the inspiration, but he did not accomplish the work. In companies fired by numerous creativity books, workshops, lectures and articles, however, the idea for a painting is often confused with the painting itself (Govindarajan, 2010). As a result, the idea is given to the department which is responsible for it with a request to implement and to sell it. But have you ever tried to paint a picture based on a Post-it note? You would probably soon give up.

To make the implementation easier, the painting should at least be sketched out, the colours determined and the painting techniques and the canvas, etc. too. Ideally, you should already have compared various sketches and plans and selected the best variant for implementation. The actual painting can *then* be done by someone else, as it was custom in the studios of italian renaissance masters.

In the corporate context, this means that if no conception work is accomplished, no ideas are likely to be implemented. Every idea initially means extra work and new problems for the implementer. If it is not even clear how the idea is to be implemented, it is often doomed to fail.

Conception does not only ensure that ideas can actually be implemented and thus have excellent potential traction. The most exciting aspects of the idea are also often only discovered during the detailed work and development, and it is these which ensure the best possible customer fit. This significantly increases the quality of the idea and that is crucial for the later success of the innovation (Forde & Fox, 2016).

A study of new product developments in 272 companies showed, for example, that in addition to the idea development process and the work with stakeholders, *concept development* was also one of the key positive influencing factors in terms of an innovation's subsequent product success, implementation time, market penetration and financial success (Markham, 2013).

We can conclude that implementation is usually only a problem if insufficient work has been done on the underlying idea (and it does not meet the needs either from the customer's or the company's perspective). If ideation is not just used as a creative idea, but as analytical preparation for the implementation too, there is a significantly greater probability that you will be able to achieve a successful implementation. So it is not creative ideas which should be the targeted outcome of ideation, but specific innovation concepts.

Only the best ideas are developed into concepts. The outcome of the ideation workshops described in the last section is usually hundreds of different, individual ideas on Post-it notes. These must be systematically recorded and completed so that a decision can be taken on this basis about the best ideas to develop into innovation concepts.

In the first step, it is important to note down **all of the idea Post-it notes produced in a complete list of ideas (in a table or in innovation management software)**. You should record every single idea here along with a title and an additional short description. Since the Post-it notes themselves often only contain just one sentence (i.e. the title of the idea), initial conception work usually takes place when the ideas are being transferred. This is about putting the idea into words again as a short description. Since this is not always easy on the basis of Post-it notes, the person with the task of creating the idea list should at least be present at the ideation workshops where the most relevant ideas are usually discussed as a whole group anyhow. When creating the list of ideas, it is also crucial to combine similar or identical ideas into a larger solution straightaway. This automatically prevents duplications too.

Once the idea list has been created, we recommend that you let as many different people from the project team as possible **comment on and develop** the individual ideas there. Finally, all ideas must be assessed intuitively by the project team on the basis of the potential goal achievement to select the best ideas for development into innovation concepts.

Now comes some hard work to **produce the innovation concepts**. In contrast to the rather creative ideation workshops, precise, analytical, detailed work is now on the agenda. This effort is worthwhile, as innovation concepts with a precise fit will emerge during this process. These should typically contain the core of the idea as well as all of the relevant information required for a basic understanding and for implementation. Conceptual work is mostly also a combination of research, your own reflections and sparring sessions to develop ideas with others as well as numerous whiteboard and computer sketches. **The following elements should be**

developed during the conception phase, whereas the idea itself and its potential implementation should be specified simultaneously step by step.

1. *Core of the idea:* the core of the idea or the solution to the pain point must be described clearly and in an understandable format. What is new? What is the customer added value? How does this solution differ from other solutions? Why do we have reason to believe in this solution? To answer these questions, ideas can be described in the *insight—benefit—reason to believe system*. *Insight* describes the pain point, for example, with a specific quotation and statistics obtained from the *customisation phase*. *Benefit* describes the specific solution as a result of an idea. And *reason to believe* is built on traction factors (in terms of existing company competencies, brands, reason to believe in the topic, etc.) and customer factors (e.g. trends and market trends) from the *configuration phase* or selected sources of inspiration from the *compilation phase* to underline the reason to believe and the meaningfulness of the idea from the customer's and company's perspective. At its core, the solution should always contain a special feature which makes it unique. At best, this special feature should already be reflected in the title of the idea. To do this, the idea must normally be developed beyond the original Post-it note. Tools such as the value proposition canvas (Strategyzer, 2017a) but also sources of inspiration and parameters from the previous process steps can provide the necessary input. Discussions with other project members or even the network about a specific idea helps to collect new input about the idea. To ensure an idea can be implemented as well as provide the best possible traction, it should also be specifically checked once again in terms of the positive and negative traction factors from the *configuration phase*. The company's traction factors should always be kept in mind throughout the entire conception process, while the idea is being developed into an innovation concept.
2. *Customer journey:* as soon as the basic idea has been established, the next step should be to describe your user experience from the customer's perspective. As a rule, a *customer journey* is useful for mapping the process or functionality of the solution step by step. Highlighting every important step the customer takes in using the solution not only helps the company to imagine the idea better, but it also checks the idea's customer fit again.
3. *Business model:* the business model is a simple description of how the solution is supposed to earn money and how the various value streams are created and connected. This is not relevant in every innovation space, but it is relevant in most cases. In addition, the idea is divided into different elements from the company's perspective to observe how they interact. The *business model canvas* (Strategyzer, 2017b) is particularly suited to this purpose, enabling all of these elements to be displayed clearly on a single page and then checked. We can use this not only to understand the idea from the company's perspective but also to ensure the potential traction of the idea.
4. *Lean business case:* an approximate estimate of costs and revenues can be made based on the business model. Particular attention should also be paid to the goals, criteria and KPIs defined at the outset. If, for example, there was a par-

2

ticularly large increase in sales, this should appear again in the business case. Depending on the idea, it can be very challenging to create an initial approximate business case. The goal, though, is not to determine all the numbers exactly in advance. Instead, it is crucial at this point to list the categories of costs and revenues which will arise and to consider their relative size. Besides using research and benchmarks for comparable solutions, experts from the company or the network can also help to carry out these assessments. On the one hand, the lean business case tests the idea's reasoning and implementation capability, but it also makes it easier for key stakeholders to assess the idea and plan resources for its implementation.

5. *Implementation planning:* to simplify the later implementation during the conception phase, we recommend that companies prepare a simple implementation plan and a market entry plan, if necessary, as part of their conception planning. In contrast to a detailed project plan, the implementation plan initially only contains the most important elements of the implementation. By supplementing these with responsibilities, approximate duration and any costs, you can already roughly check the implementation capability on the basis of the concept, making the start of implementation significantly easier too. Moreover, implementation planning also helps with making an initial assessment of the complexity of the solutions, and this may be important for selecting the concepts (◘ Fig. 2.26).

The innovation concept's content represents a good basis for implementation in terms of developing all of these elements. It should be noted that this content cannot simply be generated in a linear fashion, but is usually interlinked. We therefore recommend that you continue to return to the idea during concept development so that you can, for example, supplement or change it depending on the research results, process observations or feedback which you receive. You should also continue to review and, if necessary, adapt the customer journey, business model and lean business case and your implementation planning. As a result, concepts are developed as part of a strongly *iterative* process. And during this process, the original Post-it note is firstly developed into sketches on a whiteboard or computer and ultimately into documents or presentation slides with images, texts, tables and, potentially, interactive graphics, such as mock-up diagrams or wireframes which then contain all of the formal and functional characteristics of the solution.

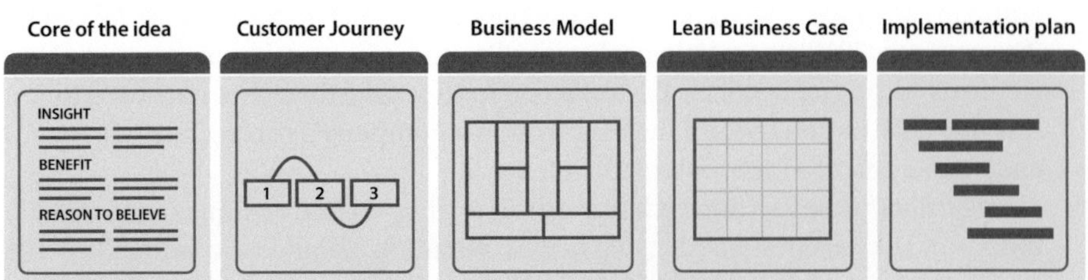

◘ **Fig. 2.26** Elements in the innovation concept. (Author's own figure)

Guest Commentary: Reyk Radojewski, Chief Financial Officer, Beiersdorf South East Asia

"As a *global* corporation that is serving *local* consumer needs in the highly dynamic health and beauty market, it is crucial for Beiersdorf to launch locally relevant innovations to its markets. While the key priority is to put the diverse and individual consumer needs into the centre of the innovation process, it is likewise important to secure a high speed to market to capture trends when they happen, not after. Therefore, operating a highly efficient and agile innovation process generates a competitive edge. In order to being able to focus and prioritize the resources tied up in the innovation process to the most impactful projects, it is necessary to translate any idea or concept into a measurable *lean business case*. In some innovation processes this can be a key challenge.

Typically, at the very early stage, where the innovation may just be a first idea, some teams might struggle with deriving a first quantification of a business case. The temptation to just 'shoot a number' or 'guess' is often very high. A good lean business case avoids this trap by focusing on some logically derived and documented underlying assumptions for any '(gu)estimation'. Along the innovation process, these assumptions can serve as great anchor points to understand, discuss and explain changes. Moreover, teams will not question and challenge the actual figures (who has not heard the following words: 'I don't believe these numbers') but will focus the discussion on the underlying assumptions and eventually sharpen those over time. That way, focusing the discussion and challenges on assumptions and mechanics of the business case leads to a more fact-based, rational dialogue rather than one driven by emotion.

Every feasible idea has a value creation potential on one side and a price tag on the other. An idea that cannot be broken down into relevant figures is not an innovation but remains an illusion. Will the estimate be 100% correct? Most likely not. But it can help to prioritize and to take investment decisions. Discussions about fact-based, plausible assumptions clearly separate ideas which only look attractive on a slide deck from the ones which really have substance and are well-thought through. Those are exactly the ideas a company is willing to invest resources on and drive them to market readiness.

Consequently, investing the extra effort into creating a *lean* business case in the early stages of the innovation process will very likely pay off later, as the benefits are evident: core assumptions are available, leading to more focused discussions. Resources are concentrated on the most impactful projects, leading to less waste. Relevant facts and figures are serving as a foundation for ongoing discussion, moderating the evolution of the innovation. And a learning mechanism is in place, allowing the comparison 'actual' vs 'plan' once the innovation is launched to the market. That way, the lean business case will allow to assess the case not only during but also long after the initial ideation phase. What are the key reasons that the innovation performed better/worse? What has changed versus the initial assumptions? Typically, these will be the questions being asked once the innovation performance is being discussed. With a good lean business case, innovation teams can get ahead of these questions and successfully steer their idea through any discussion."

Usually, the outcome of this concept work is a wide range of innovation concepts (often around ten) which give a clear picture of possible solutions. In the best scenario, each of these concepts contains the elements stipulated. However, depending on the resources available for the conception, you might, for example, pre-select some ideas based on a description of the core of the idea so that you only develop a few of them through to complete innovation concepts.

At this stage, we do not yet recommend that you develop prototypes, i.e. simple physical (or digital) versions of the solutions. The visual concept is normally adequate for further validation and selection initially. Also, with a prototype, you always run the risk that you will assess the current implementation instead of the actual idea. Prototyping is only necessary during the conception phase if you are unable to assess the functionality of the idea adequately without using a prototype.

To ensure that concepts are feasible, you should conduct a **feasibility check for each of the relevant innovation concepts**.

In addition to carrying out research as part of the conception which is already serving as an initial feasibility check, we also advise you to consult experts regardless of how complex the solution is. For solutions with technological components, in particular, we recommend that you involve internal or external implementation experts in the conception process at an early stage. These may, for example, re-examine the basic functionality of the solution, the lean business case or the implementation planning from their perspective using the existing concepts. This will not only enable you to improve the potential for excellent traction and rapid implementation, you will have also succeeded in getting potential implementers involved at an early stage.

After this basic assessment and feasibility check, the next step should be to validate the concepts from the perspective of both the target group (desirability) and the company (feasibility, viability) so that you can maximise customer fit and traction and, if necessary, adjust these again before they enter the final round of implementation selection.

2.4.3 Count Your Chickens Before They Hatch

Greek philosopher Aesop once wrote about a milkmaid in one of his fables. She went to market to sell her milk, telling her mother how she would buy a chicken with the money she would get for the milk, then sell the eggs every day, buy a new dress and find a husband. But she spilled the milk and had to learn from her mother about not counting your chickens before they hatch. In the context of the innovation process, this proverb seems to be all too true, because counting on an idea before it is even implemented seems hasty and even dangerous. After all, the journey from a good idea to its successful implementation is particularly challenging and unpredictable, especially for large companies. Consequently, fast experimentation and testing is the way to go for many companies to get their ideas to 'hatch' as fast as possible and validate their success afterwards.

The better you can assess the success of an idea before its implementation though, the lower the risk associated with that implementation. And it will be all the easier to choose which of the innovation concepts developed is to be implemented in the end. That is why we have to forget Aesop's advice here and validate any positive or negative feedback about the various innovation concepts 'before they hatch', that is, in advance, even before real-world testing. In terms of efficient innovation, you should ideally request this validation from customers as well as the relevant stakeholders in the company to ensure you achieve excellent customer fit *and* excellent traction.

This validation occurs in three consecutive steps. The first is the validation with the customer—and, on this basis, any reworking of the concept. The second is the recommendation of an assessment within the project team followed by any further concept revision. The third is the final assessment round with decision-makers. Here the concept(s) for implementation is/are selected on the basis of the goals and criteria set at the outset of the process.

A qualitative and a quantitative assessment should ideally be carried out by the customer to validate the desirability of each concept. Even if excellent customer fit has already been theoretically ensured as part of the ideation and concept work, this should be validated in practice. Qualitative feedback from the customer can also contribute to the further optimisation of the concepts and so to a further improvement in the customer fit.

- Focus groups (with participants drawn from the target group) are particularly suitable for *qualitative validation*. If various innovation potentials were generated with different pain points, several focus groups will be necessary. It is a good idea to present the innovation concepts as part of the focus group on the basis of the 'core ideas' and to have each participant intuitively assess them. A scale from 0 to 10 (0 = bad, 10 = excellent), for example, is suitable for generally assessing the idea. You should also ask whether the participant would use or buy the solution themselves. We recommend that you ask about the general relevance of the pain point from the participant's perspective (or even select the participants based on their agreement about the pain point). The logic of this is that if a participant categorises a pain point as relevant and scores the corresponding solution as bad (or excellent), the idea appears to have a poor (or an excellent) customer fit—at least for this participant. Yet if the pain point is categorised as irrelevant and then the solution is scored as bad (or excellent), this has practically no significance since the solution was designed specifically for customers with that particular pain point. You can filter out inappropriate scores like this. Qualitative validation offers the opportunity to collect comments and feedback about individual ideas over and above a pure concept assessment. This can occur either in writing via assessment forms and/or in idea discussions as part of a focus group. Qualitative feedback like this helps us to understand the individual assessments better and to adapt the concepts, if necessary, so that we maximise customer fit.
- An additional *quantitative assessment* using a larger sample from the target group (or several target groups) helps to build up a broader database for subsequent concept decision-making. There are various suitable web tools or market research providers for this which can often provide a direct pool of participants which are also a good fit. Tests with tools like eye-tracking software can supplement the database if required and can help to evaluate positive or negative feel-

ings when looking at concepts. Regardless of the market research provider or tool selected, it is a good idea to present ideas as simply as possible so that they can be understood without any further verbal explanations. In its simplest variant, you can adapt the assessment scheme used for the qualitative assessment to the quantitative assessment—supplemented by a text box for any other comments and ideas. The advantage of a quantitative assessment is obvious. Since you can relatively inexpensively assess the customer fit of ideas (and also how easy it is to understand them) using a large database, you can check with a high degree of certainty whether you can actually achieve excellent customer fit using the concepts in question. If you can, then you can count your chickens before they have hatched.

An **(initially) internal project assessment from the company's perspective** also ensures that the innovation concepts developed are actually feasible, taking into consideration the company's strengths and restrictions—and that the goals and criteria agreed at the outset of the process have been optimally considered. We really recommend this internal project validation, because it allows you to discover—and correct—the final differences of opinion in good time with all of the relevant stakeholders ahead of the final deadline.

To validate the *feasibility* of the concepts, you first need the list of traction factors from the *configuration phase.* Since it contains both positive and negative traction factors, you need a two-stage process.

- *In the first step*, you need to check which of the *positive* traction factors (i.e. strengths of the company) have been considered in the relevant concepts. The more positive traction factors you can use in the implementation of a concept, the better. After all, this means that you can potentially achieve particularly excellent traction. These factors should also be mentioned explicitly in the concepts in question.
- *In the second step*, you need to check the extent to which any *negative* traction factors (i.e. restrictions) might hinder the implementation of individual concepts. If you uncover any negative traction factors in a concept in this way, you will need to adapt the concept so that it either no longer comes into contact with the negative traction factor during a potential implementation or that the implementation is still possible in a transparent way despite this. If you cannot achieve this adaptation, you will need in the worst case to reject the concept.

Finally, you need to assess the *viability* of each concept to determine the extent to which it meets the goals and criteria set at the outset of the innovation process. The list of goals and criteria from the *configuration phase* sets the individual assessment variables in advance. The project team intuitively assesses each concept in terms of its potential to meet all of the goals and criteria based on this—rather than, as is often the case, based on how new or creative it is. It is true that you can never exactly predict the success of a concept. However, this approach can at least ensure that all of the concepts possess the necessary *potential* to meet the goals and criteria set.

In traditional innovation processes, the final round of decision-making takes place partly like in the *Dragon's Den*. If you know the television program of this name (or its American equivalent *Shark Tank*) in which start-ups pitch to investors, this situation will be familiar. An idea is worked on for a long time, only to be torn to shreds or changed completely by the decision-makers later on. This is not only the case for start-ups in their investor pitch but also for some employees when they present ideas to the decision-makers in their company. Why is this? Decision-makers are usually sceptical about new ideas at first as these normally mean extra work and risk. Added to that, each individual stakeholder has their own criteria in mind which an idea must meet. If these are not met, the idea is rejected. On top of that, decision-makers are often in a position of great uncertainty since questions about hard facts, key performance indicators (KPIs) and the feasibility of the ideas can usually not be answered at all, especially in the case of ideas developed in a purely customer-centric way. What is the outcome of this dragon's den then? That most ideas do not succeed in being implemented. Employees are frustrated because their ideas have not been appreciated, and decision-makers are unhappy, because they have not obtained any new ideas with a good fit.

Instead of a 'dragon's den', the final decision-makers' meeting should therefore aim for an atmosphere where ideas are not presented and then criticised, but where the best innovation concepts for implementation can be easily selected out of the many suitable and well-developed ones.

People should mention (without being asked) all of the important factors in the decision during the **final presentation of the innovation concepts**. This is perfectly possible. All of the information required by decision-makers to select an innovation concept is already available from the earlier detailed concept work, the feasibility examination with experts, the desirability validation of concepts with customers as well as the final check of traction factors and target achievement for the viability. The individual concepts 'only' need to be visualised and presented as succinctly and as transparently as possible. You need to opt for a healthy balance between obtaining a sufficient amount of information to make a decision and enough storytelling for the ideas. To satisfy this simultaneous desire for logic (information) and emotions (storytelling), we recommend that you start the presentation by recalling the goals and criteria set at the outset as well as the innovation potential selected on this basis before the individual ideas can be presented with their insight, benefit and reason-to-believe. You can then include other concept elements as required, for example, to explain a complex idea more clearly or to illuminate the lean business case for a complex solution. In the subsequent discussion, you can then answer further questions as comprehensively as possible on the basis of the individual concept components, thus making people feel even more secure.

The assessment by stakeholders is important for a variety of reasons. Firstly, the innovation concepts developed all fundamentally lie within the given traction space and meet all of the goals and criteria (at least, provided the concept work has been carried out correctly in all of the steps). Individual concepts usually vary in their specific potential to achieve the goals. And this is precisely what the decision-makers ultimately need to assess. Secondly, every decision-maker always holds their own subjective views too. You cannot make ideas completely objective—not with even the most stringent conceptual work. It is therefore never possible to predict exactly which concept will be better or worse in the end. Ergo, you need to conduct your assessment in a similar way. Thirdly, an assessment of all the innovation concepts developed provides you with a clear ranking of implementable concepts. Lastly, you can select at least one of these. In the end, assessing the concepts or selecting between several concepts generates an opportunity for co-determination with decision-makers (instead of just a straight yes/no option in terms of a concept for implementation; see also ▶ Sect. 2.9.1). This is crucial for securing decision-makers' support during the subsequent implementation.

Innovation concepts are firstly assessed intuitively by the decision-makers in terms of the goals and criteria set, based on the information presented. This (initial) 'gut feeling' assessment provides an important basis for the final implementation decision about the concepts.

What is the background to this? Even with making a great effort to analyse the concepts, you can never predict the success or failure of an innovation with complete certainty in advance. Ultimately, it is not possible to fully anticipate what will happen between now and when the innovation is launched, and so a certain residual uncertainty is inevitable. Intuitive assessment is helpful here as an additional source of information. All of the important factors have already been included subconsciously in decisions based on gut feelings (Sinclair, 2005). Thus, with an intuitive assessment, a broad decision is taken based on the decision-makers' experience, knowledge, skills, assumptions and feelings—rather than just on analytical models which are limited in their depiction of reality.

How exactly does this intuitive assessment work? Michael Eisner, the former CEO of Walt Disney, describes intuition as follows. When a good idea presents itself, 'your body reacts in a certain way—you get an unusual feeling in your stomach, throat or on your skin. It's the same sensation you get when you first observe a great work of art' (Hayashi, 2001).

This is specifically what happens now. Decision-makers intuitively assess each individual innovation concept against the individual goals and criteria set, for example, on a scale from 0 to 10 (0 = does not meet them, 10 = is an ideal fit). From the perspective of all the decision-makers, a clear innovation concept ranking emerges from all of the average assessments (multiplied by the respective weightings of the individual goals and criteria, if applicable). A comparison of this ranking order with that gained from the customer assessment can provide further important information. This is because customers include other factors in their intuitive assessment. So by combining the decision-maker's and customer's assessments, you usually obtain a good feeling for the potential of the individual concepts in terms of their traction *and* customer fit.

A **final decision about the implementation** can be made either during or after the meeting. Our experience shows that the original judgement reached from intuitively assessing concepts is confirmed in most cases, even after further careful consideration. And so, once you have decided on one or more innovation concepts, nothing more stands in the way of implementing them.

The task now is to get the 'implementers' on board and to tackle the upcoming implementation as efficiently as possible. And this is exactly what the *conversion phase* is aiming to do in the last step of the 5C process.

Case Study: FTI Group

New Digital Business Models to Increase Package Tour Revenues

FTI Group is one of the four largest package tour providers in Europe. During the 2015/2016 financial year, 4.7 million guests booked their holidays with this tour operator.

The tourism industry had by then been characterised for some years by a very fierce price war between tour operators. This trend was further exacerbated by the success of comparison portals and price-sensitive customers. The result was decreasing margins on more or less substitutable products. On top of this, political developments and terrorist attacks had led to declining booking figures—and thus to lower utilisation of flight contingents in countries like Egypt or Turkey. So in practice there was a need for innovations able to counteract these developments.

Configuration

At the start of the configuration phase, goals were defined as 'gaining additional customers' and 'revenue increases with existing customers'. The following criteria were agreed: Implementing the concepts should already have been contributing to significant revenue increases in the following year, and FTI Group intended to fall back on its own IT department, in particular, and on a selected partner agency to implement these. On this basis, the decision was made for the *innovation space* of 'new (digital) business models'.

As the configuration progressed, it became clear that travellers' booking decisions depended on various factors. It was therefore also important for them to be able to trust that the travel description actually matched the offer in reality. Travellers usually checked this before booking on rating portals, such as HolidayCheck. The risk still remained that the situation might change dramatically in the period between the booking date and the departure date (as a result, for example, of new hotel management, renovation work, etc.). With this information base and with the associated potential in the customer relationship, the following *innovation potential* of 'digital innovations for the early bookers target group which enables customers to trust more strongly in booking (early)' was decided.

Customisation

As part of the customisation process, it was not only decided to first study the envisaged target group of package tour travellers more closely in terms of their innovation potential but also independent travellers too. This should have helped to understand the differences between the target groups more clearly, on the one hand, while on the other, we intended to find out specifically what had been preventing independent travellers from booking the actually very convenient package tours so far.

In terms of methodology, we used focus groups. This was partly to gather a wide range of different opinions as efficiently as possible but also to observe participants close up and thus better assess the significance of individual statements. As a result, both target groups specifically expressed their fear (already identified as part of configuration via secondary research) that the framework conditions which the travellers themselves have no influence over (e.g. the quality of the restaurant, the presence of new construction sites near the hotel, etc.) might deteriorate between the booking date and the departure date. It also became apparent that there was a desire to make a travel booking to achieve what could best be described as 'peace of mind'. This important *insight* was validated as a *pain point* in further research. From the perspective of target groups in the market, no satisfactory solution for genuine 'peace of mind' existed for travel bookings at that time.

Compilation

As part of the compilation phase, we analysed the international tourist industry market in detail. A wide range of inspiring solutions regarding *best practices* were identified in general for 'peace of mind', such as purchasing flight ticket options, big data price prediction algorithms or simply even travel insurance to cover, for example, the cost of travel interruption due to illness. A white spot in the market quickly became apparent for travel and hotel bookings, in particular. Still no adequate security relating to the decreasing attractiveness of the services booked actually existed for travellers at that time. In preparation for the subsequent construction phase, additional examples from *analogous markets* were identified, including service providers who specialised in suing for compensation for a company's defective performance. In addition, *concepts for the future* were selected as inspirations that dealt with topics, such as artificial intelligence, virtual reality, mass customisation or social commerce.

Construction

We generated more than 600 ideas from the inspirations acquired during the compilation phase. They were selected gradually over the remainder of the process and then developed into innovation concepts. To help early bookers trust that the travel offer would be satisfied, we developed the concept of the 'quality guarantee'. Similar to travel insurance, this could be booked for a small additional cost to cover the trip. The advantage for the traveller was that if the recommendation rate of the 'HolidayCheck' rating portal dropped by at least 10% between the booking date and 20 days before the start of the trip, they would be able to rebook the accommodation they had booked free of charge.

The quality guarantee was the first of several concepts to be implemented within 6 months for the Sonnenklar.TV brand (a part of the FTI Group portfolio), and it is already being used today for many of the travel bookings made there (■ Fig.. 2.27).

Configuration (1) – Customisation (2) – Compilation (3) – **Construction (4)** – Conversion (5)

Mind-set	**Think inside the box**		
Section	**Ideas are not random**	**No pain, no gain**	**You can also count your chickens before they hatch**
Outcome	✓ Ideas	✓ Feasible innovative concepts	✓ Innovation concepts validated and prioritised ✓ Concept to be implemented
Methodology	1. Select and invite ideation workshop participants 2. Prime the participants by sending them tasks in advance 3. Prepare aids in advance - inspirations (from 2.2.3) - auxiliary axes or. help cards (e.g., parameters or their variants from the morphological boxes from 2.1.3) 4. Carry out a structured workshop (`multidimensional ideation') for idea generation	1. Systematically record all of the ideas (and expand and cluster) 2. Assess the ideas 3. Select the top ideas 4. Develop innovation concept ideas, incl.: - core of the idea - customer journey - business model - lean business case - implementation planning 5. Feasibility check (with experts)	1. Visualisation of innovation concepts (e.g. 10 concepts) 2. Qualitative and quantitative validation with the target group 3. Internal project validation based on the traction factors, and assessment based on the goals and criteria 4. Present and debate with key stakeholders 5. Intuitive assessment with goals and criteria by the key stakeholders 6. Selection the concept(s) to be implemented
Aid	▫ Pool of participants ▫ White spots and inspirtions (2.3) ▫ Morphological boxes (2.1.3) ▫ Run a workshop	▫ Ideas from the workshop (2.4.1) ▫ Innovation concept elements	▫ Innovation concept (2.4.2) ▫ Market research tools Traction factors (2.1.2) ▫ Goals and criteria (2.1.1)

Fig. 2.27 Overview of construction. (Author's own figure)

2.5 Conversion: Where There Is a Way, There Is Also a Will

The implementation phase generally seems to be the most difficult part of an innovation. Innovative ideas are conceived, but then reluctant implementers either fail to realise them as intended—or simply fail altogether. The implementers, on the other hand, see ideas coming their way which they cannot realise at all in that form, and so they block them from the start. The only solution is often based on the phrase 'where there is a will, there is a way', meaning 'if an idea is a good one, we will certainly find a way to implement it'. Yet this cannot be a long-term strategy as it does not allow for any planning of the innovation execution.

Fortunately, there is another option. **If the 'way' to implementation (of the innovation concept) is clear and is an optimal fit to the implementers' requirements, their will to implement grows**. Not only because this makes the implementation easier, but because the implementers also feel sufficiently valued in terms of their needs.

The *conversion phase* therefore deals with the transition from a feasible innovation concept through to its implementation as an efficient innovation—taking into account the implementers and any relevant implementation methods (see ◘ Fig. 2.28).

The following building blocks illustrate this last process step:

1. **Everyone on board**: often, ideas are kept secret until no one can avoid implementing them. These skunkworks tactics often seem to be necessary to prevent ideas being blocked at an early stage by implementers acting as the company's 'immune system'. Whereas everyone finds their own ideas convincing, this is usually not the case as regards other people's ideas. On the contrary, 'not-invented-here' syndrome now quickly strikes. Nevertheless, there is a cure for this, and that is considering all the relevant implementation factors and criteria from the outset. We already ensured this in the first step of the 5C process when identifying the traction space. Yet the challenge remains that innovation concepts are not implemented by the people who developed them previously. We should not employ skunkworks tactics to address this. Instead as far as possible, we need to get everyone 'on board' so that they become an active part of the innovation concept at an early stage. Or to put it another way, you transfer the 'psychological ownership' of the idea or the innovation concept to them. You not only need to make it as easy as possible for the implementers to implement the idea (as it was designed); they should ideally be 'dying' to implement the idea or innovation concept even. An implementation kick-off with methods aimed at assessment and involvement based on effective psychological concepts can get the implementers on board—thus putting the implementation of the innovation concepts on the road to success.
2. **The fast bird catches the worm**: as innovation concepts are an optimal fit to the traction and customer factors set in advance, they are already a perfect fit for

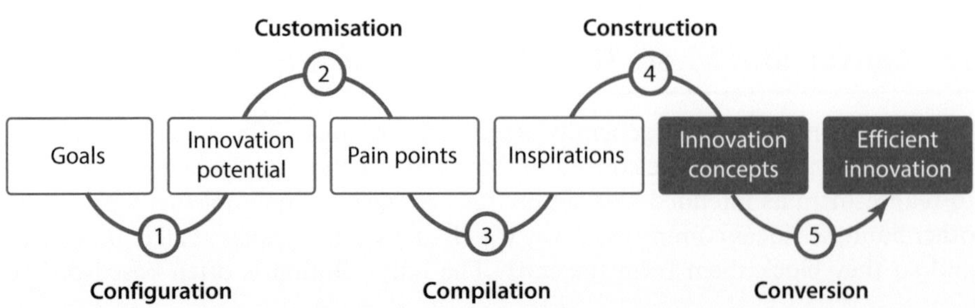

◘ **Fig. 2.28** 5C process: conversion. (Author's own figure)

the simplest possible implementation. Nevertheless, we recommend that you also minimise the implementation risk further (or maximise the chances of success) by working as cost-effectively as possible and as closely as possible with the customer. It is therefore a good idea at this point to use the lean start-up method based on iterative experimentation and testing. This is now used in a targeted way for the best possible implementation (rather than for developing ideas, as is the case in many other innovation processes). It now helps to work out the details for rapid and risk-minimising (or success-maximising) implementation, helping to stay ahead of the competition.

3. **All endings are easy**: the end of the innovation process is particularly challenging, as a rule. After all, most ideas do not take the strengths and weaknesses of the company into sufficient account either because they have been developed out-of-the-box and/or developed in a purely customer-centric way. So it is very difficult at least to implement them in the company—if it does not fail completely in the end. By systematically developing efficient innovations, we avoid this innovation frustration in the 5C process, making the end of the innovation process as easy as possible. Ultimately, the previous steps have already ensured the best possible chance of implementation and subsequent success in the market by solving the *right* customer problem at the *right* point using the company's *existing* strengths. In this way, we can achieve the company's goals in an optimum way by taking the relevant criteria into consideration. As a result, the innovation concept developed using this logic can now also be finally implemented (usually by making use of the normal company processes) and launched successfully in the market. Of course, the innovation journey does not end there. Once the innovation has been launched in the market, then the real work starts. Yet once a solution for a relevant customer problem has already been implemented at least once, this can already be judged to be a significant success—for the customer, for the employee and for the company.

2.5.1 Everyone On Board

How much do you like telling others in your company about your ideas? How often do you encounter rejection, objections and reluctance? And how easily can you be convinced by other ideas? Everyone has probably already noticed that their own ideas really make sense—but are not necessarily received as positively by others. At the same time, you yourself greet other people's ideas with scepticism. This becomes a problem if the implementer is not the person who developed the idea, but someone else. As a consequence, it regularly occurs that ideas are driven forward but kept as 'hidden' as possible until, in the best-case scenario, there is no other option but to implement them. Since nobody likes to be confronted with a done deed, this tactic usually only makes the problem worse.

Even innovation concepts with the best possible fit are initially associated with extra work, risk and uncertainty, so implementers need correspondingly great motivation to implement them successfully. People acquire this motivation when they at least partly perceive the idea as their own, that is, they take psychological ownership of the idea (Bubenzer & Rouse, 2015). This is partly achieved by involving the implementers in the innovation process at an early stage (see ► Sect. 2.1) and partly (also) by jointly assessing and determining the concepts for implementation.

The concept of *psychological ownership* is a very powerful tool for implementation success and describes a strong personal connection to an idea or innovation concept. As a consequence, considerably more commitment and effort is invested in implementing it than in other tasks. Studies show that such ownership especially exists when you have created the objects or ideas yourself or you have at least been jointly involved in developing them.

This phenomenon can be observed over and over again in start-ups. The founder and idea developer builds more and more on their idea and raises the start-up as if it was their baby. In companies, however, it is usually not practical—nor usually sensible either—for the idea generator to be the implementer too, because other teams are responsible for the implementation and may also be more familiar with it. It is therefore important to transfer the strong connection or psychological ownership associated with the corresponding innovation concept as well as possible over to the implementers responsible for managing it.

A simple experiment shows how such an ownership transfer can succeed. Professors (Baer & Graham, 2012) conducted a study on psychological ownership. They asked 100 students to review a strategy for a new restaurant and then send it to a committee. Some of the students were given what was termed a 'final concept' which they were just supposed to review. The other group of students was told that the concept was not quite finished and they should add the missing details, such as the name of the restaurant, the location, etc. The difference in perceived psychological ownership was then investigated using some psychological assessments. The group of students which had been able to make their own changes achieved significantly higher ownership scores than the other group. In subsequent tasks, it was also shown that the students with a higher ownership score were also more likely to add additional elements to the concept, i.e. to work constructively, whereas the other students removed elements of the concept instead.

This makes it clear that **ownership can be transferred by actively involving the people it is being transferred to**. Further studies show that this involvement can be achieved particularly through the following three elements: *control*, *knowledge* and *collaboration*. This is the exact opposite of the skunkworks tactics mentioned above which try to drive ideas through in secret for as long as possible.

Instead of hiding an idea, it would be preferable to get everyone on board. The more closely you can integrate implementers into the innovation concept through *control*, *knowledge* and *collaboration*, the greater the chance that the *ownership transfer* will succeed—and the innovation concepts you develop will be implemented with enthusiasm, effort and commitment.

- *Control* describes the opportunity to be involved in making decisions about the implementation. One opportunity to do this is to take part in presenting the concept and then in assessing and prioritising various concepts (see ► Sect. 2.7.4) or alternatively (or also) to be involved in deciding further details of the implementation. As part of this, implementers may, for example, propose and

select different variants of a concept, or they may decide on various implementation details together.
- *Knowledge* refers to the implementers gaining an in-depth understanding of the innovation concept. It is not enough by itself to just present or to flesh out the concept. Idea providers (or concept developers) should instead also explain the background, communicate the research results and explain the thought processes. If implementers are also given the opportunity to debate the innovation concept in detail themselves and to provide feedback, this may further improve their perceived knowledge.
- *Collaboration* offers the most important opportunity for ownership transfer. As the above experiment has shown, even work on the details of a finished concept increases this ownership significantly. Since implementers cannot—and should not—all be involved in ideation and/or conception, it makes sense to present a feasible concept but to prepare this for implementation jointly with the employees responsible for the implementation. Smaller brainstorming sessions or round tables are normally adequate for this. After all, we no longer need completely new ideas or solutions. We only have to add individual implementation details (such as names, locations, test customers, designs/colours, etc.). You also need to jointly determine the exact implementation process with the implementers.

In practice, we recommend holding a **joint implementation workshop** with the idea providers (or concept developers) and the employees responsible for implementation. This can either take place after the concept presentation to decision-makers or as soon as they have decided to implement one or more of the innovation concepts. You should invite anyone to the implementation workshop who is relevant for the upcoming implementation. Most of these will come from the specialist departments in question or the external solution providers. Furthermore, there may also be a specific implementation team for initial testing or rapid preliminary studies (see ► Sect. 2.9.2) who should also take part in the workshop.

The following steps included as part of the workshop can then ensure strong ownership transfer and the best possible start to implementation:
1. *Presentation* of this concept to be implemented (and any variants) followed by discussion and the opportunity to provide feedback.
2. *Knowledge transfer* by transferring any relevant additional documents, data and contacts as well as explaining the thought processes which led to the solution presented or to individual concept details.
3. *Joint brainstorming and discussion of implementation details*, such as names, designs, go-to-market strategies, pricing, etc. Inspirations can also be prepared in advance to assist brainstorming (see ► Sect. 2.4).
4. *Supplementing the existing innovation concept* with specific feedback as well as additional ideas/thoughts about the ready-to-implement concept.
5. *Joint drafting or completing of an implementation plan* with specific steps, timings and responsibilities as well as any relevant milestones.
6. *Celebrate the kick-off*, preferably with the support of key stakeholders and top management.

If adequate ownership transfer has taken place as part of the implementation workshop, nothing else will stand in the way of the implementation, meaning that everyone is on board. Since the specific implementation can proceed very differently depending on the innovation space, solution approach, industry or company, in the following sections, we recommend some fundamental principles able to support rapid, efficient and successful implementation.

Guest Commentary: Till Bauer, Head of Strategic Projects and Commercial Innovation, MSD Sharp & Dohme (Subsidiary of Merck & Co., Inc.)

"At MSD Sharp & Dohme, as one of the oldest pharmaceutical companies in the world, we have for many decades been faced with the repeated challenge of continuing to advance the established business with new innovations. Similarly important is the pioneering anchoring of innovations as part of the corporate strategy as well as the concerted implementation of all participants. For this reason, all internal and external stakeholders must work together to achieve success.

What is important for the innovation process itself are clear responsibilities, fast decision-making and the use of adaptable, agile methods with a clear definition of the project structure. Over and above that, innovations should be clearly anchored in strategy. And not forgetting that to ensure a high degree of customer focus, customers must be involved in the process of developing ideas and products at an early stage. If this occurs in the piloting or implementation phase, it is often too late.

To successfully transition from innovation concepts into implementation, it is particularly crucial to harmonise the various stakeholders' goals from the outset. In the light of this, a major role is played by expectation management and 'buy-in' at all relevant levels—from the customers' and the partners' side as well as that of the executive management and the operational units. Especially at innovation projects with many different stakeholders, it is important to work out the common denominator at an early stage to avoid conflicting goals later on. It is best to set your goals and criteria in cross-stakeholder teams and ensure you discuss these continuously with them for the remainder of the process. That requires trust, openness, honesty, perseverance and respect.

With implementation partnerships, it is also key to define roles and responsibilities at the earliest possible stage. A basic understanding in terms of sharing out (financial) risk is similarly important for setting mutual expectations. Close collaboration with stakeholders, such as companies, associations, institutions or individuals, within and across industry boundaries, is an important success factor for achieving this.

Ultimately, ownership is a pivotal point in the implementation of innovation projects, and you need to ensure that the executive management is fully behind it. You also need to ensure that you carry out a structured evaluation across the phases and that there is a smooth hand-over of projects. The goal is to ensure that only the most convincing projects enter the implementation phase and you avoid implementation frustration.

We ensure all of this in our innovation projects—otherwise concepts will not be a good fit in the end."

2.5.2 The Fast Bird Catches the Worm

As the proverb goes, it is usually the early bird who catches the worm. With innovations however, it is not always important to be the first with an idea. It is more important to launch innovations in the market (more) quickly than the competition and with excellent traction. Therefore, in innovation, it is the fast bird which catches the worm. The examples of negative phrases at the beginning of the book show how frustrating implementation can often be. This is now a thing of the past with customised innovation concepts taking account of all the relevant goals and criteria as well as transferring ownership to implementers. Innovation suddenly becomes easier precisely where it used to be particularly difficult—in the implementation phase.

This does not mean that you can now sit back and relax though. Ultimately, you need to ensure that the implementation succeeds as quickly and efficiently as possible while at the same time achieving the greatest possible market success with the innovation. By working as cheaply and quickly as possible while at the same time staying as close as possible to your market and your customers, you can minimise the risks associated with implementation.

Can you still remember the various start-up methods from the first part of the book? These are not focused on developing efficient innovations for corporations during the brainstorming process. They can be very helpful for implementing them though. All of these methods are about testing and iterating the simplest possible version of the solution in the market before launching it in the mass market (or the company). After all, this is usually associated with a high level of investment and the increased risk which first needs to be minimised. The innovation concept has already been finished, the decision about its implementation made and the implementers motivated by an ownership transferred. It is now a matter of testing this and making further improvements quickly, inexpensively and close to the customer. Since the innovation concept has already been validated in principle, this is especially about improving the implementation details rather than the basic testing of the idea as is often the case in other start-up/innovation processes. This lean implementation thus helps to maximise the probability of success and customer fit in the implementation phase.

The lean start-up method available for this often conflicts sharply with the ways of working used in large companies previously. In Germany, for instance, engineers and developers are proud of their 'made in Germany' quality, so at first the idea of going to market or to the customer with a minimum viable product seems for many to be strange. Yet these methods coming out of Silicon Valley are becoming increasingly popular with decision-makers in Germany and many other countries too as they greatly minimise effort and risk. Instead of working for years with a high level of investment on the perfect offer which may or may not be criticised for some detail or other after-market launch or may come to market too late, the lean start-up method allows early testing with minimum development effort and a corresponding iteration opportunity. This even goes so far as creating a minimum viable product (MVP) as the simplest version of the solution which may, in fact, just be a landing page or a video where the solution is presented without already existing up to a first version with only the main functionality. This enables companies to, for example, test general customer interest, collect initial feedback or review conversion rates, i.e. review the effort required to convert prospects into customers along with other success KPIs.

The lean start-up method is about experimentation rather than planning, customer feedback rather than intuition and iterative design rather than traditional waterfall development. And even though the 5C process partly follows other paths in *developing ideas and concepts* to ensure customer fit and traction, these principles are a relevant tool for *implementation*.

A basic process for lean implementation should also contain the most important lean start-up elements. Even if implementations follow a different process everywhere depending on the company and the type of innovation, it is worth understanding the lean start-up method and integrating it into the implementation process in order to minimise the implementation risk and increase the chances of success. Here, we recommend reading Eric Ries' book *The Lean Startup* or *The Four Steps to Epiphany* by (Blank, 2013).

The following are the main principles contained in them:

1. *Hypotheses*: depending on the idea or innovation concept, you define the hypothesis to be tested which could lead to the best possible implementation. Since the basic idea has already been validated before implementation (when working with the 5C process), this now essentially includes details of the offer, such as the price, design, functionalities, location, etc.
2. *Customer feedback:* hypotheses are tested in the market as directly as possible. In addition to simple surveys, the MVP is particularly suitable as a stripped-down version of the solution. In this way, you can, for example, advertise (as yet non-existent) products online and offer them with different functionalities, designs, etc. at different prices. Or you can display advertising to your target audience in different locations to see where the interest is greatest.
3. *Agile development*: solution development goes hand in hand with customer feedback. Starting from the first prototype or proof of concept (PoC), feedback is incorporated directly so that you can always test new, iterated versions of the solution. In this way, you follow a step-by-step approach to the final version. A popular framework for this is Scrum methodology which is used particularly in software development to facilitate an incremental and iterative approach. In non-technical implementation, these principles can also be adapted very well by focusing particularly on transparency, reviewing and adaptation during the joint implementation process.

The flexible way of working needed for such a process is usually seen in **small, independent teams with clear roles, but no formal hierarchies**. For this phase of implementation, we recommend that you do not rely on specialist departments (which will subsequently be responsible for the implementation), but instead use specific lean start-up implementation teams. These are already available in many organisations, but in other cases people work temporarily with external partners. Both variants are quite possible so long as you get the subsequent implementers sufficiently 'on board' in advance (see ▶ Sect. 2.9.1).

Once you have found the best possible version of the solution for implementation using lean start-up methods, you can now finally implement this using your specialist departments and business units and then launch it in the mass market (or the company). As a result of this detailed conceptual work and the subsequent iterative testing of the solution in the market, the probability of success for an efficient innovation is now maximised.

2.5.3 All Endings Are Easy

For traditional innovation processes, all beginnings are easy (to paraphrase the famous German writer Goethe who stated that 'all beginnings are difficult'). This is because problems usually occur especially at the end of the implementation process. Whereas great solutions can initially be imagined in a playful way at the fuzzy front end—using creative idea development—it is a great challenge for established companies to implement them due to their existing back end (PWC, 2017). We reverse this logic in the 5C process. Since the innovation concepts exactly fit the traction and customer factors set in advance, they are customised perfectly for the simplest and most successful implementation possible. At the same time, this also means that the start of the innovation process becomes more difficult. This seems a fair price to pay if it minimises the implementation risks for innovations, maximises their implementation success and avoids any corresponding frustration with the implementation for everyone involved.

With the intensive conceptual work carried out already and the subsequent agile optimisation of the solution using the lean start-up method, the **launch in the market** (or in the company) can now **generally also be carried out by the company's traditional operational departments** and/or existing suppliers and solution providers. This is because their needs and restrictions have been taken into account from the outset through the criteria and traction factors, and the implementers themselves have already been brought 'on board'; implementation now succeeds in the context of tankers too.

Launching in the market does not mark the end of the innovation though. The task now is to achieve the relevant traction in the market. After going through the 5C process, the prerequisites for this are now ideal. Ultimately, the innovation concept to be implemented has also been selected in terms of how well it can exploit the company's existing success factors or strengths to scale the innovation quickly in the market and so leave the competition trailing behind it.

Successful market implementation is achieved by exploiting the strengths of the company (or of any external partners identified). The company's resources, employees, processes, etc. identified in advance are now activated in order to develop the solution into the finished innovation. Accompanying measures, such as the classic stage-gate process or other project management tools, can assist with this. Overall however, a completely new process should not be necessary as the concept has already been customised to fit the company and its competences.

The next step is to successfully place and scale the innovation in the market. Relevant traction factors, such as networks, customer access or the brand, can be exploited optimally again in go-to-market strategies.

The subsequent scaling of the innovation in the market is also referred to as diffusion (see also ◘ Fig. 2.29). According to Rupert Everett—the father of this theory—its most important elements are, in particular, the innovation itself, communication channels, timing and the social system.

The **diffusion or adoption of the innovation** usually follow these steps:

1. *Knowledge:* discover that the innovation exists.
2. *Conviction:* become interested in the innovation with the intention of learning more about it.

2

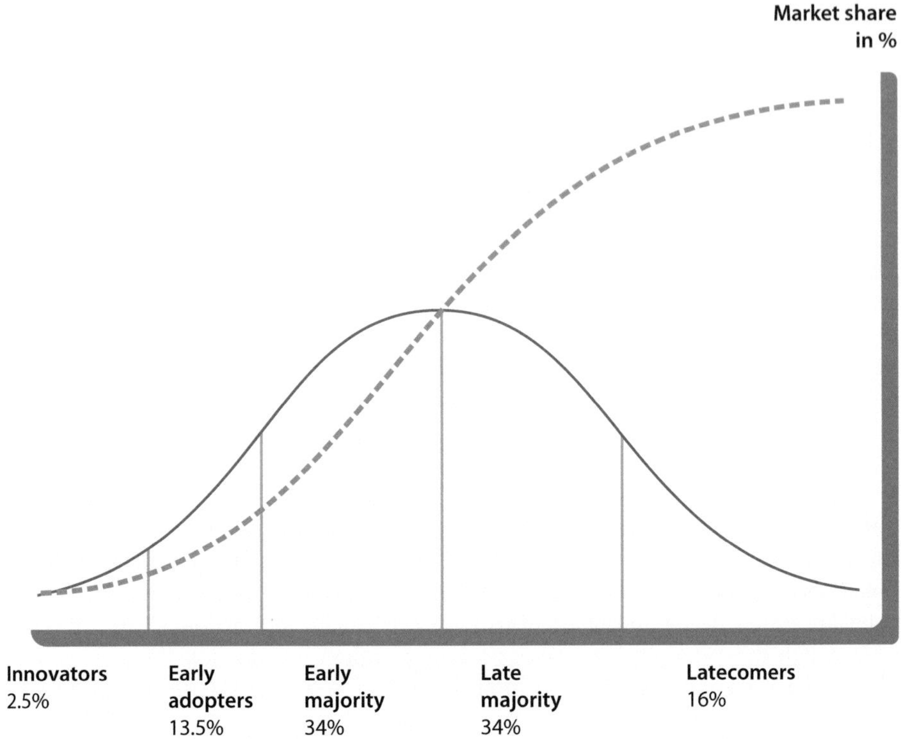

Fig. 2.29 Diffusion of innovations. (Adapted: Rogers, 2003)

3. *Decision:* weigh up the advantages and disadvantages to decide whether or not to apply the innovation.
4. *Implementation:* use/test the innovation.
5. *Confirmation:* continue using the innovation.

To positively influence these steps, companies employ various strategies, for example, using bloggers as influencers to quickly *inform* or *convince* customer groups about new innovations. Others use early adopters to provide recommendations. Uber customers, for example, were happy to recommend the company's smartphone application to other people, motivated by the incentive that both the people who had been newly recruited and those who had provided the recommendation would receive free Uber rides as a reward. Other companies offer generous test phases to make *decision-making* and *implementation* easier. Companies attempt to impact diffusion in these ways and many others.

If a corporation has developed its innovations close enough to its core business, it can now play to its strengths for diffusion. *Knowledge*, for example, can be communicated directly in this way to a large target group through the existing interfaces with the customer. The reason-to-believe of an existing brand can result in greater openness towards innovations in the *conviction*, *decision-making* or *implementation* phases, whereas operational excellence can help with positive *confirmation* of the innovation, among other things.

All of this verifies how important traction factors are for market success—and why it is so difficult to create successful diffusion as a start-up or a separate external unit. Many of the factors necessary for diffusion are simply not available after all.

It becomes clear here at least why large companies possess the best prerequisites to win the battle against disruptive start-ups with efficient innovations and so strike back. The best thing about it is that all endings are easy—once these efficient innovations have been developed using a methodology which is a good fit for corporates (◘ Fig. 2.30).

Configuration (1) – Customisation (2) – Compilation (3) – Construction (4) – **Conversion (5)**

Mind-set	**Where there is a way, there is also a will**		
Section	**Everyone involved**	**The fast bird catches the worm**	**All endings are easy**
Outcome	✓ Transfer idea ownership to the implementers ✓ Ready-to-implement innovation concept	Tested, validated solution for implementation	✓ Implemented, efficient innovation with excellent customer fit and excellent traction
Methodology	1. Invite workshop participants: idea generators and/or concept developers and employees responsible for implementation 2. Hold an implementation workshop: - present the innovation - concept - transfer knowledge completely - brainstorm the implementation details - develop/supplement the implementation plan - celebrate the kick-off 3. Approve the ready-to implement concept	1. Select the team for the implementation test 2. Carry out the implementation test using the lean start-up method: - set the hypotheses to be tested for implementation - develop the solution as a Minimum Viable Product (MVP) - collect customer feed-back for the solution (online and offline) - develop the solution in an iterative and agile way (e.g. using Scrum) 3. Identify the solution to be implemented	1. Transfer implementation responsibility to specialist departments/business units 2. Implement the innovations (using the established processes and departments in the company) 3. Potentially supplement by external partners or new competences 4. Process go-to-market strategy for excellent diffusion in the market 5. (Successful) market launch
Aid	▫ Feasible innovation concept (2.4.3) ▫ Potential inspirations for implementation ideas (2.3) ▫ Run an implementation workshop	▫ Ready-to-implement innovation concept (2.5.1) ▫ Lean start-up method ▫ Prototyping resources	▫ Solution to be implemented (2.5.2) ▫ Implementation plan (2.5.1)

◘ **Fig. 2.30** Overview of conversion. (Author's own figure)

2

Case Study: Hymer

Product Innovation in the Camper Van Segment

Hymer is the European market leader in the caravan and motorhome segments. Innovations in these markets are not only important revenue drivers; they are also relevant for long-term differentiation in a challenging, competitive environment. Yet it has been years since there were any more really big innovations, such as the sleeping alcove, the double-thickness floor or the fold-down bed. The manufacturer was all the keener to set new standards in the market in the long term with a significant new innovation like these.

Configuration

Given the above starting position and the specific goal of increasing sales in the younger, next-generation target group, the *innovation space* of 'new products' was decided at the beginning of the project. A challenging additional criterion was agreed at the same time, namely, that the product innovation should be presented to the general public as a prototype at the world's largest caravan trade show the following year.

Since revenue growth was set as the most important goal, the analysis of external factors focused on identifying the greatest sales potential. This was evident in the fast-growing segment of camper vans below 3.5 tonnes—also because these did not require any additional driving test under the current driving licence rules, so they were therefore accessible to a particularly broad target group. As this segment also fitted very well into Hymer's existing traction space, 'product innovations in the camper van segment' was therefore selected as the most exciting *opportunity space* for the remainder of the process.

More specific analysis of customer factors within the opportunity space uncovered a huge potential. More than 80% of motorhome travellers are couples travelling without children or friends. Almost all of the models in the motorhome market at that time were designed for more than two people and were thus wasting valuable interior space. On this basis, the *innovation potential* of 'product innovations in the camper van segment for two solo travellers' was chosen.

Customisation

As part of the customisation phase, insights were collected from the 'two solo travellers' target group using a wide variety of channels and methods. These included own experience when travelling in a camper van, individual interviews with campers with many years of experience, interviews on various camp sites, focus groups with 'non-campers', discussions in various forums, blogs and social media and much more. This revealed various *insights* and one particularly strong *pain point* which was that travelling in a camper van particularly is not very comfortable due to the severely limited space available. The beds are too small for two people, and the toilet is not separate from the shower. The exciting thing was that there was still no satisfactory solution in the market for that pain point.

Compilation

Analysis of international *best practices* showed that there were only a few models worldwide which were designed for two solo travellers. Those models showed that removing the rear seat for additional travellers actually allows you to achieve a significant gain in space. Individual models were already exploiting this space gain to meet the individual needs of two people travelling together, such as a larger double bed. Yet no model had so far also managed to simultaneously solve all of the demands revealed for two people travelling together. Travelling in a camper van therefore still involved compromises.

The potential pool of *analogous best practices* was huge. Many insights were gained especially from markets like micro-apartments, cruise ships, yachts, aircraft and space stations. Innovative solutions to this problem had apparently been intensively researched already for situations in which little space is available.

Looking ahead to the future generated further important inspirations, for example, from our research at trade shows, from our own external network and from the Internet regarding new technologies, such as 4D printing and nano- and UV technologies. The same applied to the targeted searches into existing patents or current research results for solar technology or even concept studies conducted by large car manufacturers.

Construction

Multidimensional ideation with multidisciplinary teams generated a total of more than 500 specific ideas for product innovation in the 'camper van for two solo travellers' segment. It quickly became clear that particularly by combining different individual ideas, we would be able to create as great an innovation as had been achieved in the past with sleeping alcoves, double-thickness floors or fold-down beds. We at first pursued a variety of different concept routes. In the end, eight innovation concepts were developed which were put through their paces in a feasibility check with internal and external experts before then being presented to the relevant target group and optimised further on the strength of the feedback. Ultimately, the 'HYMER DuoCar' concept was selected for implementation jointly with Hymer's top management based on the goals and criteria set at the beginning. This was a concept which launched a brand new floor plan into the market which made it possible to separate the toilet from the shower, offered a particularly large double bed in its vehicle class and still provided adequate space to cook, eat and relax. In short, it satisfied all of the demands of two solo travellers.

Conversion

In the conversion phase, the vehicle was initially developed through to the finished prototype together with internal specialist departments, such as design, development and marketing, as well as external suppliers and experts. This conversion had to be particularly agile due to the strict timings (the starting criterion was to present the solution at the world's largest caravan trade show in less than 12 months from the start of the project). In August 2017, the 'HYMER DuoCar' was presented to the general public at the Caravan Salon Dusseldorf in Germany. Potential customers and the trade press praised the vehicle as a 'sensation' and a 'revolution', which won the European Innovation Award of the fair. Eventually, Venture Idea supported the innovation project until the successful series production of the final 'DuoCar S'.

The perceived disadvantage of the 5C process was already mentioned at the beginning of Sect. 2, namely, that considerable effort is required to carry out this process up to implementation compared with an innovation process on a greenfield. We hope, though, that in the course of our remarks, we have been able to emphasise the advantage of this methodology. Innovations which have been developed in corporations on the basis of the 5C process enjoy a significantly greater probability of success compared with any other known innovation processes. At the same time, using the 5C process can also reduce your implementation effort while significantly increasing your implementation speed. And so it turns out that all endings are actually easy, making the difficult beginnings worthwhile.

Now equipped with the methodology, you next need to implement it successfully in your company. And in the case of established corporations, this methodology usually comes up against an existing structure as well as existing innovation strategies and methods. In the following section, we will explain in detail how you can overcome this challenge successfully and which elements are usually significant for implementing the 5C process for efficient innovation (◘ Fig. 2.31).

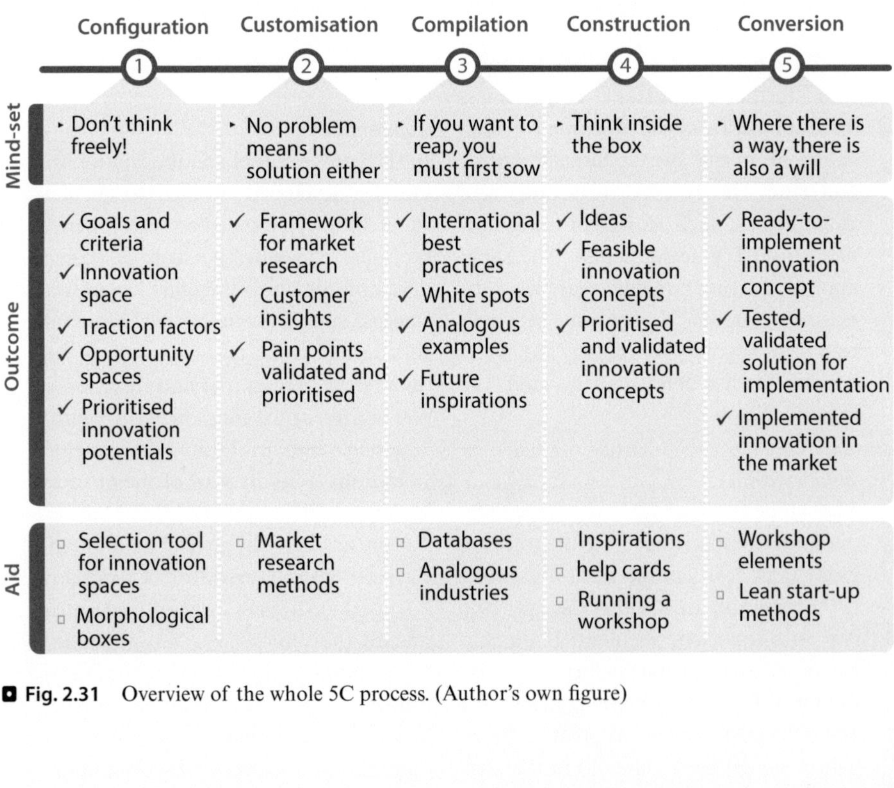

◘ **Fig. 2.31** Overview of the whole 5C process. (Author's own figure)

References

Accenture (2015). Innovation: Clear vision, cloudy execution, 2015 US Innovation Study, Online.

Agan, T. Please stop ideating, Harvard Business Review, April 29, 2014.

Almquist, L. *Prasad und Ojha: Cracking the code of innovation*. Bain & Company, October 7, 2013, Online.

Anthony, S. (2016). Kodak's downfall wasn't about technology. *Harvard Business Review*, July 2016, Online.

Baer, M., & Brown, G. (2012). Blind in one eye: How psychological ownership of ideas affects the types of suggestions people adopt, Organizational behavior and human decision processes, March 10, 2012.

Best, M (2012): Get the corporate antibodies on your side. *Harvard Business Review*, May 14, 2012, Online.

Blank, S. (2013). Why the lean start-up changes everything. *Harvard Business Review*, May 2013 issue.

Blank, S. (2014). Why corporate skunk works need to die, Forbes.com, November 10, 2014, Online.

Bubenzer, P., & Rouse, E. (2015). Your idea is also mine (now)!, Psychological Ownership and Identification with Ideas in Organizations, *Article Academy of Management*, 2015, 1.

Burkeman, O. (2010). The slow hunch of genius, The Sydney Morning Herald, Online October 23, 2010.

Chatterjee, S. (1998). Delivering desired outcomes efficiently: The creative key to competitive strategy. *California Management Review, 40/2*(Winter 1998), 78–95.

Christensen, C. M. (1997). *The innovator's dilemma: When new technologies cause great firms to fail*. Harvard Business School Press.

Christensen, C.M., et al. (2016). The hard truth about business model innovation, MIT Sloan Management review, Fall 2016 Issue, Online.

Coyne, K., Clifford, P.G., & Dye, R. (2007). Breakthrough thinking from inside the box. *Harvard Business Review*, December 2007 Issue.

Doblins. (2017). 10 types of innovation, Doblins Online, May 15, 2017. https://www.doblin.com/dist/images/uploads/Doblin_TenTypesBrochure_Web.pdf

Fichter, K. (2005). Modelle der Nutzerintegration in den Innovationsprozess, Institut für Zukunftsstudien und technologiebewertung, WerkstattBericht Nr. 75, July 2005.

Forde, A., & Fox, M. (2016). A proposed approach for idea selection in front end of innovation. *Technology Innovation Management Review, 6*(8), 48–55.

Gibbins, G. (2015). There is no 'Backend' of Innovation. What if?! Online, December 21, 2021, https://medium.com/@whatifglobal/there-is-no-back-end-of-innovation-af2da673b4ef.

Girotra, K., Terwiesch, C., & Ulrich, K. T. (2010). Idea generation and the quality of the Best idea. *Management Science Journal, 56*(4), 591–605.

Govindarajan, V. (2010). Innovation is not creativity. *Harvard Business Review*, August 3, 2010, Online.

Greenfield, R. (2014): Brainstorming doesn't work; try this technique instead, Fast company, April 29, 2014.

Hargadon, A. (2012). The challenge of innovating in brownfield versus greenfield markets, March 22, 2012, Online: www.andrewhargadon.com

Hayashi, A.M. (2001). When to trust your gut. *Harvard Business Review*, February 2001 Issue.

https://medium.com/@whatifglobal/there-is-no-back-end-of-innovation-af2da673b4ef. Accessed on December 21st, 2021

HYPE (2017a). Delivering results with full-lifecycle innovation, HYPE, Aufgerufen am 01.05.2017, Online: http://www.hypeinnovation.com/approach/delivering-results

HYPE (2017b). Delivering results with full-lifecycle innovation, HYPE, Online, July 1, 2017. http://www.hypeinnovation.com/approach/delivering-results

HYPE. (2017c). Using customer insights to fuel innovation, Hype, Online. http://www.hypeinnovation.com/download-ebook-customer-insights

2

Johnson, M.W. (2010). Where is your white space? *Harvard Business Review*, February 12, 2010, Online.

Jung, D. (2017). Die Persona-Methode für Innovations- und Veränderungsprojekte, Online, June 20, 2017. https://www.denkmodell.de/hintergrund/die-persona-methode/

Kaufman, S.B. (2011). Why inspiration matters, Harvard Business Review, November 8, 2011.

Lawrence Somerset Ltd. (2017). Customer insight and the innovation process, Lawrence Somerset Limited, Online, July 1, 2017. http://www.l-s-l.com/Documents/CustomerInsight.pdf

Lehrer, J. (2012). Groupthink. The brain Myth, The New Yorker, Online, January 22, 2021.

Lindstrom, M. (2016). Small data – The tiny clues that uncover huge trends, St. Martin's Press, February 23, 2016.

Adapted from: Loreto, V., et al. (2017): Dynamics on expanding spaces. In: *Creativity and universality in language*, 59–83, Springer International Publishing.

Lund, S. (2014). *Brick by brick: How LEGO rewrote the rules of innovation and conquered the global toy industry, part II, Chapter 7*. BusinessNews Publishing.

Markham, S. (2013). The impact of front-end innovation activities on product performance. *Product Innovation Management, 30*, S1, 77–S1, 92.

Dr. McGowan, C. (2016). Dot collecting – the habit of great creative people, October 6, 2016, Online. http://www.sodainc.com/single-post/2016/10/06/Dot-Collecting-The-Habit-of-Great-Creative--People

McKinsey. (2015). How the beat the transformation odds, McKinsey, Survey, April 2015, Online.

McKinsey and Company. How the beat the transformation odds, Survey, April 2015.

Michalko, M. (2012). Priming your creativity, the creativity post, October 4, 2012, Online.

MIT. (2017). Mathematical model reveals the patterns of how innovations arise. *MIT Technology Review*, January 13, 2017, Online.

Mootee, I. (2011). Strategic innovation and the fuzzy front end. *Ivey Business Journal*, März/April 2011, Online.

Oleynick/Trash (2014). The scientific study of inspiration in the creative process: Challenges and opportunities, Researchgate, June 2014, Online.

Persil. (2017). Why do we think "Dirt is good"?, Persil, Website, Online, July 1, 2017. https://www.persil.com/uk/dirt-is-good/real-play/why-do-wethink-dirt-is-good.html

Phillips, J. (2009). Innovation relies on synthesis, October 19, 2009, Online: http://innovateonpurpose.blogspot.de/2009/10/innovation-relies-on-synthesis.html

PWC. (2013). Breakthrough innovation and growth, PWC 2013, Online.

PWC. (2017). Reinventing innovation. Key insights from PWC's innovation benchmark, PWC 2017, Online.

RED Associates. (2017). Website, May 31, 2017: www.redassociates.com

Reinig, B.A., & Briggs, R.O. (2008). On the relationship between idea-quantity and idea-quality during ideation, Online, April 18, 2008.

Rogers, E. M. (2003). *Diffusion of innovations* (5th ed.). Free Press.

Rohrbeck, R. (2014). Trend scanning, scouting and foresight techniques. In O. Gassmann & F. Schweitzer (Eds.), *Management of the fuzzy frontend of innovation*. Springer.

Samuels, M. (2016). Why innovation labs fail and how to make them succeed, ZDNet, May 16, 2016, Online.

Schwerdtfeger, B. Innovations management: Christensen über disruptive Innovation, Haufe Online, December 7, 2016, Online.

Segal, L. (2017). Great ideas aren't enough (how Kodak missed its chance to Lead the digital revolution), LinkedIn Pulse, May 25, 2017. https://www.linkedin.com/pulse/great-ideas-arent-enough-how-kodak-missed-its-chance-lead-segal-phd?trk=v-feed&trk=vfeed&lipi=urn%3Ali%3Apage%3Ad_flagship3_feed%-3Bi6LWC8iLGd2nWSQER%2BOWDw%3D%3D

Sinclair, M. (2005). Intuition: Myth or a decision-making tool? *Management Learning, 36*(3), 353–370.

Skribsted, J.M. (2014). User-led innovation can't create breakthroughs; just ask Apple and IKEA, Fastco Design, March 3, 2014, Online.

Strategyzer. (2017a). The value proposition canvas, Online, July 31, 2017. https://strategyzer.com/canvas/value-proposition-canvas

Strategyzer. (2017b). The business model canvas, Online, July 31, 2017. https://strategyzer.com/canvas/business-model-canvas

Ulwick, A. (2002a). What is outcome-driven innovation? Strategyn, Whitepaper, Online.

Ulwick, A.W. (2002b). Turn customer input into innovation. *Harvard Business Review*, January 2002 Issue.

Ulwick, A. (2005). *What customer want*. McGraw-Hill Education, August 2005.

Wipo. (2013). Keeping things cool with frugal innovation, Wipo Magazine, online. http://www.wipo.int/wipo_magazine/en/2013/06/article_0003.html

Wyman, O. (2015). 'Car innovation 2015', Study, Oliver Wyman, Online.

Zeschky, M., & Gassmann, O. (2013). Out of bounds: Cross-industry innovation based on analogies, Springer Link, July 16, 2013.

Zwicky, F., & Wilson, A. G. (1967). *New methods of thought and procedure*. Springer.

Zwilling, M. (2011). Innovation is about execution, despite the myths, Forbes, October 24, 2011, Online.

The Innovation Machine: Efficient Innovation in Corporations

Contents

L. Sauberschwarz, L. Weiss, *The Corporates Strike Back*,
https://doi.org/10.1007/978-3-030-79114-8_3

'Get started' should now be the motto after the understanding of the 5C process. We have shown that corporations will be able to develop efficient innovations with excellent customer fit *and* traction using this methodology. These represent a long-term competitive advantage in the innovation battle.

Yet understanding the 5C process is not enough by itself if a company wants to implement efficient innovation successfully with long-lasting effect. To this end, it should first ask itself about the role which innovation currently plays and, even more importantly, about the role it intends to play in the future. Once you have created sufficient **awareness of the strategic importance of innovation in your company**, you can create the necessary framework conditions at organisational and operational level to successfully implement and apply the 5C process.

An important prerequisite for implementing the 5C process (*Configuration, Customisation, Compilation, Construction and Conversion*) is already present in most large companies, that is, the necessary motivation. According to a global McKinsey study, 84% of companies surveyed consider innovation to be the critical success factor for generating growth (McKinsey, 2017). An innovation study conducted by Accenture with top US managers also shows that only 1% of all respondents considered innovation to be unimportant for corporate success (Accenture, 2015).

This is no big surprise in the context of the ever-increasing pressure to innovate. It is not only competition and agile start-ups which are constantly providing a new stimulus for innovation. Other external factors also exacerbate the need to innovate. Management pioneer (Drucker, 2002), for example, cites the following factors as being particularly crucial:

(a) *Industry and market changes*, for example, energy transition, the liberalisation of long-distance transport, diesel car bans or the expansion of the broadband Internet—in other words, issues that are often driven by consumers or politics
(b) *Demographic and social changes* which in Japan, for example, have led to increased research in robotics as a result of its rapidly ageing society
(c) *Lifestyle changes* which strongly impact the health and fitness market, for example, through the increased need for self-optimisation or are able to change the core business of tobacco corporations through the declining coolness of smoking
(d) *New knowledge*, for example, new technologies or research results which can play a role in a company's market—such as blockchain technology in the context of companies operating in financial markets.

Companies must react to all of these stimuli. The only question is how? Companies can either decide to simply ignore them or to fend them off. Or they can view them as an exciting opportunity to get to grips with new innovations of their own. And increasingly often, they seem to prefer the latter path.

However, even if the significance of innovation is clear, it is only practiced successfully and systematically in a very few companies. Consequently in McKinsey's study, 94% of the companies surveyed stated that they were dissatisfied with their innovation success (McKinsey, 2017).

Guest Commentary: Klaus Burmeister, Founder and Managing Director, Z_punkt The Foresight Company, Foresightlab and Initiative D2030 (Germany 2030)

"Corporates' power is legendary. Whereas in the 1970s, it was multinational corporations, today it is the Internet giants or platform companies which are often caught in the crossfire of criticism due to their market power. They shape our lives with their products. Their investment decisions shape societies' future prospects. But are they also the driving forces of innovation?

This question seems justified. Traditional industrial groups often think and act in a structurally conservative way. Their market power seems more likely to slow down rapid change. In times of far-reaching system innovations, like those we are seeing in the energy and mobility sectors, these companies are coming under increasing pressure to innovate from politics, customers, new technologies and companies outside the industry. The 'diesel debate' is an excellent example in this respect. Whereas German car manufacturers—paralysed by their success—were defensively singing the praises of diesel, the People's Republic of China introduced a quota for electric vehicles in 2019. Tesla and hundreds of Chinese electromobility start-ups thus seem to be better equipped for the future.

So to make a positive contribution to innovation and progressive change in the interdependent relations between economic actors, state regulation, the scientific community and society, large companies especially need a new focus and a new strategic approach to innovation. The increasingly short corporate lifespan is proof of this. The only corporates to survive will be those which are drivers of innovation. They have the power to do this. They just need to use it."

What causes this gulf between their desires and the reality? One possible answer is given by the authors of the Accenture study (Accenture, 2015). They note that 'big' innovation goals do not fail to be realised, because of a lack of enthusiasm, self-awareness or even investment. They fail, because of the way in which an innovation is implemented. Of the companies surveyed, 82% do not differentiate between measures for incremental innovations (such as product improvements/brand extensions) and strategically significant innovations.

Strategic innovation should be anchored firmly in corporate strategy as a key component and clearly distinguished from incremental improvements. Strategic innovation describes new (growth) opportunities for the company as a whole and thus stands in stark contrast to individual, uncoordinated activities or incremental improvements. So strategic innovations provide market-differentiating changes which create a long-term competitive advantage, leading to a measurable value added for the company (Accenture, 2015). In short, they offer great strategic relevance for the company. The topic of innovation can therefore no longer be dragged along behind the company just in specialist departments or in management, but instead must be anchored strategically in the company. As Harvard professor Gary Pisano (2015) remarked, for example, 'Despite massive investments of time and money, innovation remains a frustrating issue in many companies. Innovation measures fail regularly. And successful innovators are often unable to sustain their performance in the long term—as Polaroid, Nokia, Sun Microsystems, Dell, Yahoo!, Hewlett Packard, Blackberry and many other examples show. The reasons for this go much deeper than the most frequently cited reason for failed implementation. The problem with innovation measures can usually be traced back to a lack of innovation strategy'.

Guest Commentary: Jörg Limberg, Vice President Europe Research Solutions Sales and Marketing, Elsevier, Former Vice President and General Manager Software and Solutions, Hewlett Packard

"Strategic innovation is a byword for the launch of innovations which add value (i.e. products, services, topics, organisational structures, markets, etc.) and have so far either been served in a different way, or not at all. You should always be pursuing a longer-term goal, so the focus should be on future opportunities rather than past successes. However, large companies in particular tend to compare the current situation with the past—driven by the desire that today will be the same as the good old days as soon as possible. The majority of your workforce 'only' knows a time of steady growth with the appropriate flagship products which sold well thanks to the longstanding, proven organisational structure.

To prevent this, business units, specialist departments and project teams must be involved in developing strategic innovations at an early stage. We also need to communicate across all management levels. It is only once the (planned) innovations have been communicated, explained and justified to employees in a transparent way that these will receive maximum support in their implementation.

A lot of creativity, enthusiasm and implementation ability is required for the development and implementation itself. This can be executed in specialist, small- to medium-sized organisational units in a particularly straightforward and result-orientated way. Management's skill is then to select the innovation with a good fit and implement it. It is true when they say that, 'Lots does not help lots'. Focusing is also the recipe for success here, whether it means innovating the sales concept or (re-)innovating the business model.

Even if strategic innovations are increasingly the result of stronger customer orientation today, the great advantage of corporations in terms of innovation is their tremendous implementation power/traction. Once an innovation has made it into implementation, the lever for success (scaling) is many times greater as compared to a small company or start-up. This should be taken into account in every strategic innovation process and when selecting ideas to be implemented."

Strategic innovation should fit the ideal of efficient innovation and should exploit the existing strengths of the core business. After all, strategic innovation can only contribute a relevant value added to the company if the company's innovations exhibit both excellent customer fit and excellent traction. If the innovation lacks an adequate customer fit, it ultimately has no (or insufficient) relevance in the

Fig. 3.1 Strategic innovation vs ambidexterity. (Adapted: O'Reilly III & Tushman, 2016)

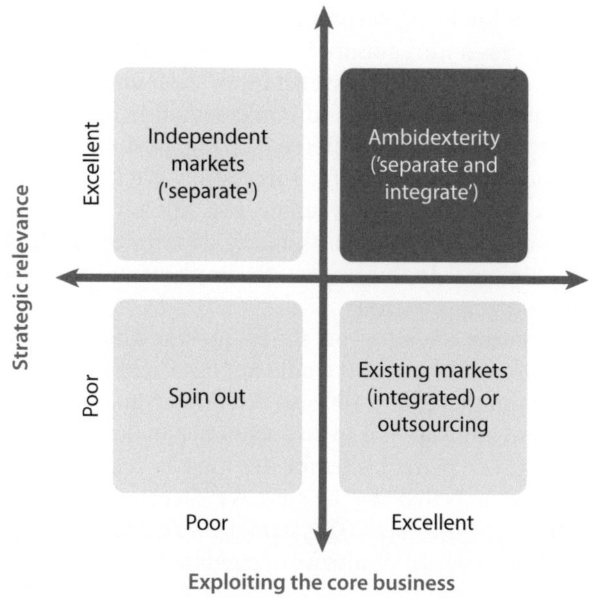

market. And even customer fit alone is not enough for strategic innovation. If the company cannot exploit its existing strengths during implementation, then it will lack the necessary traction to generate a correspondingly large value added for the company.

Charles O'Reilly and Michael Tushman add in their book *Lead and Disrupt* (2016) that innovations which are simultaneously supposed to show great strategic relevance and exploit the strengths of the core business require organisational ambidexterity (see ► Sect. 1.4) (see ◘ Fig. 3.1).

Consequently, strategic innovation cannot be outsourced to separate units. Instead, new, exploratory innovation topics must be investigated in tandem alongside the current core business and linked to it using processual ambidexterity. Customer fit is still missing from this analysis. Taking this into account is a necessary prerequisite for transforming *strategic* innovation into *efficient* innovation.

The good news is that implementing the 5C process ensures that you will achieve a high degree of strategic relevance and exploit the company's existing core competence (in terms of traction) *and* excellent customer fit with *processual* ambidexterity. Nonetheless, we also need the right *organisational* competences to do this. O'Reilly & Tushman (2007) describe these necessary, dynamic capabilities as 'skills, processes, organisational structures, rules and disciplines which equip the organisation with the skills to identify opportunities and threats and to reconfigure existing strengths to address them'.

In short, besides a process, companies also need the right organisational anchoring on the one hand, and the right framework conditions for the corresponding innovation unit, on the other. If the company creates these framework conditions, it will not only be systematically equipped to generate strategic innovations, but efficient innovations too.

The following section explains these framework conditions in detail, namely, the necessary organisational anchoring of innovation in the company, the optimal characteristics of a specialist innovation unit and the process for implementing the 5C process. As regards to implementation, we draw a distinction in the following sections between the different starting positions of companies. Different important framework conditions for successfully implementing the 5C process are already in place depending on whether you already possess a strategic innovation unit, customer-centric design thinking department and/or separate innovation units in the company. In this respect, the implementation will differ depending on your current starting position.

You can also carry out the 5C process without implementing the above framework conditions. Otherwise it would not have been possible for us, as external specialists, to carry out more than 100 successful innovation projects for corporations. Though if efficient innovation is to be anchored and developed in the company sustainably, the appropriate prerequisites for this must be created, and the company as a whole must also be innovated step by step. As (Drucker, 2002) rightly notes, 'Entrepreneurship is built on implementing systematic innovation'. To make this possible, corporations need the necessary framework conditions.

Summary

The Innovation Machine: Efficient Innovation in Corporations

Besides introducing the 5C process, the long-term implementation of efficient innovation in the company also requires suitable strategic anchoring in the organisation and a correctly designed innovation unit.

- To achieve innovation success in the long term, clarity is needed about the strategic significance of innovations in the company before the correct methodology is implemented.
- In contrast to incremental innovation, strategic innovation stands for market-differentiating changes which are highly relevant to the company as a whole.
- Besides implementing the 5C process in the long term, sustainable efficient innovation with great strategic relevance, customer fit and exploitation of the core business for traction also requires suitable organisational anchoring and a specific innovation unit.

3.1 Organisational Anchoring of Efficient Innovation

Organisational structures generally represent the biggest hurdle for successful innovations. The innovation study by McKinsey, for example, showed that 42% of companies surveyed believed that an improvement in the organisation alone would result in momentous improvements in innovation success (McKinsey, 2017).

According to a survey by the German Association for the Digital Economy (Bundesverbands digitaler Wirtschaft, BVDW), the greatest barriers to innovation were a lack of time (70%), inadequate financial resources (41.8%) and a lack of support at management level (31.6%). These are all factors which are determined substantially by the company's structures. BVDW Vice-President Harald R. Fortmann explains logically, 'It is surprising that a lack of time or an inadequate budget are cited as barriers to innovation to this extent. As a rule, innovations represent German companies' capital. Functioning innovation management is an investment in a company's future. If you neglect this today, you might never recover' (BVDW, 2014).

Guest Commentary: Timo Emmert, Head of e-Commerce, MediaMarktSaturn

"Continuous renewal with successful innovations is becoming increasingly important for an established retail company like MediaMarktSaturn. Not only because we sell innovative technologies ourselves, but also because the environment and customer needs are changing ever faster. In order to keep up with this trend, it is crucial to link innovation with the overall strategy and make it a top management issue.

To this end, we have, for example, built up a strategic project portfolio for the e-commerce division, which always shows us at a glance the relevance of existing projects and new ideas. Based on jointly defined strategic goals and criteria from the overall strategy, we first assessed and listed all existing strategic development projects in a portfolio matrix (with dimensions such as the potential impact on revenues and the corresponding effort). This makes it possible to quickly identify relevant and irrelevant projects, but above all to identify gaps where the matrix does not yet contain enough relevant projects with a high potential impact in the short or long term. These gaps can then be specifically filled by determining new opportunities from external and internal factors. In this way, the strategic innovation roadmap is defined top-down, but can be filled bottom-up by all stakeholders.

The true strength of such a focused, strategic innovation portfolio was demonstrated to us in the Corona crisis of 2020. Social distancing measures changed the external factors for us in one fell swoop, which meant that internal strengths and weaknesses were also brought to bear. Here we were now able to quickly adapt the goals and criteria, and thus also the existing projects, and to start new projects based on new opportunities and existing strengths in order to close new gaps in the achievement of our goals. For example, thanks to our strong brands, we were able to quickly redirect customers from offline to existing online channels in order to maintain demand. At the same time, it was important to maintain availability on the supply side despite dysfunctional supply chains. For instance, by using the warehouses of existing but closed stores for the online channels, we were able to offer highly requested products during the Corona crisis. I am certain that this combination of strategy and innovation will continue to secure the lead in the consumer electronics market."

To implement the 5C process in the company in the long term, you need to create organisational framework conditions with a good fit. The 5C process always ensures that work is carried out within the company's existing traction space—so you do not need to change the basic organisation and culture to be able to apply it. Yet with the right organisational framework conditions, you can also ensure that the process becomes applied successfully internally with long-lasting effect.

The support of top management and good collaboration between all specialist departments, for example, is key for taking into account any goals, criteria and traction factors in the 5C process. Certain staffing, physical and time resources are required to develop and test the concepts. The culture should also at least be a good fit in the sense that people understand and support the efficient innovation approaches and mindsets—rather than, for example, insisting on pure customer centricity or too rapid prototyping. These **fundamental factors of structures, resources and culture** need to be examined in more detail below.

For efficient innovation to meet its strategic goals, the innovation **structure** must be *anchored strategically* in the company, that is, it must be linked directly to the top management. Gary Pisano (2015) describes this in the *Harvard Business Review*: 'Innovation affects virtually every function. Only senior managers can orchestrate such a complex system. They must take responsibility for the process, structures, talent and behavior'.

This is why we recommend setting up a kind of cross-divisional function, for example, as a unit reporting to the company's board. This guarantees access to decision-makers for setting goals and criteria in the *configuration phase* as well as support from them when implementing innovation concepts. By splitting off strategic innovation from the specialist departments or business units, you also ensure that you obtain an overview of the company as a whole, you eliminate silo thinking and you avoid excessive influence by operational business interests. It also ensures that you make a clear distinction between strategic innovation and incremental innovation.

Efficient innovation as a cross-divisional function enables you to access all of the stakeholders who are relevant to an innovation project. For efficient innovation, you need a correspondingly large network within the company. Like a coral reef that is attracting fishes, the innovation function is collecting relevant stakeholders, linking them together using suitable communication channels. With their help, you can then review, test and later launch the developed innovation concepts in the market (Markman, 2012).

In terms of organisational anchoring in the company, links up to the top *and* down to the bottom are therefore crucial. The 5C process uses a top-down/bottom-up approach. Goals and criteria are initially set by top management, whereas subsequent input is collected from all of the relevant stakeholders.

Guest Commentary: Dr. Hans-Joachim Popp, Chief Information Officer, Dt. Luft- und Raumfahrt (German Aerospace Centre)

"Innovation teams must be well connected to top management as well as to the implementers. For example, there are always topics that top management definitely wants to implement, but which are not feasible in the company in the form envisaged. Regardless of the size of budget made available, they are simply not realizable. For situations like this, the innovation team must serve as the interface between the strategic goals and their implementation. After all, feasible innovations must be found within the strategic framework. If this does not happen, then budgets will be spent on unrealistic projects which result in little impact for the company in the end and are therefore doomed to failure. This is why the innovation team should be independent from specialist departments and business units so that it can assist with this strategic work conceptually as a cross-divisional function."

An outward-facing network is also important. This even enables innovation managers to involve external partners, customers and suppliers in the process. Top management or specialist departments can also support the external network required to set it up, for example, by making their contacts available to the innovation managers.

You only require a small number of **internal resources** to carry out the 5C process (depending on your team size). The reason for this is that, for efficient innovation, the largest part of implementing innovations usually takes place in specialist departments and business units rather than in the innovation unit itself. After all, it is important to exploit the company's existing traction factors as much as possible. You therefore only need to plan a budget for the innovation unit to carry out the innovation process through to concept development (or in the best case through to the end of any testing). This budget is needed to cover expenses for your own staff as well as costs related to the concept, such as access to tools and databases, events, the involvement of external experts, workshop participants, market research, materials, premises, etc.

The budget for implementing individual projects should, by contrast, come from the department(s) which will later benefit from implementing the innovation. The 5C process is ideally geared towards reflecting this budgetary separation. Ultimately, the budget available for implementing the innovation can already be included as a criterion at the beginning of the innovation process and thus taken into account during the entire process through to the finished innovation concept.

It is even possible to carry out innovation projects for which there is no available implementation budget. If at the start of the process you have determined that this is the situation, you can ensure your implementation requires no budget by employing suitable innovation concepts. Is such a scenario realistic? Completely. We ourselves have already carried out several successful innovation projects for which no implementation budget was available. Does it even make sense? From our perspective yes, especially if you need particularly fast scaling, for example, over hundreds or thousands of company store networks. In a scenario like this, if no budget is needed to implement the innovation measures (and ideally either no or hardly any time either), national or international scaling can be carried out over thousands of branches literally overnight thus enabling economic success to be achieved more quickly.

Besides, the separation between the conception budget and the implementation budget implies that the unit responsible for efficient innovation must be regarded as a cost centre rather than a profit centre. Otherwise, there might be a risk that this would be managed by individual business divisions and specialist departments with today's business interests rather than focusing on the most important innovations from an overall strategic point of view.

The human resources needed for concept development depend on the number of projects required. As described in more detail in ▶ Sect. 3.2, you need at least one full-time innovation employee to manage each individual innovation project (timewise, this employee may manage about two projects a year). The company consequently only needs to provide the appropriate number of innovation employees depending on the number of innovation projects it requires.

What is particularly relevant (in the context of corporations) is that it only requires a very small amount of time from top management or the relevant project stakeholders in the corporations. If you follow the 5C process, you will only need a few days with the decision-makers per project, with a workshop in the beginning and one at the end of each process step through to the *construction phase* (i.e. deciding to implement one or more of the innovation concepts).

The employees managing the subsequent implementation are conversely only involved at certain times during the process for targeted interviews and as part of the implementation workshop described in ► Sect. 2.5.1. They are not needed for idea generation or development. Greater commitment by them is only necessary during the final implementation phase. However, the activities needed then fit in with their day-to-day tasks if possible or can be accepted in individual objective agreements with the required employees.

The 5C process requires hardly any resources outside the innovation unit for implementation through to the development of the final innovation concepts. This also helps to avoid situations (familiar to many companies) in which innovation projects are brought to a halt because, for example, ideation workshops and the development of ideas must rely on employees who do not feel responsible for innovation, and so only take part in it or support it reluctantly—if at all.

The fundamental **culture** of the company does not need to change to ensure the successful application of the 5C process. The workforce does not, for example, suddenly need to be particularly creative or innovative to achieve efficient innovation. Still, a change is often necessary in terms of the innovation mindset of the people or the relevant decision-makers involved in the process. This is particularly the case when start-up methods like design thinking or lean start-up are currently being used in companies either to generate ideas or for concept work. In the end, it requires an iterative approach here which is close to the customer (but far from the company) and uses rapid prototype construction and testing. Once this has been internalised by the managing directors or innovation managers, for example, educational work will be needed. Ultimately, you must create an initial awareness that it makes sense to spend sufficient time on concept work and the necessary preparatory work in order to develop efficient innovation with customer fit and traction. This can be a challenge after countless 'learning journeys' to Silicon Valley to transfer the start-up culture. The first thing to explain is why a corporation is not the same as a start-up and ought not to act like one either. We hope, though, that this book will provide you with the arguments needed to support this.

The 5C process ensures that innovations are possible independently of a specific corporate culture by taking into account *cultural* conditions in the context of the *configuration phase* criteria and traction factors. In this way, the company can fundamentally remain as it is in terms of its culture. After all, the majority of its workforce is only involved as part of implementing efficient innovations. This implementation should indeed build as strongly as possible on what already exists—and on the corporate culture too. For decision-makers who are striving for large transformation or change processes, this may be disappointing at first. Yet for the implementers of innovations, it is (understandably) an immense relief if no cultural change is necessary to implement an innovation—if this can succeed at all within a corporation.

When the focus is specifically on the innovation unit or team, different standards apply. This is because having your 'own' culture which strengthens your innovativeness is, in fact, a necessary prerequisite for working successfully with the 5C process. This and other factors for the innovation unit, in particular, are discussed in the following section.

Summary

Organisational Anchoring of Efficient Innovation

Organisational structures are often the greatest hurdle for successful innovations. To implement the 5C process in the company in the long term, you need to create the appropriate underlying organisational conditions:

Structure

- Organisational anchoring by creating links to the top and bottom of your company using a top-down/bottom-up approach.
- Strategic anchoring in the company through a direct link to top management.
- Operational anchoring as a cross-divisional function to access all of the relevant operational stakeholders.
- Outward-facing links by building a suitable network.

Resources

- Minimal internal resources as efficient innovation mostly uses the implementation budgets of business units and specialist departments.
- Own budget for carrying out the process through to concept development or implementation testing.
- Set up as a cost centre rather than a profit centre to avoid operational dependency.
- Human resources depending on the number of projects desired (about two projects per innovation manager per year).
- Top management involvement is about 4 × 0.5 days per project.
- Operational stakeholders are only involved at certain times for targeted input (not for ideation).

Culture

- No change in the fundamental culture of the company as a whole
- Communicate any new perspectives and mindsets to the people and decision-makers involved in the process if they have already internalised the cultural aspects of other innovative measures

3.2 Characteristics of an Efficient Innovation Unit

To anchor efficient innovation in the company in the long term, you need to **(re) build a suitable innovation unit or team along with the appropriate organisational framework conditions**. This innovation unit is responsible for developing efficient innovations with the help of the 5C process. For this to be successful, it not only requires scientific methods but also the organisational support described in the previous section in addition to strategic anchoring. It also needs a suitable internal structure and culture, the right ways of working, specific individual and team competences as well as a way to measure success which fits the 5C process and the innovation task. Or as Peter Drucker (2002) put it, 'Innovation is primarily work, not genius. It needs knowledge. It often needs imagination. And it needs talent. But what innovation really needs is hard, focused, meaningful work. If you are not diligent and lack perseverance and commitment then knowledge, imagination and talent are no use'.

The following detailed examination of the above characteristics of an efficient innovation unit shows how you can succeed in the balancing act between creative problem-solving and analytical work which is needed for the 5C process.

The task of the innovation unit is to conceive efficient innovations. To achieve this task, you should also build up its **internal structure**. First of all, you require innovation/project managers who can take responsibility for managing the process. The team should consist of at least two to three people to enable verbal sparring (i.e. discussions in preparation for new, difficult tasks). After all, this is often needed in concept development. Furthermore, the number of innovation managers depends on the number of projects to be carried out. As a rule, one (trained) innovation manager is required per innovation project. They can carry out approximately two 5C projects a year—or one if they are still heavily involved in overseeing its implementation.

To ensure innovation managers' work is focused and thorough, it is advisable to appoint an additional manager for the innovation unit. They do not necessarily have to be more senior in the company's hierarchy. Instead, it is their task to free up innovation managers. Partly, they are responsible for maintaining regular contact with top management, but they partly also act (or at least provide support) as the public face of the company in an outward-looking role.

Managers should receive *variable* support, for example, from internal and external experts, stakeholders or consultants. Junior staff, interns and work experience students can also be deployed to provide support for research tasks but also, for example, as workshop participants to complement the team in a flexible way, thus relieving the innovation managers of repetitive work.

Agile, iterative implementation testing can also form part of the unit's tasks in line with the conversion phase in the 5C process. This is not absolutely necessary though since your own suitable teams or external partners often already exist and you can transfer this task to them. Either way, direct access to these kind of resources for iterative testing is a necessity!

As a result of innovation managers taking direct responsibility for all of the steps in the 5C process (at least through to the start of implementation testing), they are able to dig into a topic completely and thus achieve the diligence, perseverance and high level of commitment which Peter Drucker insists that innovation needs. This not only requires the right internal structure, but a suitable way of working too.

The innovation unit should be able to work in as focused a way as possible on the innovation topics. To this end, they must be allowed to work in an independent way. This should also be possible within the context of large companies since the methodology already sets out very precise steps for processing innovation projects.

No micromanagement is therefore necessary. Instead, employees working in the innovation unit should be allowed as much flexibility and freedom to work independently as possible. This is because you cannot always carry out completely different tasks in the process, such as research and analysis, idea development or market research, in the same prescribed format.

Researchers Anna Jordanous and Bill Keller (2016) have worked out the ways of working and behaving needed for creativity using a linguistic analysis of 90 academic publications. They identified 14 core attributes which included independence, freedom, social interaction and communication (see ◘ Fig. 3.2). The other attributes named also provide a good overview of an innovation unit's meaningful ways of working.

For example, innovation managers should be free to decide when and where they want to work to handle the tasks in question. Shared premises are nevertheless necessary to give the team a common venue and, for example, to hold workshops. These premises should offer various work opportunities, for example, for focus work, sparring, drafting documents or workshops. In addition to this geographical link, it is up to the innovation managers themselves to link up virtually and spar among themselves, for example, via team tools, such as Slack, MS Teams, WhatsApp or the Intranet.

◘ **Fig. 3.2** Creativity is... (Adapted: Jordanous & Keller, 2016)

On the other hand, links with other internal or external stakeholders, or exchanges required during the process, should be kept to a minimum during the project phases. Since you need a great deal of focus to achieve this work, distractions from meetings or emails are to be avoided as far as possible—except where these play a specific role in the process. Accordingly, the head of the unit serves as a contact person and point of contact during the project phases which assists innovation managers' focus. If this succeeds, efficient innovations will be developed based on highly efficient ways of working.

Yet the best structure and ways of working are not enough for developing efficient innovations if the necessary **individual competences** are missing. Even if the *work* on innovations is important, there is still a need for the relevant complementary competences, such as those mentioned by Peter Drucker, like *talent*, *imagination* and *knowledge*.

The 5C process demands that its users achieve a balance between analytical abilities and great problem-solving ability or creativity. Most people's strengths lie either in the analytical or the creative part though. Yet it is only by combining these strengths that it can be possible to work both *conceptually and analytically* as well as *perceptively and creatively*. On the one hand, it is possible to conceptually and analytically work out the potential for innovation and to design a suitable solution. On the other, perceptive, creative approaches can be used when it comes to observing customers, collecting sources of inspiration and generating ideas which are a good fit. A combination of these sorts in the innovation manager (and thus avoiding purely 'creative' types) is key to the success of the innovation process in corporations.

Ted Levitt (2002) also describes this in the *Harvard Business Review*. He noted that innovation in the hands of 'creative types' is often the worst thing that can happen to a large company. According to him, these 'compulsive idea-makers' lack any understanding of the organisational structures and processes which ideas must fit into in order to be implemented successfully. They confuse 'having ideas' with 'innovation' and underestimate the needs of the day-to-day business as well as the complexity of the organisation.

It is instead necessary to identify so-called creative generalists who are very curious and possess broad knowledge as well as analytical *and* creative competence (see also ► Sect. 2.4.2 and specifically ◘ Fig. 3.2 on creative competence). Frequently, these kinds of competence are found in the 'entrepreneurship' environment, for example, among founders who have ideally already gained experience in corporations or else among employees in incubators or accelerators.

If the iterative testing of innovation concepts also falls within the scope of the innovation unit's duties, additional kinds of competence which can be contributed by programmers, designers, etc. may be necessary. However, these people do not necessarily have to be a permanent part of the innovation unit, but can usually be overed by internal experts or external partners (and supervised by the innovation manager), if required.

Finding employees with the specific kinds of competence described above is no easy task. It is further complicated by the fact that individual kinds of competence are not sufficient by themselves for the success of the innovation unit. After all, the team must also form a unit from a social and psychological point of view.

Guest Commentary: Dave Birss, Author of *"A User Guide to the Creative Mind"* and Chief Thinker, RIGHT thinking

"My work with companies and my books revolve around researching and communicating the necessary skills and competences for developing and implementing innovations. The various roles in the process are particularly important.

Creative tasks can be divided into 'thinking' and 'acting', and they each require different skills. Creative thinking—or problem-solving—can best be accomplished by creative generalists. These people have an insatiable curiosity about everything. This characteristic provides them with the broad knowledge, experience and skills they can build on when developing new ideas. It allows them to think outside the box and gives them the resources to break out of the prevailing assumptions in their industry.

When it is time to implement an idea, it is best to rely on creative specialists. They possess in-depth knowledge, experience and skills related to their specific work. They can do this faster, better and more effectively than any generalist could.

Both roles require passion and a thirst for knowledge. The difference is just that one focuses on a specific topic and the other is topic-agnostic. But both roles are important, both contribute added value. And each is creative in their own way."

The social fabric of the innovation unit is crucial for its success in the long term. For this reason, individual employees' **social competence** should be regarded as being at least as important as their individual kinds of competence. Whereas you can continue to learn many skills and kinds of competence with time, you cannot easily remove disharmony between strong personalities. Yet this harmony within the team is exactly what is important for new ideas and innovations to constantly be developed. While each innovation manager is, in principle, responsible for 'their' own innovation topic, exchanges with other team members are still essential for discussing ideas and developing them further—and are just as important for overcoming the various challenges encountered during the innovation process.

Since innovation is always concerned with *new* approaches to solutions, it is often impossible to set any defined processes and regulations. Instead, innovation concepts emerge in an environment of great uncertainty. The solution is initially not clear for a long time and is questioned constantly afterwards. Team members need to have strong mutual trust and to feel very secure to deal with this situation and still continue to express new ideas. This requires both great social competence on the part of individual members and a good interplay between their individual personalities.

A recent Google study, for example, which examined successful teams found that out of a total of five crucial factors, 'psychological security' was by far the most important factor for team success. This in turn underlies all other success factors (Rozovsky, 2015). Psychological security refers to the opportunity to take risks without feeling ashamed or insecure. Employees in teams with a high level of psychological security are significantly more likely to commit themselves to other people's ideas. They are also assessed as being twice as effective as other employees.

Building a common identity and an **internal structure** is just as important as the social competence of individual employees and the interaction between them. These factors referred to as *group norms* in psychology include the traditions, behaviours and unwritten rules which determine how teams function when they meet. These norms may or may not be expressed verbally. In either case, they exert a very great influence on teamwork (Rozovsky, 2015). So it is therefore important that the innovation unit can build its own team culture to fit the specific requirements within the context of innovation or working with the 5C process—and do so as independently as possible from the overarching culture. All of this serves to achieve processual ambidexterity. This is the only way that the innovation unit can operate not only independently of the current needs of the day-to-day business but of the limitations of the corporate culture too.

Yet this freedom does not explicitly mean that the innovation unit can—or should—act independently of the company's goals. On the contrary, a specific success measurement must be specifically customised to the task and the unit's particular ways of working or methodology. ► Section 3.3 explains in more detail how this is specifically achieved.

While the innovation unit should be able to operate as freely and as independently as possible, the company must also still be able to measure its success. As has already been described in the context of organisational anchoring, the unit should not be set up as its own separate profit centre. Instead, it needs to be set up specifically as a cost centre for developing efficient innovations; otherwise there is a danger that the innovation unit will be too tightly controlled by individual specialist departments and business units with current, purely short-term business interests. And these will therefore be unable to focus properly on the most important innovations from an overall strategic perspective.

Measuring the success of the innovation unit should accordingly be based on the return on investment, i.e. the final revenue relative to the investment in the efficient innovations developed, rather than relative to its own unit's profitability. Success-based assessment which best fits the unit's independence and flexibility is hence possible. Yet the success of an innovation project does not only depend on the innovation concepts themselves. After all, once these have been developed, they must also be implemented and launched in the market. The innovation unit only has a limited influence over this implementation phase. It is therefore advisable to add other KPIs on top of the return on investment so that you can measure the innovation unit's success as accurately and as holistically as possible. For example, the implementation rate of innovation concepts and the total number of completed projects can be used as further success factors. In addition to general innovation success, the efficiency of the unit and the feasibility of innovation concepts can also be assessed. With regard to the implementation rate, you should at least target a rate of 50% of the projects in the long term in our experience. If you do not achieve this rate, it either indicates problems in applying the 5C process or problems with the organisational setup of the innovation unit. In terms of the total number of projects, two projects per year for each (sufficiently trained) innovation manager is realistic, as has already been mentioned earlier. If they are more heavily involved in the implementation, one project per year is more realistic.

The success KPIs should, of course, be chosen depending on how long the unit has already existed. This is because a longer construction phase may be necessary at the beginning to become sufficiently familiar with building up the 5C process and implementing the structures which are necessary for the innovation unit's work.

The following section shows how this implementation can proceed. The implementation is specified in relation to the current starting position of the company in question. Depending on whether the company is engaged in current incremental, strategic, customer-centric or separate innovation, other implementation measures may partly be necessary.

Summary

Characteristics of an Efficient Innovation Unit

To anchor efficient innovation in the company, a corresponding efficient innovation unit or team needs to be set up which can manage the balancing act between creative problem-solving and the analytical work required to implement the 5C process.

Internal Structure

- A team with at least one manager and two to three innovation managers (depending on the number of innovation projects envisaged).
- The managers primary task is to free up the innovation managers and act as a point of contact.
- The innovation manager always implements 5C projects independently.
- Other employees, interns, etc. can supplement the team in a flexible way.
- Agile implementation as part of the innovation unit—if not already available in the company or required externally.

Ways of Working

- Maintain independent ways of working by ensuring independence and flexibility.
- Plan work on the basis of the 5C process and without micromanagement.
- Shared, flexible, usable premises.
- Maintain great focus during projects. Discussions with stakeholders solely about projects.

Individual Competences

- 'Creative generalists' with analytical and creative skills. Avoid people with purely creative skill profiles.
- Additional implementers if agile implementation in the innovation unit depends on it (see above).

Social Competences

- Psychological security in the innovation unit as a result of the appropriate social competences
- Informal meetings and collaboration beforehand to test suitability

Internal Culture

- Own identity and culture to ensure processual ambidexterity
- Own group norms (traditions, behaviours, formal and informal rules, etc.)

Measuring Success

- Measure the success of innovation projects rather than the profitability of the unit (return on investment, implementation rate, number of projects implemented per year)

3.3 Implementing Efficient Innovation in Corporations

The path to **implementing efficient innovation is not identical for every company**. In practice, we were able to observe many different approaches which are currently being used by corporations to develop innovations. These vary widely in some cases. And yet they all have one crucial thing in common, namely, that you cannot systematically combine the customer's and the company's perspectives in all these innovation approaches (Deloitte & Venture Idea, 2017). Nevertheless, in some cases, they already exhibit the first important prerequisites for implementing efficient innovation or successfully applying the 5C process.

To take sufficient account of the different prerequisites for implementing the 5C process in the various companies, we have identified the following **basic scenarios** which correspondingly have different starting points for an implementation. Even though these basic scenarios just map reality in a simplified way (if only because they exist in part in variants, in mixed forms or side by side in companies), they nevertheless help to show examples of different approaches to implementing efficient innovations with the 5C process in the company:

(a) **Incremental:** no formal (strategic) innovation approaches yet exist, so innovations take place especially as a result of improvements in business units or only as a result of traditional research and development.
(b) **Strategic**: there are already strategic innovation units which focus primarily on innovations with excellent traction, for example, as a separate unit with CIO or in business development as a strategy department or similar.
(c) **Customer-centric**: the company employs design-thinking experts or maintains its own unit which can apply customer-centric methods to focus on customer fit.
(d) **Separate**: attempts are made in separate units, such as innovation hubs or incubators, to develop (more or less strategic) innovations in a customer-centric manner and to implement them outside the company.

The first scenario, i.e. a company with **incremental innovation**, is the clearest starting point. Here, no strategic innovation efforts yet exist, or only small ones. This gives us the opportunity to build up an innovation unit with the appropriate strategic anchoring from scratch. However, this is not usually the case. Instead, one (or a combination) of the other three starting situations often exists, although you need not jettison everything you have built up with years of hard work. It is also true that usually the existing innovation measures are not (yet) suitable for efficient innovations in their current format as they cannot adequately link the company's and the customer's perspectives. Since they normally satisfy at least *one* of the two perspectives well, often strategic, customer-centric and even separate innovation units already have many of the necessary prerequisites for efficient innovation, so these 'only' need to be supplemented accordingly.

Strategic innovation units are focused on the company's overall strategy and are therefore linked closely to its core business. As a rule, they combine a number of different methods and measures to identify and process new strategic opportunities. With the help of often traditional, one-dimensional, stage-gate processes, idea management and, if need be, open innovation, they focus on topics with excellent traction or on the need for innovation within the context of the core business (Pisano, 2015).

At organisational level, these units already have sufficient strategic anchoring in the organisation and good access to all relevant stakeholders. Still, they do not (yet) possess the necessary characteristics *within* the innovation unit to enable the 5C process to be applied successfully. With a well-positioned strategic innovation unit, selected innovation topics for the core business can be processed very successfully, therefore, although disruptive topics can often only be implemented outside the company. Yet with a 'simple' addition to the composition and the way that the innovation unit works, the 5C process can be implemented and applied in the existing organisational structure to enable efficient innovations with excellent traction *and* excellent customer fit in the future.

Customer-centric innovation is usually organised in separate 'expert' units which offer, for example, method workshops and tools for specialist departments (Deloitte & Venture Idea, 2017). Specific customer-centric ideas and innovations are usually developed jointly with the employees in specialist departments. The focus is hence on communicating and jointly applying methodological knowledge as well as changing mindsets and corporate culture. The goal is often for employees to learn to think more 'from the customer's perspective'. The methodology is extremely well suited to doing that although with customer-centric innovation, a strategic link is often lacking not only from a methodical perspective but from an organisational one too. This is due to the fact that strategic tasks can usually not be solved by customer-centric innovation methods alone. Also in the case of customer-centric innovation, the projects should by definition start explicitly from the customer's needs rather than from the company's needs.

So we can conclude that in the case of customer-centric innovation, innovation teams already exist which contain some of the characteristics and competence needed for implementing the 5C process. Besides the methodology itself, however, there is generally a lack of strategic anchoring in the organisation as well as clear alignment with the company's strategic goals.

Separate innovation units, such as innovation hubs, have the primary task of founding new spin-off companies. This is related to their goal of developing projects as far outside the core business as possible (or projects which even stand in the way of the core business). Due to their strong focus on disruption, they are, in fact, strategically independent of the company as a whole, but are organisationally very highly dependent. Generally, these units build up a complete culture of their own. Its employees usually possess the personal, methodological and social competences which resemble the characteristics required for an efficient innovation unit.

Paradoxically, separate innovation units, in particular, are therefore particularly well suited to applying the 5C process. To do so, they would ultimately 'only' have to change their task or goal to efficient innovation then map this organisationally and build up the methodology in order to carry out this new task. If these separate entities were to use the 5C process to develop and test innovations which exploit the company's existing strengths (rather than setting up separate businesses), they could deliver a crucial value added for their company in the future.

After all, they would then succeed in producing efficient innovations with excellent customer fit *and* excellent traction (Weiss & Kanbach, 2021).

A study by O'Hare (2008) also shows that this can lead to the long-term success of these separate units. O'Hare establishes that innovation hubs are more successful the more closely they are linked to the core business. The innovations developed in this way can focus on topics which are strategically more relevant (to the company as a whole) and can thus achieve better traction with the innovations developed there since these can be better linked to the core business again during implementation.

Depending on the company's status or scenario, a successful efficient innovation implementation can already take place in the short to medium term. Ultimately, in most cases, you can build on existing competences in the company. As can be seen from our previous remarks, these differ depending on the starting position although in any case no framework conditions already exist for the organisational implementation nor for setting up the efficient innovation unit. The 5C process itself must (understandably) first be learned in any event and then applied.

► Section 3.3.1 firstly describes the integrated implementation of the 5C methodology in the company, i.e. for a scenario in which the topic of innovation is either not addressed in practice at all or only in terms of incremental innovation and any research and development. In the following sections, we specify the adjustments which are necessary in terms of the organisational anchoring of efficient innovation and the setting up an efficient innovation unit when strategic innovation (► Sect. 3.3.2), customer-centric innovation (► Sect. 3.3.3) or innovation in separate innovation units (► Sect. 3.3.4) is currently practiced in the company. Since implementation of the 5C process should proceed in an identical way in all cases in terms of the training phase, this is only described in more detail in ► Sect. 3.3.1.

The reader can therefore check for themselves which scenario offers the closest fit to their own company and then select the relevant section.

Summary

Implementing Efficient Innovation in Corporations

To anchor efficient innovation in the long term, the underlying conditions described earlier must be implemented depending on the existing starting position of the company in question.

- Implementation of the underlying conditions (as per ► Sects. 3.1 and 3.2) depends on the company's specific starting position in terms of the innovation approaches currently practiced.
- Basic scenarios for any existing innovation approaches: incremental, strategic, customer-centric and separate.
- If (only) incremental innovation is currently practiced in the company, we recommend that you rebuild an efficient innovation unit from scratch which has the appropriate strategic anchoring in the company.

- If innovation has already been strategically anchored (by strategic innovation units), then major organisational prerequisites for the implementation of efficient innovation will have already been created.
- If the company practices customer-centric innovation, then a few of the fundamental characteristics of an efficient innovation unit will already exist.
- Separate innovation units, in particular, can easily be converted into 'efficient innovation units'.

3.3.1 From Incremental Innovation to Efficient Innovation

Frequently, the topic of innovation is not anchored sufficiently strategically in the company even though most large companies have already recognised the strategic importance of innovation for their long-term success. In the McKinsey innovation study mentioned earlier, for example, only 30% of companies state that they have clearly defined, strategic innovation priorities (McKinsey, 2017). This number may have changed in the meantime, but one look at their practice shows that it is certainly not 100% yet either. This is not usually due to companies' ignorance though. Instead, the reasons for this are usually due to the complexity of the topic, the unsuitable approaches or methods used and, in part, the lack of pressure to innovate (if the business is currently still operating successfully).

Implementing the 5C process for efficient innovations in your own company offers the opportunity to strategically anchor the topic of innovation quickly and comparatively simply (using few resources and without any cultural changes or transformations, etc.), thereby achieving innovation success in the long term. Like this, you can minimise your risk and effort when setting up a strategic or efficient innovation unit in your company.

Guest Commentary: Björn Sprotte, Chief Executive Officer, OSM Maritime Group

"Many innovation efforts fail, because the link between innovation and the focus on customer needs as part of the overall strategy of the company is too weak. Furthermore, there is often a lack of commitment on the part of top management. In the shipping industry, this effect is exacerbated by a—compared to other industries—fragmented and traditional industry structure, the focus on reactive day-to-day business and demonstrating the beneficial financial impact of innovative approaches. This often prevents innovation from taking a leading role within corporate strategy. Instead, many companies in the shipping industry tend to pursue a strategy of cautious, continuous improvement in small gradual steps. While some companies are commencing to promote new opportunities, there is still a large unfilled space for innovation in large companies in the shipping industry. For example, it is often difficult to identify concrete potentials of digitalization for the individual areas of shipping and to use them profitably and collectively. These kind of strategic innovation topics can only be achieved by strategically positioning the topic of innovation with top management.

However, there are individual pioneers who proactively develop innovations and thus have a positive influence on the development of the entire industry. At OSM Maritime Group, we are currently taking advantage of the changes in the wake of the Corona crisis to use innovative methods for the training of our crews and to exploit new opportunities by means of holistic, digital competence management and virtualization of courses and simulations. But this only works, because this topic is led by the overall strategy and thus takes place in a targeted innovation process—ingredients that many companies in the industry still lack. The shipping industry therefore still has great opportunities to exploit huge potential in the future through efficient innovation."

The scenario described here matches that of companies in which the topic of innovation has so far only been addressed in terms of incremental innovation in specialist departments and any research and development department. This means that there has not yet been any formal strategic anchoring of innovation in the organisation as a whole and there are still no dedicated innovation units. The setting up process described below can therefore be based on the blueprint in ▶ Sects. 3.1 and 3.2—supplemented by an explanation about 5C process training.

The topic of efficient innovation must first be set up (for the first time) or anchored in the company organisationally and strategically. After all, in this scenario no (or only a few) **structures** yet exist for strategic innovations which could otherwise be relied on. It is therefore all the more important that the implementation is based on a joint decision by the company's board or managing directors. In this context, it is also a good idea to nominate a board member or a managing director to be a long-term sponsor of this topic. Like this, you can ensure that efficient innovation will also be given a high priority in the company in the long term. At the start of implementation, a joint configuration (see also ▶ Sect. 2.1) is offered by involving the company's board and managing directors. This can either be carried out together with the designated head of the innovation unit or initially by an external specialist. The configuration outcome (in terms of listing the most relevant innovation potentials for the company in order of priority) enables you to draw up an initial innovation roadmap. Based on this, you can then take more specific decisions about the size of the unit you need (depending on the number of projects planned) and any other resources. Innovation topics or potentials should initially be identified in the medium to long term to allow sufficient time to implement the 5C process in the company. When repeating the configuration phase (at least once per year), you can then include shorter-term innovation potentials.

The new corporate unit responsible for efficient innovations should be integrated into the company as a cross-divisional function. You therefore need to define the specific area of the unit's responsibility as precisely as possible. At the same time, there must be clear borders between the company's other strategic and operational units. Where the unit's topics overlap with either the strategy department or with other departments, you should, for example, specify its exact responsibilities and at the same time decide on the future involvement of the innovation unit in strategy planning, M&A issues, research and development, etc.

You must also gradually build up and constantly expand the internal and external networks required. For this, you need to create processes for internal exchange within the company via, for example, the intranet, townhall meetings, regular updates, contact databases, project databases and similar collaboration measures.

As far as your external network is concerned, general rules or options for collaboration with external parties (e.g. with regard to sharing information) must firstly be specified. Existing company contacts must be activated and catalogued and new contacts built up by, for example, attending trade shows and events.

To build up the **resources** required, it is particularly important to plan these in a timely way as part of the company's budgeting decisions. After all, no separate budgets and resources probably exist yet for (strategic) innovations, so it is important to ensure that planning managers are involved at an early stage.

The actual operation of the innovation unit initially requires budgets for personnel and premises. In addition, you need to determine the extent to which existing resources—like IT specialists, designers, financial experts, external partners, etc.—can be involved in conception and implementation. This would conversely have to be taken into account when planning the specialist departments concerned.

As far as budget planning is concerned, a decision should also be made on implementation budgets for efficient innovations in terms of the operational business units, whereas the topic of efficient innovation should also be anchored in the target agreements of business units.

Implementing the 5C process for efficient innovation does not require any change in the **corporate culture**. However, it is important to create a general openness to the new strategy on the part of both the company's management and the employees. This requires sufficient education to take place within the company about the goals and the planned organisational anchoring of the 5C process for efficient innovation as well as the way that it will operate. This is all the more relevant if other innovation measures have already been carried out without any (or with too little) success. It is then necessary to distinguish efficient innovation from any previous approaches in a transparent manner to head off employees' frustrations and defensive attitudes. It is particularly helpful for the various business units to gain an understanding of the specific benefits of efficient innovation and that although the new innovation unit is addressing new customer needs, it does so while depending on the goals, criteria and existing strengths of the core business.

Finally, a clear separation needs to be made between efficient innovations, product improvements occurring in the business units, and the work in the research and development department. Setting up a strategic unit for efficient innovation does not mean that no new ideas should be developed and pursued anywhere else in the company. Instead, the unit should be understood to be supplementing the existing innovation efforts with a plannable and strategic component.

A dedicated unit for efficient innovation must be created (for the first time) in this scenario. Depending on the existing resources and responsibilities, the precise scope of its duties and **internal structure** must first be defined to achieve this. The fundamental focus of the unit has, in fact, been established in terms of developing efficient innovations using the 5C process. You still need to review which of the activities envisaged in the process will be carried out by the innovation unit itself and which should be the responsibility of other internal or external resources. It is a good idea to fall back on existing resources within the company or any external partners especially for implementation tests and planning (see ► Sect. 2.5.2) as well as for support for market research, trend research or for business case calculations. In terms of designing the innovation process efficiently, you should at least build up the resources you need within the innovation unit to perform the first four steps of the 5C process (i.e. up to the end of concept development phase).

You can then determine the short- to medium-term size of the innovation unit depending on how you chose to divide up the activities and the number of planned innovation projects (in line with the innovation roadmap). As the unit needs to be set up (for the first time), a suitable manager should be identified or recruited first. They can then appoint suitable employees to head up the individual innovation projects. In the best scenario, they already have a few people they trust who they can work with efficiently. Generally though, new staff must be recruited (and trained). When assembling the team, particular attention should be paid to its dynamics (see ► Sect. 3.2). Further resources, such as workshop participants, experts, network partners, tools, databases, materials, etc., required to implement individual process steps can be organised by the manager and/or individual employees in the unit as required.

The innovation unit needs the greatest possible flexibility in terms of its **ways of working**, a circumstance which is not easy to implement in large companies where the work processes and ways of working are usually fairly inflexible. This means that an exception to the rule usually has to be made for the innovation unit. This is because the employees in the unit require a certain degree of freedom (as explained in ► Sect. 3.2), for example, in relation to the use and design of the premises, working hours, home-office rules, work materials or travel plans. This also includes, for example, being allowed to use new (virtual) tools for collaboration even though regulations forbidding this prevails in the company as regards data protection and mandatory attendance. One great side effect is that the innovation unit can be used not just to develop efficient innovations but also to be a test laboratory for new ways of working.

If the innovation unit is to be exceptional in terms of its ways of working, this also means that other employees in the company should not be affected by them if possible. You can ensure this by, for example, the unit manager acting as the (first) point of contact with the company. When communicating and collaborating with employees outside the innovation unit, the manager should then adhere to the company's usual ways of working.

As regards **individual competences**, you must find generalists with creative *and* analytical competence to be employees in the innovation unit. This is particularly challenging if no suitable profiles exist in the company. After all, this specific combination of competences has seldom been needed before, so you will probably not be able to fall back on your usual recruitment advertising and channels. Instead, it is now a matter of opening up new ones to search for suitable profiles, for example, through personal networks, attending specific events and directly searching for consultancies, start-up networks or innovation units in other companies.

When selecting employees for the innovation unit, you should pay particular attention to their **social competence**. As we explained in ▶ Sect. 3.2, it is important to experience a certain harmony between the personalities in the team and sufficient psychological security so that the unit employees can develop new ideas and innovations efficiently. To guarantee this psychological security within the innovation unit, it is necessary to select employees whose personalities blend well with the others, i.e. they are 'on the same wavelength'. To check this, we recommend, for example, that potential employees get to know each other *informally* as an add-on to the traditional recruitment process—or even better, through a practical (test) collaboration. It usually becomes quickly apparent how individual people work together in their day-to-day routine. For example, we deliberately invite new applicants to ideation workshops to see how they interact with others in the ultimate discipline—idea development—even at the end of the workshop day.

You should encourage the innovation unit to build up its own **identity and culture** to help with its ways of working and its social unity. However, as the innovation unit is intended to have its own culture, this also means that this may, or should, be created independently of the main corporate culture. In fact, employees working in the innovation unit need to know the company's culture so that they can take this into account for the innovation concepts. Being familiar with the corporate culture also helps people to know their way around in the company or even when collaborating with colleagues outside their own unit. It should be stated clearly though that the innovation unit is allowed to build its own identity and culture which may differ from that of the company as a whole.

Besides establishing independent and flexible working as well as open communication, events which occur outside of people's day-to-day working lives are vital for building an **internal culture**. Even if this is otherwise more unusual in the company, the innovation unit should actively encourage and demand activities like team evenings, outings or shared breakout sessions. These are precisely what helps the team to establish the required group norms (see ▶ Sect. 3.2) and to work together in a trusting, and thus successful and efficient, manner.

To manage the innovation unit in the long term, a **success measurement** must be established which ideally fits the required goals and activities. The most important measurement criterion is the return on investment (ROI) of successfully implemented innovation projects (or even, the return on innovation). Besides that, the total number of innovation projects carried out (up to the end of concept development) and their specific implementation rate is also crucial. These measurement criteria should be included in the planning and scoring tools used in the company to track KPIs.

Implementing the innovation unit usually forms part of the company's long-term strategy, so it is not essential to measure its success at the beginning, particularly, because you should initially plan in a certain amount of time for **setting up the innovation unit**. Clear measurement criteria should be set for the unit no later than the second year so that it can be managed effectively in the long term.

As soon as innovation managers have been found for the new innovation unit, they can begin their 5C process **training phase**. In the best scenario, (new) employees will already possess a certain amount of innovation expertise. The specific methodological knowledge required to develop efficient innovations using the 5C process is generally not available and must be built up gradually.

Managers can either learn about the 5C process by themselves, for example, using this book and any other documentation, or they can acquire it from the on-the-job training provided by external specialists during the implementation of 5C projects. The advantage of on-the-job training is that the first innovation projects are already being carried out right from the time when the unit starts, thereby enabling companies to achieve short-term innovation successes too.

The 5C process knowledge should ideally be transferred completely as part of three successive innovation projects:

1. *First innovation project*: implementation of an efficient innovation project by a 5C expert. One or more trainees take part in tandem in all workshops and all decisions. They also receive a detailed explanation or guidance about each individual step carried out as part of the 5C process for that specific project.
2. *Second innovation project:* joint implementation of the project by a 5C expert and the trainee. The trainee manages a subproject, takes an active part in all discussions and also takes over individual activities within the project steps up to the development of the innovation concepts. Individual activities are always planned by the 5C expert jointly with the trainee.
3. *Third innovation project:* the trainee becomes an expert themselves. They completely take over the project management for a 5C project. The 5C expert is still available to take part as a discussion partner for all of the important steps. They provide regular feedback plus offer their support if required. By the time that the third project has been completed successfully, the employee has usually achieved the status of a 5C expert themselves. From then on, they can independently apply the 5C process as a innovation manager and train new employees themselves. This is how the team can be gradually expanded from its own ranks. From this point on, training refresher sessions are only required sporadically either if there are any innovations within the methodology or for refresher purposes.

We recommend that you also use your own 5C experts to communicate the mindset required for efficient innovation more widely throughout the company. This is partly so that a better understanding of the innovation unit's work and goals can be built up and partly so that new impetus for smaller innovation projects can be generated in specialist departments. Since the implementation of efficient innovation projects with the 5C process does not, as such, require any development work in the specialist departments and business units, but can influence what is to be developed, experience shows that the level of frustration with innovation is low. This automatically increases the desire for new ideas and innovations.

With the implementation measures described in this section, the 5C process for efficient innovations is successfully implemented. This creates an important building block for establishing strategic innovation competence in the company. Other strategic innovation competence—for example, in the areas of the innovation culture, mergers and acquisitions or forecasting—will not be considered further here. It could, though, be relevant for the company as an additional building block. Ultimately, each additional building block can potentially help to further enhance the company's strategic innovation competence.

Summary

From Incremental Innovation to Efficient Innovation

Many companies do not yet possess satisfactory strategic innovation measures. Using the following basic setup, they can therefore implement efficient innovation as a new strategic function with a suitable innovation unit and methodology.

Structure

- The company's board decides to implement the new cross-divisional function with top-down or bottom-up organisational anchoring.
- Identify a board member to act as a long-term sponsor.
- Carry out configuration with top management to plan the innovation roadmap and hence the number of projects required per year.
- Ensure operational anchoring of the new cross-divisional function with access to all relevant stakeholders and clearly define its area of responsibility.
- Set up or expand internal and external networks, e.g. using suitable communication channels.

Resources

- Plan the new resources needed to develop efficient innovations early (internal budget).
- In the long term, plan the implementation of resources in the business areas (this is possible, but not necessary as the 5C process can always incorporate the current budget as a criteria).
- Determine the opportunities for internal specialist areas and external partners to be involved in developing (and implementing) efficient innovations.
- Plan the human resources needed (see also ► Sect. 3.3.2).

Culture

- No change in the overall culture of the company as a whole.
- Communicate the new innovation strategy.
- Explain the significance of strategic innovation outside the operating business.
- Communicate the efficient innovation approach and any distinction between the innovation measures already in use.
- Communicate any important building blocks to strategic and operational stakeholders, so they can understand the process requirements better.

Internal Structure (Innovation Unit)

- Define the area of responsibility in detail to differentiate between the existing departments (e.g. agile implementation, use of specialist departments, etc.).
- As a minimum, build competences and resources so that you can independently develop the innovation concepts (process steps 1–4).
- Determine the size of the innovation unit required in the short to medium term depending on the number of projects planned in the innovation roadmap (see ► Sect. 3.1).
- Appoint a suitable manager who then builds the rest of the team, especially the project managers, in line with the stated requirements.

Ways of Working (Innovation Unit)
- Define, approve and implement any new processes and regulations needed to provide independence and flexibility (e.g. home-office, travel, overtime, work materials, etc.).
- Provide suitable premises.
- Review and, if necessary, adjust the regulations concerning internal and external exchanges (e.g. email and telephone policy, meetings, etc.).

Individual Competences (Innovation Unit)
- Identify and motivate 'creative generalists' with analytical and creative skills (internal or external candidates).
- External: display adverts on suitable recruitment channels (e.g. networks, events, universities, start-up hubs, other companies).
- Provide reasoning about the benefits of efficient innovation: Process new innovations using the corporation's strengths

Social Competences (Innovation Unit)
- Ensure psychological security in the innovation unit by testing social competence as part of selecting employees.

Internal Culture (Innovation Unit)
- Create own identity and culture, potentially, separate from the company as a whole through a suitable framework.
- Create group norms, particularly also through informal activities.

Measuring Success (Innovation Unit)
- Draw up new KPIs and goals for measuring project success, e.g. the return on investment, implementation rate, number of projects implemented per year.

Set-Up Phase
- The company's board decides to implement efficient innovation.
- Carry out configuration to plan the innovation roadmap.
- Create the underlying organisational conditions (► Sect. 3.1).
- Set up the efficient innovation unit (► Sect. 3.2).
- Hand over the innovation roadmap to the innovation unit.

Training Phase
- Independently build up the competences needed using suitable documentation or training provided by external (and subsequently, by internal) specialists.
- Step-by-step training provided by 5C experts in tandem with trainees:
  1. First project: expert implements and explains/documents the project.
  2. Second project: expert and trainee implement the project together.
  3. Third project: trainee is the innovation manager; the expert is a sparring partner.

3.3.2 From Strategic Innovation to Efficient Innovation

Efficient innovation makes it possible for companies which previously (only) operated **strategic innovation to achieve not only excellent traction *but* excellent customer fit too**. The background to this is that strategic innovation describes the central or overarching management of innovation measures for rejuvenating selected strategic topics or, in some cases, the strategy of the company itself (van Someren, 2005). These strategic innovation units generally apply a combination of different innovation methods (see ► Sect. 3.3). When selecting the appropriate innovation methods, strategic units usually focus on those that enable excellent traction. Comparatively little consideration is given to customer fit in the work of strategic innovation units as a result. Why is that? It is simply because when innovation methods are selected, you currently have to decide to pursue either excellent customer fit or excellent traction. This is because no method has so far been able to produce sufficient processual ambidexterity (see ► Sect. 1.4). With strategic innovation, you should innovate while focusing specifically on the strengths of the core business. The focus here is therefore on traction. This consequently means that you have specifically complied with the first part of the definition for efficient innovation, 'as close to the core business as possible, as disruptive as necessary'. However, more disruptive ideas that satisfy future customer needs and trends are often not processed at all or are only pursued outside the company (without traction) as it is not possible to integrate disruptive, customer-centric ideas adequately.

The 5C process makes it possible to achieve processual ambidexterity and hence a simultaneous focus on excellent traction *and* excellent customer fit. This makes the methodology ideal for use in corporations which so have far relied (or had to rely) on strategic innovation with excellent traction. Since strategic innovation has by definition already been anchored strategically in the existing organisation, **additions or changes in terms of the existing innovation unit itself are required particularly for implementing the 5C process for efficient innovation** and, of course, for providing appropriate training for future innovation managers of 5C innovation projects.

Strategic measures have already been implemented into the **structure** so that usually innovation already enjoys close links to the company's board and managing directors. This important prerequisite for efficient innovation is therefore already in place. After implementation has been decided, we recommend that you win over the company's board and managing directors responsible so far for innovations as sponsors of efficient innovations so that you guarantee long-term support for efficient innovation.

Configuration (see ► Sect. 2.1) is necessary at the start of implementation. Since strategic innovations are already being worked on, the existing or planned opportunities, potentials and projects should be included in this context within configuration as potential opportunity spaces or innovation potentials. You must then also study these in terms of their potential to achieve excellent customer fit and excellent traction. On this basis, you can then decide whether these should be pursued further using the 5C process or need to be completely reconsidered.

From those configuration phase outcomes (specifically, the potential innovation projects roadmap), you can then estimate which—and how many—new resources are required to develop efficient innovations. This planning also includes separating them from other strategic and operational units although this separation is usually easy as strategic innovation already exists in the company. After all, there is already a clear boundary between strategic and incremental innovation, so you just have to embed the new methodology in the innovation strategy. In the best case scenario, there will already be an adequate internal and external network for innovations, and their implementation to build on so you can quickly start specific work on efficient innovations.

The transition from strategic to efficient innovation does not usually require any additional corporate **resources**. The steps and activities needed to carry out the 5C process should in principle be covered by using existing resources for strategic innovations. This also applies—particularly—to personnel resources and premises. We recommend that you start by exploiting the available posts and existing premises. As a rule, new resources are only necessary if efficient innovation is to be set up in addition to the strategic innovation projects or corresponding unit planned already.

When transitioning from strategic to efficient innovation, it is also advantageous if channels and processes are already in place for involving stakeholders from the business units. Innovation is often integrated in the implementers' objectives and incentives (if not, this should occur later). Various specialist departments are available to provide support. Depending on how the strategic innovation function is understood in the company, there may already be a good link to potential external implementation partners, start-ups and other companies which could be involved in the 5C process at the appropriate points. Overall, the key resources already exist so the process can be introduced with very little lead time.

Guest Commentary: Thomas Weiler, Vice President Innovation Portfolio and Strategic Programs, Deutsche Telekom

"Deutsche Telekom facilitates innovation through a strategic innovation unit to develop novel products and technologies and enter into new partnerships with software and hardware providers. The interplay of various organizational aspects is particularly crucial here: centralized and decentralized, local and global, organic and inorganic perspectives must be sensibly linked to bridge customer needs on the one hand and the company's resources and competencies on the other hand towards a meaningful outcome. It is the task of the innovation unit to maintain oversight and to orchestrate the entire system in a goal-oriented manner in order to set and successfully execute on strategic priorities. To this end, it can, for example, support local initiatives via a corporate innovation platform with a budget. Expertise can also be provided, for example, by assigning the best data analytics, security or design experts to a team. This way of topic-specific collaboration enables Deutsche Telekom to better satisfy the needs of various markets overall.

The company structure and particular setup can be both a blessing and a curse and needs to be leveraged to the maximum. In comparison, Google has—despite all its platform assets and data capabilities—no established personal sales channels to small- and medium-sized businesses in Germany and therefore still struggles to understand their problems and challenges on an individual level. Meanwhile, Deutsche Telekom can provide this target group with appropriate solutions by combining local understanding and central core competencies. Conversely, a purely local presence has its obvious limits. For example, regional telecommunications companies such as Deutsche Telekom's smaller subsidiaries seem less attractive and less equipped to enter into all required product and technology partnerships or investments themselves, but they can benefit from the headquarters acting as a global player, deploying an international partnership management and scouting office for worldwide cooperation agreements. The combination of market insight and customer exposure in Southern and Eastern Europe—markets often neglected by Amazon and Co. for their relative size and effort to adapt, e.g. in terms of language—with the technological capabilities, resources and sophisticated innovation toolbox from headquarters can thus be turned into a 'winning formula'.

In order for this to work in practice, all components of corporate innovation governance need to be geared towards joint objectives, and functionally interlinked:

- Board-level decision committees such as the group-wide 'innovation and product council' determine strategic priorities such as 'home experience', 'voicification platform' and 'digitization of customer service' and remove roadblocks for swift execution.
- Implementation is expected to be goal-oriented, with a common interest, ambition and focus being created via comprehensible objectives and key results (OKRs).
- Strategic planning is performed to transparently allocate resources onto priorities, balancing sustainable commitment with roughly 2/3 of central budget being put onto preset priorities annually and 1/3 remaining flexible to address intra-year opportunities.
- Mission-critical internal skills are bundled in an 'innovation hub' and grouped in chapters and scrum teams, forming the executing force behind the innovation program.
- Teams are engaged via a bottom-up ideation process and able to 'pitch' their concepts to the respective decision makers—complementing the necessary top-down guidance on goals and opportunities.
- The portfolio is steered in a 'venture capital-like' investment logic, determining priorities annually and readjusting them during the year, building upon success metrics that are specific to either the 'explore', 'build' or 'scale' maturity stage.
- Not to forget, formal as well as informal communication and community-building up to the regional functional areas in sales and technology are crucial to align all the necessary contributors on which success in the market ultimately depends.

If all those factors can be successfully addressed, the strategic orientation of innovation efforts allows local opportunities to be exploited with the advantages of the group as a whole."

Innovation is already anchored from the top-down through the implementation of strategic innovation. It is now important to make the new methodology or the reason for the transition from strategic to efficient innovation sufficiently transparent (this should not be difficult using our earlier explanations). This also includes communicating a basic understanding of the 5C process to clarify the differences with previous processes in collaboration with the innovation unit. No fundamental change in **culture** is needed for the implementation, as we have already noted several times.

As a rule, the existing unit for strategic innovation already has a suitable **internal structure**. Its general responsibilities include developing (strategic) innovations, possibly including responsibility for the test phase or even for the implementation itself. Often, access to databases and internal and external experts, potential workshop participants, etc., is available. The unit itself usually already includes several employees, including managers and project managers who in the future can be deployed to develop efficient innovations using the 5C process. It goes without saying that you could instead build up another separate efficient innovation unit using the 5C process. We do not recommend doing that in the long run though. Ultimately, you need to develop innovations with excellent traction *and* excellent customer fit to ensure the success of the company in the long term even though at the outset it may make sense to supplement the existing unit with external 5C experts. They can assist employees with implementing the first 5C projects as well as training them to become 5C experts.

The 5C process can also be introduced gradually (i.e. run alongside other existing innovation methods at first). However, it is better to transition directly to the 5C process although measures like open innovation, employee initiatives, start-up investments, etc. can, of course, supplement these (even in the long term).

The most flexible **way of working** in the (subsequently efficient) strategic innovation unit probably still needs to be established. Due to its particularly close proximity to the core business, the way of working in the (strategic) innovation unit is more likely to closely match that of the rest of the company. Yet due to its proximity to the company's board and managing directors (and with their assistance), this is fundamentally a good starting position to offer more freedom within the innovation unit in future. The freedom to be flexible is one thing, it is quite another to also live this in reality. It is the unit manager's responsibility, in particular, to shield their innovation managers, on the one hand, while on the other, to proactively encourage them to be independent and flexible. Ideally, the sponsor should not only grant them this freedom, but even proactively demand it from employees in the innovation unit. If you ensure a sufficiently flexible way of working, the framework conditions for the innovation unit will fundamentally be ideal—so long as you have suitable employees in terms of their **individual and social competence**.

In a (strategic) innovation unit, you will probably find only a few generalists who possess the required creative *and* analytical abilities. Given the unit's previous focus, you can more or less assume that most employees' competence, in particular, will be analytical. You now have two options. Either you try to foster and build up the necessary creative competence among existing employees or you need to look for the specific employees to complement the existing team, as described in ► Sect.

3.3.1. Since the strategic innovation unit often has a larger number of employees, there is a chance to either find or quickly develop the two or three innovation managers required to start an efficient innovation unit in the existing pool of employees. In the long term, the posts needed could then be filled by developing additional employees or recruiting new ones. The other human resources needed—such as experts to support the implementation tests—should normally already be available in a (strategic) innovation unit.

The high level of psychological security required to implement the 5C process probably still needs to be built up. This is simply due to the fact that the *strategic* innovation unit has so far been operating in a certain comfort zone (compared to efficient innovation). There are comparatively low levels of uncertainty surrounding the topic of innovation in strategic innovation units due to their close proximity to the core business. Overly great psychological security (see also ► Sect. 3.2 for a better understanding of this term) was simply not necessary. When selecting new employees, the innovation unit manager therefore has the challenging task of testing the existing team in terms of personality fit and social competence while also keeping an eye on the overall team structure (see also ► Sect. 3.3.1). Under some circumstances, this may be the greatest challenge on the journey from strategic innovation to efficient innovation.

Even if a certain **team culture** already exists, it is worth supporting it in a positive way. You should proactively encourage team cohesion through collective activities, such as team evenings, outings or breakout sessions and through building shared group norms especially after transitioning from strategic to efficient innovation or following any uncertainty in the team associated with this. Often, trusting and successful collaboration ultimately only becomes possible like this.

The transition from strategic to efficient innovation may also require an adjustment to the **way success is measured**. This is because the success of (strategic) innovation units is not defined in the same way in every company. In some cases, it is measured by the implementation of new innovations or even by the number of ideas or any qualitative factors generated, for example, in employee surveys (perceived innovation power, clarity of innovation measures, number of ideas, business needs being met, customer satisfaction, etc.) (PWC, 2017).

As a consequence, this means that if the previous agreements about objectives do not yet meet the success criteria for an efficient innovation unit recommended in ► Sect. 3.2 (i.e. the return on investment for the innovation projects, the number of innovation projects carried out through to working on the innovation concept, as well as the implementation rate), these should be adjusted accordingly and previous goals erased if necessary. A transition phase can be useful here though.

Previous analysis shows that transitioning from strategic to efficient innovation actually only requires a few larger adjustments and may even be carried out without additional resources. The only really critical aspect of that transition seems to be how suitable the existing employees are for taking on a innovation manager role for the implementation of the 5C process. Various options for solutions have already been discussed above for this point too. In conclusion, you would only need to train employees (as described in detail in ► Sect. 3.3.1) to transform them into 5C experts and successfully complete the transition from strategic to efficient innovation.

3

Summary

From Strategic Innovation to Efficient Innovation

Companies operating strategic innovation already possess many of the organisational prerequisites required to implement efficient innovation, but still need to make adjustments, particularly with regard to the innovation unit.

Structure

- The company's board decides to implement efficient innovation as a supplement to, or basic methodology of, strategic innovation.
- Use the existing cross-divisional function.
- Use the existing sponsor for strategic innovations on the company's board.
- Carry out configuration with top management to plan the innovation roadmap and hence the number of projects required per year including the existing and planned projects.
- Use the existing operational anchoring of the strategic cross-divisional function with access to all relevant stakeholders, and clearly define the area of responsibility.
- Use and potentially expand the internal and external networks, e.g. using suitable communication channels.

Resources

- Review the resources planned to develop innovations (internal budget).
- Review the planned implementation resources in the business areas.
- Use and, potentially, expand the opportunities determined for internal specialist areas and external partners to be involved in developing (and implementing) efficient innovations.
- Review the planned human resources.
- Initially use the existing resources.

Culture

- No change in the overall culture.
- Communicate the new innovation strategy.
- Communicate the efficient innovation approach and any distinction between the innovation measures already in use.
- Communicate any important building blocks to strategic and operational stakeholders to provide an understanding of the process requirements.

Internal Structure (Innovation Unit)

- Define the area of responsibility in detail to differentiate it from existing strategic innovation measures.
- As a minimum, build up competences and resources to independently develop innovation concepts (process steps 1–4) as a supplementary team.
- Recommendation: introduce efficient innovation as the basis for innovation development for the existing unit as a whole, and supplement it through further (existing) strategic innovation measures (e.g. investments, open innovation, etc.).
- Review the innovation unit size required in the short to medium term depending on the number of projects planned on the basis on the innovation roadmap (see ► Sect. 3.1).

- Select a suitable manager, preferably from the existing unit who will then select or supplement the rest of the team, especially the innovation managers, in line with the stated requirements.

Ways of Working (Innovation Unit)
- Review the processes and regulations to provide independence and flexibility (e.g. home-office, travel, overtime, work materials), and implement these.
- Review and, if necessary, adjust the regulations on internal and external exchanges (e.g. email and telephone policy, meetings, etc.).

Individual Competences (Innovation Unit)
- Select 'creative generalists' with analytical and creative skills from the existing unit or supplement them.
- If they need supplementing, display adverts through suitable recruitment channels (e.g. networks, events, universities, start-up hubs, other companies).
- Provide reasoning about the benefits of efficient innovation: generate new innovations with the corporation's strengths.

Social Competences (Innovation Unit)
- Boost psychological security in the innovation unit by testing social competences as part of employee selection.

Internal Culture (Innovation Unit)
- Reinforce the unit's own identity and culture, potentially independently of the company as a whole using a suitable framework.
- Reinforce the unit's own group norms, especially through informal activities too.

Measuring Success (Innovation Unit)
- Adjust any KPIs and goals for measuring project success (return on investment, implementation rate, number of projects implemented per year).

Set-Up Phase
- The company's board decides to implement efficient innovation.
- Carry out configuration to plan the innovation roadmap.
- Create the underlying organisational conditions (▶ Sect. 3.1).
- Set up the 'efficient innovation unit' (▶ Sect. 3.2).
- Hand over the innovation roadmap to the innovation unit.

Training Phase
- Independently build up the competences needed using suitable documentation or training by external (and subsequently, by internal) specialists.
- Step-by-step training provided by 5C experts in tandem with trainees (see ▶ Subsection 3.3.1):
  1. Project: expert implements and explains/documents the project.
  2. Project: expert and trainee implement the project together.
  3. Project: trainee is the project manager; the expert is a sparring partner.

3.3.3 From Customer-Centric Innovation to Efficient Innovation

Customer-centric innovation has already been *in vogue* for years, and justifiably so. It not only generates ideas—especially with the help of design thinking—which have excellent customer fit but also helps employees learn about new ways of working, how to deal with uncertainty, playful development and a customer-first mindset (HPI, 2017). Committed ambassadors in the company advocate consistently, focusing on the needs of the customer. Employees are trained in applying design thinking, and in the best scenario, a customer-centric innovation unit is not only set up, but the entire culture of the company is also transformed into being more customer centric.

All of these are successes which no company either wants (or should want) to reverse. At the same time though, it seems necessary to change or expand the current customer-centric innovation. After all, customer-centric innovation implementation successes are lacking in strategic issues all too often, especially in complex corporations. This is exactly where the 5C comes in to now ensure excellent traction for innovations as well in addition to excellent customer fit (which is currently already being achieved with customer-centric innovation). This will build on the existing customer-centric innovation competence and now ensure that the company will in the future be in a position to produce efficient innovations with excellent customer fit *and* excellent traction using the 5C process.

Guest Commentary: Stefan Heidrich, General Manager, Maybelline New York/Essie, L'Oréal

"Maybelline New York makes trends wearable. The brand democratises international trends around lipsticks, etc. and makes them accessible to a wide range of consumers. Consumers with their individual needs and desires are always the focus of our actions. Innovations at all levels play an important role in being successful in this market. Whether you are thinking about new technologies in our products, new service tools or even new sales points where customers can find us, all of these building blocks are part of the innovation spectrum. Agility plays a key role here. The market for decorative cosmetics especially is extremely dynamic and strongly supply-orientated. Trends and new brands come and go very quickly, trends from other countries are international in a short time, and the desire for innovative products is enormous.

To understand the needs of our consumers even better, we work in multifunctional teams for each category made up of representatives from various departments, such as Category Management, Marketing, Sales, Market Research and Controlling. These teams develop the 'golden rules of the category'. In this way, the focus is not on brand strategy or products, but on the needs of end consumers and the growth of the category for retail. All measures are centred around these two goals.

Our strong orientation towards our consumers also results in us increasingly incorporating them into our product development. We travelled around the world with five 'trend squads' as we call them, that is, social media influencers with a wide reach. They let themselves be inspired in different metropolises of the world and designed their own make-up collections. The looks were then presented in the Maybelline show at the Berlin Fashion Week. A unique initiative in the market to date."

In companies with customer-centric innovation, the topic of innovation is usually already on the agenda of the top management and is therefore being considered in the **structure**. However, innovation units which are supposed to concern themselves with new innovations using customer-centric methods are often not sufficiently well anchored strategically. This is also due to the fact that the methodology is only to a very limited extent suited to alignment with strategic goals and criteria. Instead, design thinking units generally assist specialist departments and business units to generate new ideas and innovations jointly. Combining customer-centric methodology with participants from the operational business usually means that the overall strategic component is missing.

To carry out the implementation from customer-centric to efficient innovation, you usually first need to take the innovation topic onto a higher level strategically therefore. Since a decision to implement efficient innovation must be made at the company's board and managing director level, it should be possible to realise this transition (provided the efficient innovation has been approved). One further structural change is also essential. The innovation function or department must transition from a profit centre to a cost centre (if it is not one already) and also become independent of the operational business units. If there continues to be a need for customer-centric innovation workshops for the business units, the resources needed for this can certainly be maintained at operational level.

At strategic level, an innovation roadmap must be drawn up as part of the configuration phase (see ► Sect. 2.1) to identify the most relevant innovation potential for the company both now and in the future. Existing projects or knowledge from customer-centric innovation can be very useful for considering opportunity spaces and innovation potential. After all, this also needs the best possible knowledge about the potential customer(s). Once the innovation roadmap has been created, you can take a decision on this basis about the resources required in the future for an efficient innovation unit (see also ► Sect. 3.3.1 on detailed resource planning).

Collaboration with the specialist departments and business units usually changes too as a result of the transformations at organisational and strategic level. This must be redefined as needed. Yet efficient innovation can build very well on existing collaboration, because it is precisely this internal network which is used to implement the 5C process. This also applies to the external network which is often already linked very well in the context of customer-centric innovation methods and is therefore also available for efficient innovation.

If the 5C methodology is to be built up in addition to the existing design thinking units, you will need to replan your **resources**. This can occur as described in ► Sect. 3.3.1. For a scenario where efficient innovation is intended to replace customer-centric innovation, you need to determine whether this has been regarded as a cost or profit centre so far. Since the latter is often the case, you must now change this so that you can take sufficient account of the future strategic goal setting of the innovation unit. If customer-centric innovation has already been set up as a cost centre, you can presumably simply redirect the budgets for this.

In any case, it is a good idea to exploit their premises as they are often already very well equipped. The same applies to the existing internal resources (e.g. in the specialist departments) used to support the various activities within the 5C process.

3

The topic of **culture** should be treated with very great sensitivity if customer-centric innovation has been used so far. A 'customer-first' culture has often been built up in the company over many years. You now need to communicate why this is not enough by itself and why the company with its existing core business must be elevated to the same level of importance as its customers. There is a danger that employees will feel frustrated, especially those who were previously supporters of design thinking, etc., but only if they get the feeling that the previous successes have now become obsolete. If, on the other hand, people understand that customer-centric innovation is just the first important step towards efficient innovation and now 'only' needs to be supplemented by the previously missing company perspective, it would become clear that what has been built up so far is important and can still be used. And furthermore understand that the transition to efficient innovation now makes it possible to not only develop innovations which are relevant to the customer but to launch them in the market with excellent traction as well.

Design thinking experts are always more likely to be trainers and facilitators than innovation managers, so the previous unit's **internal structure** will have to be adjusted. This is because innovations have not been developed independently by a customer-centric innovation unit so far, but jointly with the company's operational employees. You should examine in detail whether the previous design thinking experts are also suitable as 5C experts—and therefore innovation managers—for the independent implementation of innovation projects.

This is different in terms of rapidly testing the implementation of efficient innovations as part of the conversion phase (see ► Sect. 2.5). You can assume that the kinds of competence needed in the context of customer-centric innovation are already available. After all, prototype development, iterative testing and agile development are significant components of customer-centric innovation development.

Access to other necessary resources, such as internal and external experts, databases, materials and tools, should also be provided as far as possible. The work with workshop participants who do not come from the relevant business unit may simply be new, meaning that a corresponding pool of participants would have to be built up. Companies often need to fall back on multidisciplinary participants here too.

A manager for efficient innovations should first be appointed to set up the new internal structure and the resources needed. Whether this should be the previous customer-centric innovation manager depends on whether the previous unit has been transformed or supplemented. Besides setting up the internal structure, including the human resources, this manager would also be responsible for ensuring a flexible way of working, adequate psychological security and the appropriate team culture required.

The previous **way of working** with customer-centric innovation should, as far as possible, already fit that required for efficient innovation. Some factors will need to be improved though. Ultimately units had usually been very closely linked to the operating units before and had therefore been more dependent on, or influenced by, their way of working. To strengthen their ability to be independent and the flexibility they require for working with the 5C process, it is the manager's task to shield the efficient innovation unit as best as they can from the operational business. This is completely new for previous design thinking experts as they have been used to being in extremely close contact with a wide range of employees and departments within the company and working together on ideas or innovation projects. Working with the 5C process requires a lot of focus, though, and maximum concentration by the designated innovation managers as regards the challenging task. For the sake of efficiency, project managers should therefore be able to work with as little disturbance as possible, at their own pace and according to their own needs. This also applies to organisational regulations, such as working hours, home-office, etc. where this has not already been implemented as part of customer-centric innovation.

In the best case scenario, design thinking experts will already be generalists with creative and analytical competence. In the end, working with design thinking fundamentally requires similar **individual competence** to the 5C process for efficient innovation. You should, for example, think of the need to talk to customers and analyse their needs, on the one hand, and, on the other, develop new ideas based on these needs. The challenge when transitioning from customer-centric to efficient innovation therefore has less to do with the specific competence of individual employees. It is more that customer-centric innovation ways of thinking and behaviour which have been internalised over a long period of time could result in a certain blockade mentality among employees. Design thinking experts may have little understanding of the fact that corporate goals and criteria should now be used as the starting point for the innovation process instead of the customer's needs, as has been the case until now. This is why it is important to not only explain the differences between mindsets and methodology in terms of customer-centric vs efficient innovation. Really, people need to understand and re-internalise the usefulness of the transition from one to the other. Experience shows that this will succeed better with some employees and worse with others. We therefore recommend that you identify as users of the 5C process those employees who in the best scenario have themselves already reflected on the limits of design thinking in corporations and are therefore particularly open to new approaches. It may then be possible to very quickly succeed in building up an active team for efficient innovation with these employees.

Psychological security as part of **social competence** is not a mandatory prerequisite for working with design thinking. You should therefore check its current status in the team. Design thinking experts are usually trainers or facilitators and do not need to be (fully) responsible for the ideas and innovation concepts developed. In this way, the psychological security they require (see also ▶ Sect. 3.1) is significantly lower than is the case when working with the 5C process. After all, here an individual innovation manager works independently and takes responsibility themselves for developing successful innovation concepts. So for the transition from customer-centric to efficient innovation, you must check whether the composition of the (new) team can meet the objective of psychological security in terms of its personalities.

As regards the **internal culture** of the innovation unit, design thinking already offers a large number of positive factors including, for example, building a good failure culture, accepting experimentation and using many playful elements. Working with design thinking has already established innovation-friendly group norms and thus created an important prerequisite for introducing the 5C process. It is therefore (only) a matter of continuing to maintain the norms which have been already established. These ensure that even in an uncertain situation (as is always the case in the context of innovation), new ideas and concepts are being developed continuously and shared readily with others.

The previous goals for **measuring success** which have been used by the design thinking department are probably not suitable for developing efficient innovations. After all, that usually involves internally communicating methodological knowledge, a 'customer-first' mindset and assistance with developing new ideas and innovation concepts. With regard to the latter, especially, the focus is often (erroneously) on the number of new ideas and concepts rather than on their implementation success. We therefore need to adjust our success criteria to the number of projects, the implementation rate and the return on investment of implemented innovations (see also ▶ Sect. 3.2).

In the end, it is a matter of retraining the existing design thinking experts to become 5C experts. Even though some methodological competence—especially with regard to determining the customer perspective in the customisation phase—is already available with employees, we nevertheless recommend that you undertake complete **training in the 5C process** in line with the process described in ▶ Sect. 3.3.1. This is the only way to ensure that all of the interrelationships within the process can be grasped fully and internalised for later application. Moreover, you should set a sufficient period of time for implementing the methodology before you begin to measure the success of the new unit.

The greatest challenge in transitioning from customer-centric to efficient innovation lies in anchoring it strategically within the company. This strategic anchoring has not been achieved adequately so far. With the personnel resources and other resources which already exist, there are already very good prerequisites available for future work with the 5C process for efficient innovations. The same applies to the existing team culture. It is only the psychological security in the team which you need to check more carefully. And so a transition from customer-centric to efficient innovation can be carried out very quickly if necessary. By supplementing the new methodological competence, this will in future make it possible to develop *implementable*, efficient innovations in line with the 5C process which possess excellent customer fit *and* traction in the market.

Summary

From Customer-Centric Innovation to Efficient Innovation

Companies with customer-centric innovation have already laid good foundations for efficient innovation, but still need a more strategic focus on innovation through suitable underlying conditions.

Structure

- The company's board decides to implement or change the cross-divisional function with top-down and bottom-up organisational anchoring.

- Use the existing sponsor of (customer-centric) innovations, if one is available.
- Carry out configuration with top management to plan the innovation roadmap and therefore the number of projects required per year.
- Use the existing operational anchoring to access any relevant stakeholders, although redefine the area of responsibility.
- Use and, potentially, expand internal and external networks, e.g. using suitable communication channels.

Resources

- Change from a profit centre into a cost centre, if necessary.
- Review the planned resources to develop efficient innovations (internal budget).
- Review the planned implementation resources in the business areas.
- Use existing opportunities for internal specialist areas and external partners to be involved in developing (and implementing) efficient innovations.
- Review the planned human resources.
- Use the existing premises.

Culture

- No further change is required in the culture as a whole, but refer to cultural changes already made as a positive factor.
- Communicate the new innovation strategy.
- Communicate the efficient innovation approach and any distinction between the innovation measures already being used.
- Communicate any important building blocks to strategic and operational stakeholders, so they can understand the process requirements.

Internal Structure (Innovation Unit)

- A team with at least one manager and two or three innovation managers (depending on the number of projects required) from the existing customer-centric innovation unit or as a new, supplementary team.
- Select or recruit a manager, depending on the above team composition.
- Select or recruit a innovation manager, depending on the above team composition.
- Use and, potentially, supplement other existing employees and resources.
- Use the existing agile competences.

Ways of Working (Innovation Unit)

- Build or improve independent ways of working focused on independence and flexibility.
- Introduce work planning based on the 5C process without any micromanagement.
- Alter exchanges with internal and external stakeholders to improve the focus in projects. Hold discussions with stakeholders solely about projects, the manager acts as a point of contact.

Individual Competences (Innovation Unit)

- Review the analytical and creative skills to identify ‘creative generalists’.

- Avoid purely creative skills profiles, particularly by communicating the new methodology requirements (from the customer's and company's perspective).
- Use the existing agile implementation in the innovation unit.

Social Competences (Innovation Unit)
- Test social competence for psychological security in the innovation unit.
- Introduce or improve the use of informal meetings.

Internal Culture (Innovation Unit)
- Use the identity and culture created without needing to transfer this to the company as a whole.
- Reinforce the unit's own group norms (traditions, behaviours, (in)formal rules).

Measuring Success (Innovation Unit)
- Change the KPIs and goals to measure the success of the innovation projects (return on investment, implementation rate, number of projects implemented per year).

Set-Up Phase
- The company's board decides to implement efficient innovation.
- Carry out configuration to plan the innovation roadmap.
- Create the underlying organisational conditions (► Sect. 3.1).
- Set up the efficient innovation unit (► Sect. 3.2).
- Hand over the innovation roadmap to the innovation unit.

Training Phase
- Independently build up the competences needed using suitable documentation or training by external (and subsequently, by internal) specialists.
- Step-by-step training provided by 5C experts in tandem with trainees (see ► Subsection 3.3.1):
  1. Project: expert implements and explains/documents the project.
  2. Project: expert and trainee implement the project together.
  3. Project: trainee is the project manager; the expert is a sparring partner.

3.3.4 Efficient Innovation in Separate Innovation Units

The separate innovation units (or corporate venturing units) discussed in detail in the first section of the book are the current 'hype' in the innovation market. They have managed to catapult the issues of innovation and disruption right to the top in many corporations. To provide protection against disruptive start-ups, investments worth millions have been poured into building innovation hubs, digital labs and incubators whose primary task is to turn into (disruptive) start-ups themselves. Yet, these separate units (unfortunately) simultaneously imply separation from the core business or the actual company—and hence a loss of traction in implementing innovations (Weiss & Kanbach, 2021).

This does not seem to detract from the attractiveness of this strategy though. Many of the world's top companies, as well as hidden champions and other established companies, run their innovation labs. However, while some show moderate success, more often they fail to deliver on their promise as tangible results fail to materialise (Forbes, 2019). Consequently, these separate units must now be turned into successful innovation machines using existing resources for efficient innovations with a strong focus on implementation.

Guest Commentary: Carsten Stöcker, Senior Manager Blockchain and Machine Economy Lighthouse, innogy Innovation Hub, innogy

"In the innogy Innovation Hub, we traditionally focus on customer-centric innovations and spin-offs into new start-ups. Especially when it comes to blockchain and other disruptive technologies, this strategy quickly reaches its limits though. To be successful here, you need the strengths of the entire corporation which are lost when you spin off into a start-up. At innogy, for example, we have established business relationships, access to IT resources, legal support, connections to politics, etc. Even potential partners often only talk to us, because we are from innogy and not from an unknown start-up.

So in the future, it will be necessary to link the innovation hub even more closely to the core business strategically."

Separate innovation units, such as innovation hubs or labs, offer excellent prerequisites for implementing the 5C process. They tend to have a direct line to the company's board. They have an independent way of working with great innovation competence and a good team culture. Besides developing ideas, they can even perform rapid implementation tests. However, the goals and the methods used to achieve them often clutch at straws, because the organisational or strategic anchoring is missing. Instead of pursuing the goal of innovating as far away from the core business as possible, the separate innovation units ought to deliberately exploit the core business to achieve excellent traction when implementing innovations and do so while simultaneously ensuring excellent customer fit and the necessary degree of disruption (see ► Sect. 1.3). This will succeed in the future if the 5C process is used in separate innovation units to successfully combine the company's perspective with that of the customer.

To implement the 5C process, the separate units must be moved back closer to the core business in terms of their **structure**. It is then necessary to develop efficient innovations taking into account specific strategic goals and criteria, instead of setting up purely customer-centric start-ups which contribute hardly any added value to the company as a whole. The most important success factors for this implementation are described below.

The support of top management is already very clear in companies with separate innovation units. As a rule, a sponsor already exists among the company's board and/or managing directors—often the CEO even—who can lend their support to the implementation of efficient innovations too. The top management has made a relatively headline-grabbing and costly strategic decision in setting up innovation hubs so that every change of direction needs to be 'sold' very well. It is therefore all the more relevant to build the implementation of efficient innovation on the firmest possible existing foundations. And to ensure that the company's board which is responsible for this has internalised the concept of efficient innovation sufficiently and can communicate it just as well.

Once these communicative foundations have been laid, you can begin to make the changes to the **strategic and organisational anchoring** of the separate innovation unit. What is new, in particular, is integrating the unit as a cross-divisional function with a strong link to the core business and the corporate strategy. After all, the strategy pursued so far has been to keep as far away from the existing company as possible (to be a speedboat vs a tanker).

The strategic link is made (relatively) automatically by applying the 5C process. In the end, the relevant goals and criteria for the company, as well as its relevant traction factors, are determined jointly with top management as part of the configuration phase (see ▶ Sect. 2.1). Potential opportunity spaces are assessed on this basis. This naturally also applies to the innovation projects in the separate innovation unit so far or those already been planned. It quickly becomes clear which potential unit projects can ensure the necessary strategic and organisational link to the company—and which cannot. Furthermore, it is then obvious which other opportunities are likely to offer greater potential to become an innovation success as they provide both excellent customer fit *and* excellent traction. As a result, no further organisational changes at all are necessary in the best scenario in terms of the separate innovation unit.

Separate innovation units already possess sufficient **resources** to implement the 5C process for efficient innovation. That includes not only the financial resources needed, but also its own well-equipped premises and adequate personnel resources. The network—especially the outward-facing network—which has already been established in the separate innovation units is often excellent too since it generally includes intensive collaboration with start-ups, research institutes and other companies. It is only the *internal* network which may need to be improved as often too weak a link exists with the stakeholders in the core business' operating units due to the separation which has occurred.

The number of resources available in the separate innovation units is even set too high overall in terms of efficient innovations. So in addition to their development capacities, these units generally possess a large implementation budget for investing in their own start-ups—in the hope that this investment will gain in value as a result of external investors coming on board. The focus on generating profit through your own start-ups—and thus also the need to finance them—does not apply if efficient innovations are (mainly) implemented using resources from the core business and any external partners. Consequently, the budget set aside for investments in your own start-ups can in future benefit business units for the implementation of efficient innovations. In the innovation unit itself, (only) resources remain for concept development and initial implementation tests. The unit is therefore transformed from a profit centre into a cost centre. This has the further advantage that the innovation unit can then focus entirely on achieving strategic goals—instead, for example, of chasing after goals like 'founding at least 30 start-ups per year' which generate no (or hardly any) value added for the company as a whole, as shown in the study of the German business magazine 'Capital' (Kreimeier, 2017).

When transitioning from a separate innovation unit into an efficient innovation unit, it is vitally important to bear in mind that the employees and the unit manager, in particular, may initially feel fairly unhappy. The long-term pressure to found start-ups with a valuation in the hundreds of millions has been removed, so has the budget to attempt this. So it is important to not only hand back a certain amount of responsibility through the new strategic role but to also clearly communicate this new role—as well as the associated opportunities for employees and the company.

Innovation hubs, labs, etc. already possess a good **failure culture** which invites experimentation and uses failures to learn from them. This is an ideal prerequisite for working with the 5C process—and for transforming it into an efficient innovation unit. You can certainly point to many successes in the separate innovation unit, such as the methods learned to develop and implement customer-centric ideas, new ways of working, the external network and the learning successes from dealing with start-ups and new technologies. However, a few things are not functioning yet either, first and foremost, achieving the primary goal of 'rescuing' or replacing the company's core business with new start-ups. Even if this is a long-term goal, you can already predict that it will not be achieved in many units with the current start-up methods and the separation from the core business. Accordingly, the existing failure culture probably also helps to transform this failure into a relevant insight, namely, that the 5C process for efficient innovation will in the future enable the innovation unit to make the company as a whole more successful in the long term through efficient innovations.

In terms of the **internal structure** of the separate innovation units, these are already ideally positioned to develop and implement efficient innovations. So in most cases, it is only the role of the unit described above which needs to be changed and the 5C process then be implemented.

Since separate innovation units normally consist not only of idea and concept developers, but implementers and 'doers' too, you should check at the outset which employees are best suited to leading and implementing efficient innovation projects. Depending on the number of projects to be completed, the rest of the employees can either support the unit with the individual process steps through to concept development, or they can take specific responsibility for either the conversion phase (see ▶ Sect. 2.5.2) or for long-term project management during implementation with the business units.

Other necessary resources, such as the tools, database access, expert networks, etc., required are already available in sufficient quantities so that the work on efficient innovations can start immediately, in principle. Even 'external' participants are already available for the ideation workshops (see ▶ Sect. 2.4.1), because, by definition, all employees in a separate innovation unit are already operating outside the core business.

The **way of working** in separate innovation units is generally already independent and flexible as a result of the dependence on start-up methods. When setting up units especially, they often battle to take over as few of the bureaucratic processes and regulations from the company as possible. Much freedom therefore already exists which can be used in an ideal way for developing efficient innovations.

You should now encourage them to link to the core business rather than seek even greater flexibility and independence.

The separate innovation units already possess a wide choice of employees with the appropriate **individual competences** to apply the 5C process for efficient innovation. Of course, not every employee in the previous unit is equally suited to this task, and you must now identify generalists who possess both creative *and* analytical competences (see ▶ Sect. 3.2). These are ideally suited to the role of an innovation manager for efficient innovation projects using the 5C process. As already described above, other employees in the previous unit can especially be deployed in the future to transform innovation concepts into innovations or to support their implementation. In the long term, fewer resources will tend to be needed (than currently exist in the unit), since the company's internal resources are more closely integrated into the implementation of innovations as a result of the stronger link to the core business.

As a rule, a high level of psychological security and an innovation-friendly **team culture** already exist in separate innovation units. This relates to their deliberate focus on experimentation, their desire to learn together and their constant discussions in (and also often outside) work. This kind of environment provides the ideal prerequisites for working on efficient innovations. You just need to check whether the new core team for efficient innovations has already been assembled appropriately in terms of the fit of the various personalities and social competences, and whether the best possible basis for trust can exist within this team.

You should change how you **measure success** for mapping the innovation unit's modified goals. As this is a critical point, the strategic, organisational and communicative factors described above should therefore be put in place beforehand so that you can build up the understanding required to measure success. You can then modify the success criteria for the innovation unit in line with the amended task as well as the modified goal. In the future, the unit should then be measured by the total number of projects per 5C employee as well as by the implementation rate of these projects and the return on investment of the implemented innovation projects. Often fuzzy goals, such as the number of new start-ups, the disruption caused to the core business or the invention of the 'Uber for branch x', will now be a thing of the past, and nothing will stand in the way of implementing the 5C process to achieve excellent innovation success. Since most of the prerequisites for the 5C process for efficient innovations are already in place with separate innovation units, the transition to measuring success based on the above goals will occur in the short term, essentially as soon as the methodology has been implemented.

In many respects, separate innovation units therefore already offer the ideal prerequisites for developing efficient innovations especially with regard to existing personnel resources, ways of working and the existing team culture. By changing the strategic goals and the stronger links to the core business associated with this and by providing the relevant training in the 5C methodology (see ▶ Sect. 3.3.1), the existing innovation unit can rapidly become a successful innovation engine for developing efficient innovations.

Guest Commentary: Jun.-Prof. Dr. Dominik Kanbach, Junior Professor in Strategic Entrepreneurship, HHL Leipzig Graduate School of Management

"The cooperation of established companies with start-ups is nowadays an essential part of corporate innovation activities. Initially the prevalent model of start-up cooperation has been corporate venture capital which has seen a significant growth rate in the 2010s. Since the mid-2010s, new forms of start-ups cooperation have emerged: activities such as corporate accelerators, incubators, innovation labs or other forms of start-up engagement.

Our strategic entrepreneurship research group at HHL Leipzig Graduate School of Management continuously conducts empirical studies on the landscape of these activities across industries and companies since 2015. We focus especially on understanding these different corporate innovation and venturing modes and their underlying objectives, as well as the organizational configurations and approaches. From our recent research projects, we can identify five main trends in the development of start-up engagement activities that show how corporate venturing can (and needs to) become more efficient in delivering tangible value for the established companies.

First, after some time in operation, many activities have been significantly adapted or closed down. Overall the landscape of start-up cooperation activities is under continuous change and adaption.

Second, especially activities with loose and open cooperation with start-ups have been widely terminated or adapted. Especially the earlier trend of bringing start-ups into corporate programs with the intention to look for potential cooperation projects along the way has almost completely disappeared, pointing to a lack in value created.

Third, corporates consequently tend to become more concrete in their focus on specific technologies or business models they look for in start-ups. Most of the companies initiating cooperations with start-ups have now defined strategic focus areas for external innovation.

Fourth, cooperations are more and more connected with concrete innovation projects as a result. By doing so, corporates ensure a closer connection with the core business. For instance, departments formulate demands for innovative solutions in their respective fields of responsibility, and exactly for these demands external start-up cooperations are initiated. Thereby, a 'pull effect' from within the company is created overcoming the frequently observable resistance of working with start-ups in the context of pushing start-ups into the organization.

Fifth, in order to identify and recruit start-ups with the best fit for a cooperation, the trend goes towards outsourcing the external scouting process. Specialized companies supporting corporates in getting into contact with start-ups appears to be a more promising way to partner with outstanding start-ups then to just advertise a potential cooperation on the corporate website.

Overall, it is observable that cooperations from established companies and innovative start-ups have become an integral part of corporate innovation activities and will continue to be so. However, the relationships and the forms of cooperation are under change, and corporates engaging with start-ups must continuously review and adjust their activities in order to be able to achieve desired results."

The precise implementation naturally depends on the details of how the innovation unit is built up and anchored in the organisation. This applies to all of the business scenarios considered here as well. A precise inventory of the company is always required before the methodology is implemented. The scenarios described here, though, already provide an overview of the relevant factors when implementing the 5C process for efficient innovation and thus provide you with a feeling for the changes necessary in each company scenario. The goal of all of this is to enable corporations to win the battle against disruptive start-ups in the long term in future by using efficient innovations.

Summary

Efficient Innovation in Separate Innovation Units

Separate innovation units offer very good prerequisites for efficient innovations. The underlying conditions necessary for efficient innovation can be set up relatively quickly in the company if they are enhanced by the right strategic perspective and the 5C process.

Structure

- The company's board decides to change the organisational anchoring of the (thus far) separate innovation unit as a cross-divisional function linked into the core business.
- Use the existing separate innovation unit sponsor with more transparent reasoning about the need for efficient innovation, and use the resources which have already been built up.
- Carry out configuration with top management to plan the innovation roadmap and hence the number of projects required per year.
- Establish stronger operational anchoring to access all relevant stakeholders, including redefining areas of responsibility.
- Use and, potentially, expand external and (especially) internal networks, e.g. using suitable communication channels.

Resources

- Change from a profit centre into a cost centre.
- Review the planned resources to develop efficient innovations (internal budget).
- Transfer the planned implementation resources into the business areas (and balance the strategic significance with budget managers).
- Expand the opportunities for internal specialist areas and external partners to be involved in developing (and implementing) efficient innovations.
- Review the planned human resources.
- Use the existing premises.

Culture

- No change has (so far) been needed in the culture as a whole.
- Communicate the new innovation strategy.
- Communicate the efficient innovation approach and any distinction between a separate innovation unit (emphasising the successes already achieved).
- Communicate any important building blocks to strategic and operational stakeholders, so they can understand the process requirements.

Internal Structure (Innovation Unit)

- A team with at least one manager and two or three innovation managers (depending on the number of projects required) drawn from the existing separate unit.
- Select a manager focused on a suitable profile (not only a 'doer' or a 'creative').
- Select an innovation manager drawn from the separate innovation unit.
- Use and, potentially, supplement other existing employees and resources.
- Use the existing agile implementation competences.

Ways of Working (Innovation Unit)

- Use existing independent ways of working focused on independence and flexibility.
- Introduce work planning based on the 5C process and focused on new, closer collaboration with the core business.
- Increase exchanges about the project with internal stakeholders.
- Limit exchanges with external (and internal) stakeholders outside of project work: the manager acts as point of contact.

Individual Competences (Innovation Unit)

- Review the analytical and creative skills to identify 'creative generalists' (in comparison to the existing founder types and creatives).
- Communicate the new methodology requirements (from the customer's and company's perspective).
- Use the existing 'agile implementation' in the innovation unit.
- Reduce any resources in relation to further implementation or launch on the market through even greater use of internal corporate resources.

Social Competences (Innovation Unit)

- Use the social competence already built up for psychological security.
- Improve the use of informal meetings and selection as regards previous collaboration.

Internal Culture (Innovation Unit)

- Use the identity, culture and group norms created (if necessary, have less of a focus on start-ups).

Measuring Success (Innovation Unit)

- Change the KPIs and goals to measure the success of the innovation projects instead of the profitability of individual separate start-ups (return on investment, implementation rate, number of projects implemented per year).

Set-Up Phase

- The company's board decides to implement efficient innovation.
- Carry out configuration to plan the innovation roadmap.
- Create the underlying organisational conditions (► Sect. 3.1).
- Set up the efficient innovation unit (► Sect. 3.2).
- Hand over the innovation roadmap to the innovation unit.

Training Phase

- Independently build up the competences needed using suitable documentation or training by external (and subsequently, by internal) specialists.
- Step-by-step training provided by 5C experts in tandem with trainees (see ► Subsection 3.3.1):
  1. Project: expert implements and explains/documents the project.
  2. Project: expert and trainee implement the project together.
  3. Project: trainee is the project manager; the expert is a sparring partner.

References

Accenture. (2015). Innovation: Clear vision, cloudy execution, 2015 US Innovation Study, Online.

BVDW. (2014). Faktor Mensch wird beim Innovationsmanagement viel zu wenig berücksichtigt, BVDW- Study, November 12, 2014, online.

Deloitte & Venture Idea. (2017). Beyond the innovation buzzwords, study. www.venture-idea.com/beyond-the-innovation-buzzwords

Drucker, P. F. (2002). The discipline of innovation. *Harvard Business Review*, August 2002 Issue.

Forbes. (2019). Innovation lab 2020: What innovating the future looks like, Online, January 18, 2021. https://www.forbes.com/sites/forbesbusinessdevelopmentcouncil/2019/07/10/innovation-lab-2020-what-innovating-the-future-looks-like/#5b31d9171b5f

HPI. (2017). Was it design thinking?, HPI Academy, Online, July 31, 2017. https://hpi-academy.de/design-thinking/was-ist-design-thinking.html

Adaptiert von: Jordanous, A. & Keller, B. (2016). Modelling creativity: Identifying key components through a corpus-based approach, auf: *PLoS One*, *11*(10), e0162959, October 5, 2016.

Levitt, T. (2002). Creativity is not enough. *Harvard Business Review*, August 2002 issue.

Markman, A. (2012). How to create an innovation ecosystem. *Harvard Business Review*, 02. December 02, 2012, Online.

McKinsey. (2017). Growth & innovation, McKinsey, Online, July 31, 2017. http://www.mckinsey.com/business-functions/strategy-and-corporate-finance/how-we-help-clients/growth-and-innovation

O'Hare, J. (2008). Innovation hubs: Why do these innovation superstars often die young?, DS 48: Proceedings DESIGN 2008, the 10th international design conference, Dubrovnik, Croatia.

Adapted from: O'Reilly, C. A. III (2016). Lead and disrupt. *Stanford University Press.*

O'Reilly, C. A. III, & Tushman, M. L. (February 19, 2007). Ambidexterity as a dynamic capability: Resolving the innovator's dilemma. *Harvard Business School.*

Pisano, G. P. (2015). You need an innovation strategy. *Harvard Business Review*, June 2015 Issue.

PWC. (2017). Reinventing innovation. Key Insights from PWC's Innovation Benchmark, PWC Online.

Rozovsky, J. (2015). The five keys to a successful Google Team, Google, November 17, 2015, Online: https://rework.withgoogle.com/blog/five-keys-to-a-successful-google-team/

van Someren, T. C. R. (2005). Strategische Innovationen. Gabler Verlag.

Weiss, L., & Kanbach, D. K. (2021). Toward an integrated framework of corporate venturing for organizational ambidexterity as a dynamic capability. *Management Review Quarterly*, 1–42.

Further Bibliography for Excurses

Buber, R. (2009). Qualitative Marktforschung – Konzepte, Methoden, Analysen, Gabler.
de Bono, E. (1999). Six thinking hats, Back Bay Books, Revised and updated.
Duncan, K. (2016). Das Buch der Ideen, Midas Management Verlag AG, 4. Auflage.
Gassmann, O., Frankenberger, K., & Csik, M. (2014). The business model.
http://agilemanifesto.org
http://theleanstartup.com
http://wirtschaftslexikon.gabler.de/
http://www.businessmodelgeneration.com
http://www.debonogroup.com/six_thinking_hats.php
http://www.inknowaction.com/blog/innovationsmanagement/ethnografie-alsmethode-im-front-end-des- innovationsprozesses-488/.
http://www.innovationsmethoden.info/methoden/lead-user-methode
http://www.monheimerinstitut.com/aktuelles/80-ethnographische-methodenin-der-marktforschung-gruppendiskussionen-verhaltensbeobachtungoptimierungen-innovationen-inhomevisits.html
http://www.onlinemarketing-praxis.de/glossar/tracking
http://www.sdi-research.at/lexikon.html
https://de.wikipedia.org/wiki/Lead_User
https://hbr.org/ideacast/2016/04/understanding-agile-management.html
https://hpi.de/school-of-design-thinking/design-thinking/mindset.html
https://www.scrumalliance.org/why-scrum
https://www.stage-gate.com/resources_stage-gate.php
Kreimeier, N. (2017). Deutschlands beste Digilabs. Capital online: https://www.capital.de/wirtschaft-politik/ranking-digitalisierung-deutschlands-beste-digital-labore-lufthansa-daimler-man-9067. Accessed 27 Dec 2021.
Magerhans, A. (2016). Marktforschung – Eine praxisorientierte Einführung, Springer.
Navigator, Pearson Educated Limited.
Osterwalder, A., & Pigneur, Y. (2010). *Business model generation*. John Wiley and Sons.
Ries, E. (2011). The lean startup, Crown Business.
Rustler, F. (2017). Denkwerkzeuge der Kreativität und Innovation, Midas Management.
Verlag, A. G., 5. Auflage.
Windolph, A., & Blumenau, A. (2016). Brainstorming: Alles.

The End Is Not Nigh

Content

L. Sauberschwarz, L. Weiss, *The Corporates Strike Back*,
https://doi.org/10.1007/978-3-030-79114-8_4

The need for innovation will increase even further in the future driven by increasingly fast social changes, new technologies and the associated changes in customer needs.

Yet many large companies have now become tired of the journey. So many innovation measures have already been tested and so many new innovation strategies pursued—only to see them rejected again or their current results viewed with dissatisfaction. The feeling has slowly crept in that tankers are simply unable to move fast enough to keep up with all of the speedboats. After all, there have often been enough attempts to implement innovative customer needs and technologies within the existing company—only to see them fail all too often. Any remaining hope of keeping up with the competition by owning your own speedboat seems to be further destroyed with every new study about innovation hubs, labs, etc.

Armed with this book and the concept of efficient innovations, we therefore hope that corporates will once again be inspired to take the next steps on their innovation journey. Our years of research and practical experience have shown us that innovation succeeds even in highly complex business environments if you combine the customer's perspective and the company's perspective using this 5C process (*Configuration, Customisation, Compilation, Construction and Conversion*).

Regardless of the point which companies are at today, it is worth starting the next stage of the journey now. Companies in which innovation has so far only taken place incrementally or as a result of the efforts of their research and development department can in future innovate successfully in a strategic and efficient way. Corporates which already know how to exploit the strengths of their core business in their strategic innovation efforts can now optimise how they consider their customer's needs. Innovations by customer-centric innovation units can finally be implemented within corporations and, as a result, can obtain the necessary traction in the market. Separate innovation units, such as innovation hubs, labs, etc., will no longer often leave behind a company which has empty coffers and little innovation success, but will in future produce efficient innovations to win the battle against disruptive start-ups in the long term. And so this book closes with the prelude to an exciting journey, the time when the corporates strike back.

Further Bibliography for Excurses

Buber, R. (2009). Qualitative Marktforschung – Konzepte, Methoden, Analysen, Gabler.

de Bono, E. (1999). *Six thinking hats*, Back Bay Books, Revised and updated.

Duncan, K. (2016). Das Buch der Ideen, Midas Management Verlag AG, 4. Auflage.

Gassmann, O., Frankenberger, K., & Csik, M. (2014). The business model navigator, Pearson Educated Limited.

http://agilemanifesto.org

http://theleanstartup.com

http://wirtschaftslexikon.gabler.de/

http://www.businessmodelgeneration.com

http://www.debonogroup.com/six_thinking_hats.php

http://www.inknowaction.com/blog/innovationsmanagement/ethnografie-alsmethode-im-front-end-des- innovationsprozesses-488/

http://www.innovationsmethoden.info/methoden/lead-user-methode

http://www.monheimerinstitut.com/aktuelles/80-ethnographische-methodenin-der-marktforschung-gruppendiskussionen-verhaltensbeobachtungoptimierungen-innovationen-inhomevisits.html
http://www.onlinemarketing-praxis.de/glossar/tracking
http://www.sdi-research.at/lexikon.html
https://de.wikipedia.org/wiki/Lead_User
https://hbr.org/ideacast/2016/04/understanding-agile-management.html
https://hpi.de/school-of-design-thinking/design-thinking/mindset.html
https://www.scrumalliance.org/why-scrum
https://www.stage-gate.com/resources_stage-gate.php
Magerhans, A. (2016). Marktforschung – Eine praxisorientierte Einführung, Springer.
Osterwalder, A., & Pigneur, Y. (2010). *Business model generation*. John Wiley and Sons.
Ries, E. (2011). *The lean startup*. Crown Business.
Rustler, F. (2017). Denkwerkzeuge der Kreativität und innovation, Midas Management Verlag AG, 5. Auflage.
Windolph, A., & Blumenau, A. (2016). Brainstorming: Alles.

Supplementary Information

L. Sauberschwarz, L. Weiss, *The Corporates Strike Back*,
https://doi.org/10.1007/978-3-030-79114-8

Index

T

U

V

W

MIX
Papier aus verantwortungsvollen Quellen
Paper from responsible sources
FSC® C105338
FSC
www.fsc.org

If you have any concerns about our products,
you can contact us on
ProductSafety@springernature.com

In case Publisher is established outside the EU,
the EU authorized representative is:
Springer Nature Customer Service Center GmbH
Europaplatz 3, 69115 Heidelberg, Germany

Printed by Libri Plureos GmbH
in Hamburg, Germany